CRASH OUT

CRASH OUT

THE TRUE TALE OF A HELL'S KITCHEN KID
AND THE BLOODIEST ESCAPE IN SING SING HISTORY

DAVID GOEWEY

Crown Publishers / New York

Endpapers photo: *Courtesy of the Ossining Historical Society*

Title page. ii–iii: *Courtesy of the Ossining Historical Society*

Part I photo. Page 1: *Courtesy of the Museum of the City of New York*

Part II photo. Page 97: *Courtesy of the Ossining Historical Society*

Part III photo. Page 179: *Courtesy of the Ossining Historical Society*

Published in the United States by Crown Publishers, an imprint of the Crown
Publishing Group, a division of Random House, Inc., New York.

www.crownpublishing.com

Crown is a trademark and the Crown colophon is a registered trademark of
Random House, Inc.

Library of Congress Cataloging-in-Publication Data

Goewey, David.
Crash Out : the true tale of a Hell's Kitchen kid and the bloodiest
escape in Sing Sing history / David Goewey. —1st ed.
1. Riordan, Whitey, 1915–1942.   2. Sing Sing Prison.   3. Escapes.
4. Shopping Bag Gang.   I. Title.
HV8658.R56G64   2005
365'.641—dc22   2005007531

ISBN 1-4000-5469-9

Printed in the United States of America

DESIGN BY LEONARD HENDERSON

10 9 8 7 6 5 4 3 2 1

First Edition

For my parents

Officer J. Robert and
Lorraine M. Goewey

AUTHOR'S NOTE

THROUGHOUT THE BOOK, all dialogue in quotation marks is taken from court transcripts, police statements, newspaper accounts, or interviews. Any scene or dialogue not containing direct quotation is nevertheless derived from multiple source materials.

CONTENTS

PROLOGUE

Sing Sing Correctional Facility, Ossining, New York

April 14, 2003

IN THE CHILL OF AN early spring dawn, Sing Sing prison gathers to honor its dead.

I am standing in the narrow parking lot in front of the prison's Administration Building, where a small crowd has assembled. The color guard, wearing tartan kilts and starched white shirts, tune their bagpipes. Nearby, the honor guard ready their AR-15 assault rifles for a twenty-one-gun salute. Several officials, including the prison superintendent, first deputy superintendent, and an Ossining police representative, are already seated around a podium on the building's concrete steps. Uniformed staff (corrections officers nowadays—not guards) line up rank and file at the parking lot's south end near the old stockade gate. The memorial service is a tradition. Every spring for the past sixty-two years, Sing Sing pauses to remember the officers killed during the worst break in the prison's 178-year history, on Easter night 1941.

A few weeks before the memorial service, I had telephoned the first deputy superintendent and politely requested an invitation. I mentioned my brother, who had recently retired as a lieutenant after thirty years working Sing Sing, and added that I was writing a book about the escape. The first dep said he'd get back to me.

What I didn't elaborate on over the phone was that I had grown up in a prison guard family—the grandson, son, and brother of Sing Sing officers. I'd been going to Sing Sing since I was four years old, accompanying my father when he'd drive over to pick up his paycheck. *His* father had been summoned from sleep to help search for the fugitives the night of the break. Even my mother's side boasted pedigree. Her uncle was assistant principal keeper under Sing Sing's famed warden Lewis Lawes. Like it or not, this place was in my blood. When I called back again a few days later, the first dep said, simply, "Yeah, you can come. Dress warm."

That was good advice. The sun barely clears the massive gray walls, and the breeze off the Hudson River is cutting. But that's April in Ossining—more promise than gift. I look around; little seems to have changed since my childhood. I spot the guard tower where I used to deliver sandwiches to my older brother Ken. Since he couldn't leave his post even to come downstairs, he'd lower a metal bucket on a rope. Down by the river is the old Death House. My grandfather used to tell horror stories of an executed prisoner he'd lifted from the electric chair, whose knee tendons were so hot they left burn marks on my grandfather's forearms. The two-story Administration Building is seventy years old and looks exactly as it did when I climbed its steps as a kid, tightly holding my father's hand.

Warden Lawes constructed the limestone building in 1928, a grand headquarters from which he could manage the most infamous prison in America and also write his bestselling books. On the hill behind the Administration Building you can see the upper floors of the old hospital—another Lawes creation, at the time a state-of-the-art facility. The escape that killed the officers we've come to remember began in the hospital, triggering the disgraceful end to Lawes's twenty-year career at Sing Sing.

That morning, the convicts are not mentioned by name; their ignominy is obvious to everyone present. But for me, the fugitives are there, too, haunting the event, shadows behind the somber reverence. I see them fleeing while the rank and file musters by the old stockade gate, stopping just yards from the rusting trestlework that carries utility lines across the railroad tracks below—Sing Sing is probably the only prison in the world to be cut in half by busy commuter and freight lines.

That peculiarity worked to the killers' advantage, after the murder in the hospital.

Directly across the Hudson, light from the rising sun spreads across the wooded Palisades, igniting the basalt cliffs that drop to the river. The Hudson is a mile wide at this point, four miles at a northwest diagonal past Croton Point toward Haverstraw Bay. Men locked in cellblocks A, B, and 5 have spectacular, frustratingly open views through the bars. If you wanted out (and there isn't a man imprisoned in Sing Sing who doesn't), you might imagine coasting unobserved, west across the river. The killers did.

The rifle shots echoing off the walls startle me—three volleys, like a firing squad perfecting aim. Then the flag is lowered to half-staff, and the bugler plays taps. The officials make brief speeches about sacrifice. The ceremony disperses. The families leave for home; the officers go back to work. Sing Sing returns to the business of mass incarceration, just in time for the morning count.

Perhaps murderous outlaws don't deserve memorials, but their lives cry out for a closer look. The convicts whose actions shadow this April tradition tell a larger story—of Depression-era New York and of a gang of immigrant sons bonded by Hell's Kitchen loyalties rooted in a firm waterfront faith. First-generation Irish mostly, but also English, Greek, Jewish, and Italian, they planned carefully and worked hard for their alternative version of the American good life. They might have been factory workers raising families, or even policemen. But something else drove them through 1930s New York, when everyone was looking for a way out. Even once behind Sing Sing's walls, they kept dreaming. Their common ties lasted short lifetimes and made them buckets of money when most people struggled for a dollar. Toward the end of the thirties, before the Second World War erased their names, their exploits were inked in bold black headlines, and their infamy was confirmed in the predawn hours of Easter Monday 1941.

The story begins, then, in the final spring of an endless decade, at the peak of a holdup gang's white-hot celebrity, with a group of West Side boys who transcended their wildest dreams, only to find themselves backed to the edge of a wide dark river.

PART ONE

THE SHOPPING BAG GANG

There must be something wrong with society
if we have so many prisoners.
—Mayor Fiorello LaGuardia, 1935

CHAPTER ONE

ROBBERS

May 15, 1939

JOSEPH "WHITEY" RIORDAN, convicted thief, strong-arm, and current hiring boss on New York's waterfront, stepped outside his family's Isham Street apartment at dawn like it was any other workday. The Monday morning sky was clear, turning blue, with the night still close to the pavement. On spring days like this, Whitey could smell the new leaves in the breeze drifting down from Inwood Hill Park up the street—damp woods skirting the tidal flats on Manhattan's northern tip. The city's wildest park remained almost unchanged since the time of the American Revolution. You could still catch sight of deer, even fox, in the deeper groves. But now the year-old, gleaming steel Henry Hudson Bridge, spearing out of that wilderness into pricey Riverdale, gave New Yorkers another way out—an escape route north to the suburbs.

Whitey Riordan saw limitless possibility, too. But right here in Manhattan. By six that evening, he could be richer by a thousand dollars, maybe two thousand. Across Isham Street, Good Shepherd Church rose in thick granite blocks, lights from an early Mass sparkling through the stained-glass windows. When the Riordans moved uptown, Whitey's mother, Elizabeth, loved the thought of living across from the church. A lifelong Catholic, she must have hoped the cross and steeple right outside the front door would influence her wayward sons. Whitey probably shrugged it off—his money had helped their move, and his mother hadn't kicked then.

To the east, radio antennas on apartment rooftops etched the sky above Broadway. A few blocks beyond those buildings, on the Harlem River shore at 212th Street, Manhattan's last working farm prepared fields for the produce they'd send down to markets on Ninth Avenue, in Whitey's old neighborhood of Hell's Kitchen. A city boy at heart, the thought would have made him smile—Inwood seemed a continent, a whole lifetime away from the brick tenements and back alleys of his childhood.

Whitey often caught a car ride down to the docks with some other longshoremen from the neighborhood. Today, though, he preferred the IND subway. He could easily afford the nickel fare, and the fewer people with knowledge of his routine that Monday, the better. Only recently had the A train tunneled this far north, following the crowds of mostly Irish New Yorkers like the Riordans, escaping Hell's Kitchen's trash-strewn confines for Inwood's leafy air. For Whitey, though, the future was still rooted downtown on the West Side waterfront.

As hiring boss, or stevedore, Whitey shaped crews at Pier 90 on the North River, as the Hudson was then called, at the end of West Fiftieth Street. The job was one of the best on the docks. Out of the hundreds of men who gathered at the pier gates for the shape-up at 7:55 every morning and 12:55 every afternoon, Whitey chose crews of twenty or so to load and unload the passenger liners that steamed into port. Then he spent the rest of the afternoon playing cards or shooting the breeze in the dock office or union hall on Twelfth Avenue. Today, though, he'd have to hotfoot it right after the noon shape. His partner, John "Patches" Waters, and the gang were meeting at Little Joe's around two thirty, and Whitey didn't want to be late.

The boys were on a roll. In the past seven months, they had pulled half a dozen armed heists and swiped riches far beyond their imaginations. Just the thought could make a thief's adrenaline surge. But the gang—Whitey, Patches, Willie the Greek, Lulu, Rusty, and Mac—all understood by now that precision timing was the key to their success. Anyone sloppy enough to be late to a job lost out.

Quick exits from dockside weren't a problem, not for Whitey, anyway. If he had to go, he went. He didn't need to punch a time clock—he was an inside man and lived by other rules. A husky young tough with thick blond hair that inspired his nickname, Whitey put rough longshoremen to work and took no lip about it. Besides, dock boss David "The Beetle" Beadle, who ran the loading for the Cunard White Star Line, was a reasonable man. So long as Whitey cleared it first with the Beetle—no details whatsoever—and kicked back a percentage from any unnamed outside interests, the young stevedore could do as he pleased. Their arrangement was nearly as old as the shipping industry itself. Though the target of numerous probes throughout the 1930s, most recently by the New York Police Department's Riverfront Squad and the city's district attorney, Thomas E. Dewey, waterfront rackets were as deeply entrenched in the West Side as the pilings that anchored the tarred wood piers in the muddy Hudson.

That May morning, the train racing downtown underneath Eighth Avenue, Whitey could only have wondered at the straight-johns crowded around him, red-faced in their neckties, *Daily Mirror*s under their arms. How did they do it? Locked in office jobs if they were lucky—in the unemployment office if not—and saddled with hungry kids, they had nothing to look forward to. Certainly not living life on their own terms, that was for sure. Despite his gutter beginnings, Whitey had it made over them. He had found his own way, was playing another angle, as Patches put it. Thanks to Patches, Whitey was looking at another big score, more than enough to spend and still pad things for quite a while. Add that to his plum dock job, and twenty-four-year-old Whitey Riordan was on top of the world.

———

The bartender at the Yankee Tavern on Ninth Avenue wouldn't have been surprised to see Patches Waters that Monday noon, squinting around a cigarette and penciling figures on a sheet of paper. The elevated IRT—fifty-five feet above the street and right outside the door—thundered past regularly, rattling the bottles against the mirror behind the bar. But it took a lot more than that to distract Patches from his accounts. He frequently took in over $80 a week—more than sixteen hundred nickels converted to bills—from the two pinball machines he leased to the tavern. Combine that with the other machines that Patches had running in bars and candy shops around the West Side, and he stood to make over 250 bucks gross a week. Not fantastic, but not bad, either—twenty-eight-year-old Patches was just starting out with this pinball racket, after all.

Back in 1933, Mayor Fiorello LaGuardia had cracked down on gambling. While the flashbulbs popped, LaGuardia took a sledgehammer to a pile of slot machines, then ordered his men to dump the ruins into Long Island Sound. But the "Little Flower," as the mayor was nicknamed, probably hadn't figured on a kid's game like pinball taking the place of the slot machines so quickly. Patches Waters, his associates, and hundreds of other enterprising businessmen (as Patches thought of himself) rushed to fill the barroom corners left empty by the busted slots, many signing leasing deals with Amalgamated Vending, a shady distributor on Broadway. Now pinball gaming was a favorite of drinkers and school kids alike, and the mayor's office estimated that the racket took in more than $20 million a year citywide. Patches wasn't seeing that kind of cash, but he was doing all right. Certainly he could afford $2 for a cheeseburger and a very good tip. Besides, he had other means.

The job later this afternoon—the Harlem branch of the Consolidated Edison Company—would be another big score. The take could be as much as two grand per man. Definitely the rewards of a misspent youth. As for his past, Patches wouldn't have had trouble putting a dollar figure to that, either. Some nickel-and-dime stuff when he was a kid, charges dropped. Fourteen months at the Catholic Protectory for attempted burglary when he was fifteen—didn't get a cent from that job. Two years at Elmira Reformatory for a $6 holdup when he was seventeen. All told, his entire childhood probably came in under $10. Penny-ante. While Tammany Hall and Mayor Jimmy Walker were fleecing the city for millions all through the twenties—everybody from the mayor to the neighborhood cop to the borough dogcatcher had his hand out—teenage Patches was stealing his share, too. The only difference was that Patches, and thousands of other young goons breaking midnight windows, were marched before judges as crooked as themselves. The street thugs were sent away, while the official looters were rewarded with titles, became "Your Honor" and "Esquire." Well, nobody ever said life was fair. That's why you had to live for today.

By the time he was of legal age, Patches was seeing real money. Over $2,000 for his part in a Westchester bank holdup four years ago, when he was twenty-five. The good times didn't last, though (they hardly ever did), and he served forty-five months at Sing Sing on a subsequent gun charge. When he got out a year and a half ago, he was determined to set himself up nicely. And now here he was with a flush, nearly legitimate business, and a very profitable racket on the side. His quick prosperity could be glimpsed in the bar-back mirror—the stylish sharkskin suit, the white shirt collar flared across the lapels—the sharp appearance a *Daily News* photographer would snap in a few weeks' time. Patches's life was finally clicking along, cherries straight across, and tonight looked to be just as sweet.

Patches needed to meet the boys at Little Joe's apartment on East Twenty-fifth by two thirty. If a similar caper—the Con Ed office on Audubon Avenue in Washington Heights the previous December—was any indication, today's job would call for a celebration. Maybe he'd stop by Gert's house afterward, take his girlfriend out to dinner and dancing, make a night of it. Perhaps a movie, too—the sunlight outside flickered through the El tracks like a picture show projector. Like most crooks, Patches must have craved a stickup's razor thrill, the adrenaline edge when an impending job would rev inside him all of a sudden, thudding against his chest. This was the way of the world.

If you didn't play an angle, somebody would play it for you.

———

The target would be packed. Twelve tellers, plus about five managers, clerks, and other floorwalkers, not to mention a hundred pencil pushers manning the desks in the brick building's second floor, and who knew how many customers. The Consolidated Edison Harlem branch office, its plate-glass display windows fronting one hundred feet of busy sidewalk on West 125th Street, seemed no simple knockover. But that depended on where you got your information.

Jake the Butch, a gem burglar with an eye trained for perfect setups, had cased the branch for the gang. It looked to him to be a prime touch worth the risk. According to Jake, the local utility company's combined operations could work to the gang's advantage. It was a cash business. A dozen tellers' cages lined the west wall, and a spacious floor area showcased electrical appliances for sale. Customers could mail in their utility bills, if they wanted to. But Con Ed enticed the strapped and busy New York consumer with a convenient shopping experience—pay while browsing the latest GE "Flat Top" electric refrigerators (such an advance over the old-fashioned, domed Monitor Top). See something you like, all shining chrome and porcelain, you could tack on payments to your monthly bill.

Depending on how the gang played the crowd, the showroom could provide the ideal diversion for a quick heist. The merchandise piled high in the front windows blocked the passerby's view, and the showroom's rear exit opened onto a small weedy lot on a quiet residential street, across from Mount Morris Park—perfect for idling a getaway car. The gang could slip in and out, hidden in plain sight the whole time. It seemed too good to be true, but Jake's intelligence was usually sound. Though not a holdup man himself, Jake had sold the gang his slant on the December job, and that had come off like silk. His information wasn't cheap. Three hundred bucks, nearly $4,000 to a twenty-first-century crook. But if Jake was right, his take would be worth the investment.

There was no reason to notice the large Buick sedan with Massachusetts plates as it eased out of the afternoon rush-hour traffic and coasted to a stop at the curb outside the office at 32 West 125th Street. The block between Fifth and Lenox Avenues was bustling. A mixed crowd of pedestrians—Caucasian shoppers from Morningside Heights and Manhattanville and African American employees done working for the day in the strip's Italian and Jewish-owned restaurants and stores—browsed the shop windows as the dinner hour approached. Some stopped to buy popcorn, peanuts, or steaming sweet potatoes from the pushcarts that teetered up and down the sidewalk on squeaky, cast-off baby carriage wheels, thickening the air with a mixture of grease and kerosene smoke. The sedan's doors swung open and five men climbed out. The lively crowds swarmed around the men as they gathered for a moment on the sidewalk. If anyone *did* observe them, no one mentioned it to police afterward.

The late afternoon sun, hazy behind a southerly flow that had raised the temperature all day, slanted across the street and fell on the opposite sidewalk. Just outside the Con Ed office, though, the shade was cool, and you could smell the Atlantic Ocean in the breeze. Above the main entrance, a blue and orange 1939 New York World's Fair flag flapped idly. As the Buick drove off into the honking traffic and disappeared around the corner of Fifth, the men, dressed neatly if anonymously in browns, grays, and blues, exchanged glances. They shifted the paper bags folded under their arms but said nothing. One last quick look left and right to check for cops. Then they shouldered their way through the pedestrians and entered the office as a group.

Office manager James F. Kane sat at his street-side desk in the northeast corner, forms spread before him and a fountain pen in hand, trying to explain a billing change to a frustrated customer. Like many New Yorkers that third Monday in May, Kane had hoped to get off work with enough energy to take the wife out to Flushing and the newly opened World's Fair. Lately all the major dailies, most prominently the *New York Times* and the *Herald Tribune,* had devoted pages and pages to scheduled events and detailed stories about the many exhibits. The publicity was working, and the whole city was abuzz. None other than First Lady Eleanor Roosevelt was being honored at a luncheon that very day, her appearance putting the presidential imprimatur on the event. The busy First Lady still had time to write a popular syndicated column, "My Day," which was a must-read for any conscientious hostess. If she could make time for the fair, certainly anyone else could. Kane likely hated to disappoint his wife, but the increasingly baffled customer at his desk was wearing him down. All of a sudden, an evening at a damp, crowded fairground probably seemed more of a chore than a stirring night out.

Built on a thousand-acre wasteland in Queens, the $155 million World's Fair extravaganza was three times as expensive as Chicago's Century of Progress Exposition in 1933. As if to justify such expenditure in a time of slender means, the fair's planners tried to strike up patriotic appeal, timing the opening for April 30, 1939—the 150th anniversary of George Washington's inauguration. Patriotic or not, a lot of good Americans sweating at day jobs like Kane wanted to see what that kind of money could buy.

The fair's board of directors—a who's who of local corporate interests, including Kane's own top boss, Consolidated Edison Company's Floyd L. Carlisle—predicted that entrance turnstiles would click four times a second, 60 million spins for the '39 season. The start was modest but admittance steadily picked up, and three weeks in, the fair was easily the biggest thing in town if not in the nation. Just the day before, three hundred thousand people—the largest crowd to date—had shelled out 75¢ apiece (a quarter for kids under twelve) to crane their necks for a glimpse of the World of Tomorrow, where curious wonders like the television set, white fluorescent street lighting, and a seven-foot-tall performing robot named "Elektro" were making their official American debuts. These visitors to Flushing could view the accomplishments exhibited by a record sixty nations, with the exception of Hitler's Nazi Germany.

Manager Kane, though, like many Con Ed employees, would have been eager to see his company's own spectacular exhibit: the "New York City of Light," a block-long, three-story-high animated model, where a full urban day blinked on and off in a twelve-minute panorama of snaking trains and buzzing factories, culminating in a thunderous electrical storm that illuminated a miniature metropolitan area stretching from Westchester County in the north all the way down to Coney Island. The Kodak snapshots coworkers passed around the branch office didn't do it justice, those who had seen it said.

But the red-faced customer sitting before Kane came first. The small clock on the manager's desk showed 4:43—seventeen minutes until a police officer would arrive to escort Kane and the day's receipts down the street to the bank. For now, though, there was work to finish. That late in the afternoon, as all accounts would later indicate, the office was still crowded with perhaps a hundred people. Customers were in line paying utility bills, opening accounts, or conversing with clerks at desks scattered across the floor space—enough to make any sagging worker sigh. A fast exit to the World of Tomorrow would have to wait for another day.

Meanwhile, just inside the front door, Herbert J. Davis, the branch office's floor man assigned to direct customers, turned to answer another question. A short, stocky fellow scowled from beneath a charcoal fedora. He reached into his navy blue suit coat pocket and mumbled something Davis couldn't quite make out. As Davis leaned in to listen, he saw the thick, short-barreled revolver held low in the man's hand. The gun was pointing at Davis's stomach.

"I said, don't move and don't let anybody out," the man growled.

Davis froze, watching helplessly as his assailant's partners flowed around them and were swallowed up in the sea of patrons. The men moved fast, not at all like customers coming to shop or pay bills. Too late, Davis remembered the company memo months ago notifying the Harlem office of an assault and robbery at the Audubon branch the previous December. As floor man, Davis was the first defense. Though unarmed, he could have said something, called out to wait or stop. But the gun pressed into him hard, and he couldn't find the breath.

With the floor man incapacitated, the gang threaded around the salesmen's desks in the middle of the big room. One man stopped near the front of the customers waiting in the tellers' line. His face, mild as a banker's but for a busted nose, was partly shaded by a brown fedora. He brandished no weapon but stuffed both hands deep in the pockets of his dark gray suit, standing casually with his legs apart. The customers barely gave him a second glance.

One of the remaining three men (though some eyewitnesses would later swear they saw only two—it was hard to say for sure with the crowd) reached through and clicked the switch on the waist-high gate to the tellers' cage, as Jake the Butch had instructed. The three slipped inside. Veteran teller Edna Wisker, sitting before her open cash drawer, heard footsteps rushing down the line of stations and felt movement behind her. The hard barrel of a handgun pressed into her ribs, and she looked up to see a man in a brown nylon windbreaker standing very close, close enough to smell the Lux detergent he used on his clothes. His pock-marked face looked warm to the touch.

"This isn't the time to scream," he whispered.

Even the most levelheaded person cannot predict how she will react during an armed robbery. A teller through the most lawless days of the thirties, Mrs. Wisker had luckily never been a victim herself. But she must have imagined various scenarios a hundred times. After the robbery on Audubon Avenue, while commuting to work from her home in the Kingsbridge section of the Bronx, she had to wonder what she would do if today were the day.

Yet when it actually, unbelievably, did happen to her, logical thought came to a stop. Later, in her breathless statement to the police, she would explain how she just could not make sense of the situation. She had wanted to ask the man what he thought he was doing in the cashier's cage, where he clearly did not belong. But the gun in her back paralyzed her, made her lips numb.

And in a flash he reached into her drawer and scooped the cash into a green striped paper shopping bag looped around his gun hand. Edna looked up along the row of tellers and saw another young man, with a shock of blond hair and in a similar brown windbreaker, moving methodically, doing the same to Jessie's and then to Mary's cash drawers. Edna turned back to her own station, but it was now empty and the man gone, down at Helen's station and then to Eleanor's. Behind them all stood yet another fellow, thickset and with a swarthy complexion. He wore a brown suede jacket and held two pistols close to his belt. From where in the world had they all come? Her head felt light, she really could have used a drink of water, and then everything went black.

At that moment, Herbert Davis, still waylaid at the entrance by the stranger close to his side, couldn't quite see what was going on through the crowd. He couldn't hear anything above the office's typical late afternoon buzz, either. To your average New Yorker it probably looked like business as usual—a phone ringing somewhere, dozens of customers milling around the floor displays, others standing in line with their noses buried in afternoon editions of the *New York Journal and American* or the

New York World-Telegram. To Davis, aware of a danger no one else seemed to notice, it must have felt like a nightmare. During last December's holdup, the robbers had slugged a male cashier. The thug beside him appeared capable of worse than that. But the need to do something, and the impotence, would shame anyone. Where the devil was Kane? Davis started to crane his neck toward his boss's desk but gasped instead when the gun muzzle jabbed harder into his ribs.

No, was all the man said.

And then they were gone. Davis sensed the gunman brush around him, saw him disappear toward the rear of the office, past the customers. Other figures darted through the crowd after him. Davis watched the rear exit door open wide for what seemed like minutes, as if a stream of people were leaving. Then someone, it sounded like one of the cashiers, started to scream.

———

Down on the fringe of the old Gashouse District, Emilio Spagniolo—known to his friends, and to the police, by his alias "Little Joe Salvatore"—spent most of that Monday afternoon perched at a small table by the front windows of his first-floor, one-bedroom apartment. He flipped through the *Journal and American* sports pages and peeked out at East Twenty-fifth Street through the lace curtains his wife tried so hard to keep clean—the gas tanks towering at the end of the block put Rose Angela in grumbling competition with the fumes and soot. The Yankees were in Philadelphia shellacking the Athletics, but Little Joe could hardly listen to the game. The guys had said to wait for them, that they'd be back, but they didn't say when.

Short and slight, with dark good looks and a generous disposition of which people often took advantage, Little Joe was feeling aggrieved. As he'd later tell police, it was bad enough that he'd let his old friend Thomas "Lulu" Gentles, whom he'd known since grade school on the Lower East Side, talk him into keeping all the guns at the apartment—about a dozen revolvers, plus that goddamn shotgun. The agreement meant Little Joe had to be at the gang's beck and call every time they wanted to pull a job.

Today, for example, he'd had to set aside the whole afternoon, give Rose Angela some dough and tell her to get lost, see a double feature or something, because the guys were coming over. She was about the only thing Little Joe had any control of anymore.

Waiting at home all afternoon cut into the lucrative numbers operation he worked for. It meant that Joe couldn't spend the afternoon taking bets up at the pool hall on Thirty-fourth Street, his informal office. As a numbers runner, Joe earned a fixed percentage of the nickel and quarter bets he collected, anywhere from 20 to 24 percent. Joe held on to the wagers before running the money and the bets over to his controller. The bettor's odds were long, about 1,000 to 1, but that didn't dampen interest. The payoff was 600 to 1, so when your number hit, you took home $30 on a nickel bet. With that kind of action, Joe didn't like missing out. Of course the guys would pay him for his time, but that was almost beside the point. Thirty-three-year-old Little Joe had responsibilities to a large, well-managed—and well-connected—organization; he wasn't just a simple gun "drop."

Furthermore, the arrangement had begun to cause problems with Rose Angela. The guns in a blue briefcase, the shotgun in a long cardboard box like a florist's, and then some bulletproof vests that Lulu had brought over (yet never seemed to find any use for) were all hidden away in the bedroom closet. Little Joe sweated whenever his wife put away the laundry. If she took too long, or got too close, he'd say something to distract her, she'd answer back, and then they'd fight. It wore down a man's nerves. As he'd later testify, he had never wanted anything to do with the guns. And he told that to Lulu's face last November, when Lulu showed up out of nowhere at Little Joe's door one cold evening after supper.

"I want you to meet a friend of mine," Lulu had smiled. "This is a fellow I did six months with. Willie, this is Joe."

They shook hands. William Athalias was a stocky young guy, tall with dark, heavy-lidded eyes and curly black hair bright with Vitalis. Joe pegged him as a fellow *paisano* or perhaps a Greek. Little Joe knew, of course, that Lulu had been convicted of extortion along with a couple of other men, but Joe had never met any of the partners. The job—shaking down a West Side bookie—had piqued Little Joe's sense of irony, given his own line of work.

And here was Lulu with that irresistible glint in his tapered brown eyes, which meant a favor was in the asking. The clatter of dishes ceased. Rose Angela came to the entryway to say hello. With his dimpled chin and wavy hair, Lulu was probably about the only friend of Joe's she could stand. Lulu fancied himself a chef and kept meticulous notes from *Good Housekeeping,* always writing down ingredients in his careful script. And swapping recipes didn't hurt when smoothing things over with his cronies' wives.

Lulu told Rose Angela that he had to borrow her husband, and he mentioned taking a drive. Joe suggested they head up to the poolroom; he was on his way there, anyway. Joe was going to walk, but the men had a car, the cracked upholstery musty from too many cigarettes. In the backseat, Little Joe watched the lighted storefronts on Second Avenue glitter past.

"Joe, would you want to hold something for me?" Lulu, in the passenger seat, rested an elbow on the seat back, his chin couched in the crook of his arm.

"What is it?" Little Joe asked, no doubt suspicious of the answer.

"It's nothing to be afraid of."

"I don't want to take any chances. After all, I am taking numbers and I don't want to be fooling around."

"There's nothing to be worried about." A slight note of exasperation had crept into Lulu's voice, a cold edge Joe had heard before.

"What is it?" Joe asked at last.

"Pistols."

"I don't want any pistols!"

"Do me a favor," Lulu coaxed in that familiar tone he used to close a deal.

Guns, for Christ's sake—a favor that carried real weight, heavy enough to pin him. Worse than that, Lulu acted as if Little Joe wouldn't say no. Generous Joe hated feeling put-upon like that. He'd remember it, too, the way Lulu counted on Joe agreeing, even before the subject was broached. Later on, bent over their pool cues playing eight ball, cigarette smoke curling into the green-shaded lamps above the tables, Lulu seemed to have forgotten the matter. He was all bluff and laughs, first beating Little Joe, then Willie. But Joe knew the topic would return again and again until he finally said yes.

Yet despite this initial reluctance, Little Joe's role would have been exciting at first, especially when the gang started making the news. For seven months, the boys slowly muscled their way through the inside pages to command front-page banner headlines. Sharing column space with Hitler's march into Prague and District Attorney Dewey's racketeering prosecution of Tammany boss James J. Hines, the boys had made the big time. Reporters dubbed them the "Shopping Bag Gang" and the "Paper Bag Bandits" for their method of disguising their guns and loot in nondescript paper sacks. The guys may have groaned about the pansy sound of their moniker, but who really cared? They were making too much money to kick hard about a thing like that. A nickname in the newspapers meant recognition, a professional trademark.

The glamour had really started to shine the previous December. The evening newsboys were broadcasting the story, shouting the *Journal and American* headline: "FIVE EDISON BANDITS VANISH LIKE MAGIC." Joe only had to press 2¢ into the kid's palm to feel his own pulse pick up as he read the story. Twelve thousand dollars was taken, about what he saw the guys divvy up that afternoon; a sawed-off shotgun was used, just like the one in his closet. By all accounts, the Shopping Bag Gang was making the grade. And Little Joe was right there with them.

After that, Little Joe joined in the tense solemnity when the men dropped by to grab weapons for a job. This was big work, and Joe's role was important. That was maybe the most thrilling part—his position as the drop was so essential to the gang. The men, wanted by police, refused to walk around armed and run the risk of arrest for violating the Sullivan Act, the state's gun law. Yet they needed iron on a moment's notice. By willingly providing this service, Joe elevated his standing in Lulu's eyes and proved his loyalty. But lately, with all the demands this undercover responsibility made on his time, and the pressures on his marriage, Little Joe's life often didn't seem like his own.

The plastic clock above the sofa inched toward five twenty—Rose Angela would be home anytime after six. The last thing Little Joe wanted was a big introduction scene. No, this was it, the fun and games were over: he'd pull Lulu aside tonight and tell him he had to find another place for the guns.

A car door slammed outside. Joe drew back the curtains. A cab was pulling away, and Lulu and Willie were climbing the stoop to the brownstone. Little Joe got up to let them in. Clearly the job had been a success. Willie's color was up, his speech fast. Lulu, chain-smoking cigarettes, kept setting up straight lines for Willie and then wheezed with laughter as he knocked them down one after another. Little Joe retreated to the kitchen and took his time with some cold bottles of beer from the icebox.

From the first, Willie seemed to have an easiness with Lulu that Joe never felt. Joe always tried to be Lulu's equal, offering betting tips, doing what he could to help out. When Lulu considered you a pal, after all, you were introduced around, an arm draped across your shoulder like a yoke. And once you were in, you were needed—and expected to provide. But it was hard to strike a balance with Lulu; the more you gave, the more he took.

But Lulu and Willie looked to be real partners. Unlikely that Little Joe had ever felt that way about anybody he'd done time with. Those two years in the Virginia State Penitentiary at Richmond when he was a kid—a trumped-up charge that elevated a drunken teenage prank into a felony attempt to wreck a train—had convinced Little Joe that prison was not a place where you met pals. Small guys had it tough behind the walls, and friends weren't what they seemed. But Lulu was different. A New York City policeman for five years before his arrest, his confidence was overpowering. Lulu wasn't big, but he was convincing—and like all cops, he liked to control. People responded to his toughness and helped him get his way.

Little Joe came back from the kitchen, handed out the beer, and sat down in the armchair opposite the sofa. On the radio, relief pitcher Jawn Murphy was completing the Yankees' third no-hitter in their series against the Philadelphia Athletics, an operation begun by right-hander

Wes Farrell. Announcer Clem McCarthy called the score at 3–0, against a subdued hometown crowd. It would have been a reflex for Little Joe to calculate an idea of the action on that spread. Tough to do under the scrutiny of Willie and Lulu, but in any case, the take would have been more if he'd been able to hang around the poolroom longer. They listened in silence as the Yankees won. Finally, a knock on the door jarred Little Joe out of his chair.

Through the peephole, Eugene "Rusty" Mello peered back from under his gray fedora. Thuggish as a B-picture extra, Rusty sidled in, a paper bag stuffed under his arm, a smile cracking his face. It didn't improve his looks at all. Rusty lived all the way over on the west end of Twenty-fifth Street, in Chelsea, close to the docks. That tough a neighborhood— maybe it accounted for Rusty's permanent scowl.

Rusty had been the bagman after the December score. Joe was up at the pool hall around eleven that night when the manager waved him over to the phone. Rusty's gruff voice told him to come over to the Yankee Tavern, Ninth and Twenty-ninth in Chelsea. The guys had some money for him.

The place was narrow and dim, stinking of sawdust and spilled beer. Rusty was the only one around, tucked into a back booth along the wall, hidden in the smoke. Little Joe sat down and ordered a whiskey.

"Here's some money," Rusty slid a wad across the tabletop. "For you."

Little Joe counted out $385—$200 for holding the guns, the rest money he'd loaned the guys for expenses.

"Take this, too." Rusty reached under the table and slid a long cardboard box onto Joe's lap. It was the shotgun.

Little Joe thought it was a joke, but the frown on Rusty's face wasn't funny. Joe's smile faded. How was he supposed to get all the way back home, nearly to Second Avenue, with a sawed-off shotgun and almost $400 in his pocket, at midnight no less? Better not to ask. Joe didn't wait to finish his drink—he just wanted to get the trip over with. On the corner, he hailed a cab, the long box under his arm, maybe a grin plastered to his face, like he was surprising the wife with flowers. From that moment on, Little Joe realized now, the whole arrangement had seemed lousy with risks.

John "Mac" Hanley arrived at the apartment next. Lulu and Willie started up with the wisecracks again, and Rusty grumbled a greeting. Mac slumped in the only other chair, at the table by the window. He held a brown fedora in his lap, his sandy hair brushed vainly over his balding pate, two mild blue eyes staring flat before him from behind his busted nose. The hands on the kitchen clock edged past five thirty.

There were more footsteps in the hallway and another knock at the door. Joe let in the last two gang members, Joseph "Whitey" Riordan and John "Patches" Waters, who clasped a paper bag under his arm. Lulu, Willie, Rusty, Mac, Patches, and Whitey—the gang had all made it back safe, and they got right to the point.

The seven of them crowded into the bedroom at the rear of the apartment, the claustrophobia relieved only by one window looking onto the alley. Little Joe turned on the overhead bulb. Rusty and Patches tossed their bundles down on the white bedspread. The men took the guns out of their pockets and placed them on the bed, too.

"Keep these here until we come back," Lulu said.

It was a perfect opening. All Little Joe had to do was open his mouth and tell them he didn't want the guns anymore. But then he looked at the half dozen weapons, the men shoulder to shoulder around his bed about to divide a pile of stolen loot. He let the moment pass. He pressed around Rusty and Mac, retrieved the blue briefcase from the closet, gathered up the guns, and stowed them away again. Patches and Rusty opened their paper bags and dumped cash onto the bed. Meticulous as bank tellers, they separated the bills into denominations, then added up each stack. The total came to about $11,000. The guys started to laugh.

Lulu counted off the top, folded a thick wad, and held it out over the bed to Little Joe. "Here's two hundred dollars."

In singles. Little Joe put the lump in his pocket. It looked as if he had an orange in his pants. Lulu, Willie, and Mac then peeled bills off their take and handed them to Joe, payback for money he'd loaned them. It was just like them—every time they needed cash, Little Joe was forthcoming without complaint. He never questioned, of course, where all the swag went. But when it came time to settle, they paid him in small, hard-to-conceal bills.

The men took the remaining $9,800 and figured their cut at $1,550 apiece (over $20,000 in twenty-first-century coin). That left $500 to cover expenses: Jake the Butch's surveillance fee, plus a percentage for what was known as a street tax—a $200 slice for the Katz brothers, the local crime bosses, whose Harlem neighborhood housed the scene of the robbery. Their work over, Lulu folded up the paper bags and handed them to Joe. The men filed out as Joe stuffed the bags behind the brief-case in the closet. In the living room, nobody took a seat. It was time to go, after six o'clock; Rose Angela could come in anytime.

With business complete, the men left as they'd come, in pairs, a few minutes apart. Lulu and Willie, Mac and Rusty; finally, Little Joe was alone with the last two, Whitey and Patches. These two unnerved him most.

Whitey and Patches had the easy familiarity of a natural pair, like Lulu and Willie. But unlike those loudmouths, these two communicated in more than just words. Physically different, they seemed to fit together. Where Whitey was all brawn and rough around the edges, Patches was thin, with the cold polish of a hungry businessman. Whitey had a sullen diffidence and didn't seem particularly bright, but Patches was direct and smart, with a high forehead that looked packed with brains. Despite a weather-beaten face, Whitey was still a kid, his blond hair always in his eyes, his hands pushing it back into shape—this part of himself that wouldn't listen. Patches was the adult—economical, in control—his pale blue eyes fixed in a thousand-yard stare and slightly off-center, as though focused at different levels, gauging different perspectives for the best advantage.

Discussing the details of a job was off-limits, especially with the tight-lipped West Side Irish like Patches and Whitey. And of course Lit-tle Joe didn't want to know more than he already did. Too dangerous. But he could guess. He figured them for the brains behind the February job, for instance, when Willie had come over practically at dawn for four revolvers. Later that evening, Joe read in the *Journal and American* about a Cunard Line dock teller being robbed on a Brooklyn street. Four guns meant four guys, and since Whitey and Patches worked the piers, it must have been their scheme. Different from the gang's usual holdup, certainly; in fact, there was no comparison—one victim, as opposed to a hundred or so.

Finally, Whitey and Patches must have figured that enough time had passed since the others had left, and moved to the door. Nods all around, and then they were gone. Little Joe took the lump of cash out of his pocket, put it away in his bedroom bureau. He still hadn't extricated himself from his responsibilities—the guns were still in the closet; in fact, he was in just as deep as ever. And it might be a while before he saw the guys again—he never really knew, that was the thing. Maybe he should call Lulu, the next day or so. But he was feeling easier now—the gang was gone, he'd avoided a scene with his wife, and he had $350 in cash; that was some relief.

The bedside clock read six twenty. The evening editions would be coming out soon, with a real banner headline for sure. Joe's little secret—possessing gritty inside details that the reading public would never know.

Whitey and Patches split up outside. Partners, maybe they discussed a drink; but Patches would have had other plans. Whitey would have been used to that, Patches with about a dozen irons in the fire. Anyway, it probably wasn't a good idea to be seen together. They'd know that without a word. Best to get to where they were going and lay low for the night. They'd talk tomorrow, most likely, maybe grab a beer then. Patches waved down a cab. Whitey headed west.

Cars honked their way west across East Twenty-fifth Street, go-getters finally making their way home from the office. Neon light spilling across the sidewalks, turning faces vivid red and pink. Food stands on the corners were always two and three deep at this time, the smells of coffee, pizza, hotdogs with sauerkraut—dinner a weird goulash for the poor drudges. When you're hungry, though, it all smells good, and Whitey hadn't eaten in hours. Whatever his mother had made for supper, there might not be anything left—his brothers, Andrew and John, still lived at home, too. He'd have to hurry if he wanted a meal. He hailed a cab at

Broadway and settled back for the long ride up to Inwood. Robbery was grueling—the tension building for hours, then draining away. It wore a man out. He had an unbelievable fifteen hundred dollars, though, right in his front pants pocket. Yes, Whitey Riordan had come quite a way from the old days in Hell's Kitchen, even if his mother might not see it that way.

—

CHAPTER TWO

COPS

As WHITEY RIORDAN CABBED it uptown to his mother's home-cooked meal, a manhunt was already gathering on his trail. The police radio alarm shortly before five on that May evening in 1939 alerted all cruisers to "watch for six men in a car, all heavily armed. Use precaution." Assistant Chief Inspector John J. Ryan fought his way to Harlem, his driver weaving around the rush-hour traffic snarls on Eighth Avenue. Once on 125th Street, Ryan faced a familiar scene. Patrolmen on the sidewalk barricaded the Con Ed office from a growing crowd. A pack of reporters, pushing against the locked arms of police, recognized Inspector Ryan's sharp nose and silver widow's peak and shouted questions about likely suspects.

Ryan wouldn't have been at all surprised by the commotion—cops and robbers always attracted crowds. Enterprising reporters scanned the police bandwidth and raced the cops to the scene. Sirens, flashing lights, yelling reporters—all drew pedestrians, neighbors, and the smoking pushcarts that trawled the fringes of the crowd. Whitey Riordan likely would have been drawn, too, if he'd been passing by, and hadn't been the cause of the disturbance. Growing up downtown in Hell's Kitchen, he would have jostled with other neighborhood kids when the cops brought out the hangdog husband for knifing the wife. The circus atmosphere around a crime scene livened up tenement lives, cast neighbors as players in the story unfolding in the flashbulbs' glare. Fame was catching.

No doubt about it, crime was a spectator sport. Lately the public seemed obsessed with gangsters of all stripes—from street-level gunmen to crooked politicians in mahogany-paneled rooms. All that spring, New Yorkers had mobbed the courthouse steps in Manhattan's Foley Square, itching for news of the racketeering trial of Tammany boss James J. Hines, pitted against famed District Attorney Thomas E. Dewey. In one corner stood Hines, a Harlem native with wide popular appeal, who was a feared political leader tied to mobster "Dutch" Schultz's criminal empire. In the other corner was Dewey, a fiercely ambitious Michigan transplant, with picture-star good looks, mustachioed like Errol Flynn. A partisan Republican, Dewey saw smashing New York City's corrupt Democratic machine as the high road to political office. His first action against the Tammany leader had ended in a disastrous mistrial two years before. But the district attorney was undeterred. Dutch Schultz had been dead from assassins' bullets since '35, and his current gangster heirs were unwilling to talk, but Dewey kept the case file open. The second action against Hines finally ended in his conviction in March '39; Tammany supporters hissed D.A. Dewey's victorious exit from the courthouse, but cheered when the defeated Hines appeared. Still, the district attorney got his wish, and within four years climbed his career ladder straight to the governor's chair, while Hines went off to Sing Sing.

A juicy trial and a local heist weren't the only newsworthy attractions. Even the most mundane aspects of police work were guaranteed draws. Just a few months earlier, in February, all the New York papers had detailed John Ryan's recent promotion to the rank of assistant chief inspector. Thirty-six years on the force, eight citations for "meritorious service," as Police Commissioner Lewis J. Valentine told reporters, Ryan was an honest, capable policeman. Newly situated directly under the commissioner, Ryan was the top cop's crime scene representative, with command over the entire Harlem district. The *Journal and American,* and the *Daily Mirror* even ran the story with pictures. The old cop couldn't have been crazy about his grainy depiction, but what could he do? The flashbulbs bursting in his face announced that publicity was part of the job.

An officer held open the branch office's door, and Ryan stepped through. Inside, the police had a firmer hand than they did on the noisy street; a methodical investigation was underway. Witnesses to the robbery were separated into small manageable groups and questioned. An ambulance had been summoned for the only casualty, cashier Edna Wisker, who by then had been revived from her faint. She was sitting at the manager's desk with a glass of water and a man's handkerchief pressed to her cheeks, talking in gasps to plainclothes detectives. Ryan surveyed the scene. He already suspected a connection between this heist and one the previous December. That, too, was a Con Ed branch, up on Audubon Avenue, and the suspects were still at large with their $12,000 loot. Initially, though, Ryan likely worried that this investigation might prove just as fruitless. Hard to believe, but most witnesses, including office manager Kane, claimed to be unaware that anything had even occurred.

But by nightfall, some promising leads had emerged. Floor man Herbert Davis and tellers Helen Del Monte and Eleanor Pavelka all agreed in their descriptions of the assailants and the attack. Reviewing detectives' notes, Ryan saw the accounts closely matched those taken from witnesses to the Audubon raid. The Assistant Chief Inspector was becoming convinced that the afternoon holdup was indeed the work of the same gutsy, lightning-fast gang whom the newspapers had variously nicknamed the Paper Bag Bandits or Shopping Bag Gang.

But even Ryan had to admit that if the Shopping Bag Gang was in fact responsible, this time they had outdone themselves in nerve. They struck just fifteen minutes before a regularly scheduled patrolman arrived to escort the manager to the bank with the day's receipts. As a matter of fact, Ryan wouldn't be surprised if the robbery had been coordinated with this rendezvous in mind, just for kicks—he put nothing past the perversity of crooks. But the gang also got lucky. The neighborhood beat cop who passed by at about the same time each day—4:35 P.M.—had coincidentally been called over to Madison Avenue to investigate a traffic accident. Ryan had to admit that a certain amount of dumb luck often accompanied this kind of bravado. But the Assistant Chief Inspector was good at spoiling the luck of thieves. At an age when he should have been retired to Daytona Beach, sixty-three-year-old Ryan still got a charge cracking tough cases. Take the Rubel armored car stickup. It took five years to solve, but he and his cops saw it through. What could be better than that?

A plainclothes detective behind the tellers' cage beckoned to the Assistant Chief Inspector. As Ryan walked behind the waist-high gate, he noted the empty cash drawers hanging open. These boys were thorough. The detective who had called him crouched beside an open cabinet door under the marble counter, his face as blank as a sidewalk. A paperbound stack of crisp bills, must have been $10,000, sat untouched on a shelf inside. How about that, Ryan said. Maybe these guys aren't so thorough after all. He clapped the detective on the shoulder, told him to make a note, and get the manager. Ryan wouldn't have been shocked to find that the officer had smoothly palmed the money into a jacket pocket. A pile of cash—almost twice a detective's annual salary—was a great temptation, the loss easy enough to blame on the thieves. Still, maybe it boded well for the investigation—one honest cop to another.

In the city's early years, that much integrity was a rare virtue.

————————

From the late 1800s through the first decades of the twentieth century, the story of New York City was pockmarked by one scandal after another, as policemen and crooks, politicians and clergymen battled for control of the streets. When Ryan became a policeman in 1903—the same year as his future commissioner—the force was still recovering from one of the most humiliating and bizarre corruption scandals in its fifty-nine-year history: the Lexow Committee's investigation into police corruption in a midtown red-light district known as the Tenderloin. Politically sponsored graft and vice were nothing new in America's largest city, certainly. For nearly a century, Tammany Hall had run New York City as its own private game preserve. At its best, Tammany catered to the street-level needs of millions of hardworking New Yorkers, especially new immigrants, through its social wing, the Tammany Society. But the real power was its political organization, the New York County Democratic committee, which had dominated city politics since the early 1800s. Back then, when Irish immigrants flooded into the city, sparking violent reactions from the hyper-patriotic, nativist Know-Nothings, Tammany Hall provided lawyers to the immigrants, who were undoubtedly blamed when the clashes got bloody. Tammany even helped the Irish obtain naturalization papers, cutting days of red tape off the allotted waiting period. The city bosses asked only that those they helped, help them in return—by constantly voting Democratic, as many times as necessary.

Buying voter loyalty with handouts, Tammany came to control New York's twenty-two electoral divisions, known as wards. Filling city government with its own partisans was a payoff relay for crony advancement and forged a closed-mouthed inner guard that protected the city fiefdom from Albany's meddlesome inspectors. Calls for reform typically went unanswered. The infamous "Boss" Tweed, Tammany's diamond-loving, mid-nineteenth-century leader, used to pay political opponents thousands of dollars to stay home when reform measures came up for vote in the state senate. The corrupt system was deep-rooted, with power netted in a briar patch of deception and violence. Tammany wielded the mostly Irish police force, for instance, as its own private shillelagh, protecting the profitable sex industry and other vice rings.

But in 1892, the Tammany "tiger" was wounded by an unlikely crusader: a middle-aged Presbyterian minister named Charles H. Parkhurst. Reverend Parkhurst's zeal touched off a firestorm of revelations that not only exposed the seamy activities playing out on the streets but also led to a sensational investigation that captivated the entire nation. The reverend's mission ultimately paved the way to the defeat of the Tammany mayor in the next election.

Parkhurst started it all one February Sunday when he climbed the pulpit at the Madison Square Presbyterian Church with heated eyes and a shocking new text for his sermon: the police-sanctioned sex trade. Tall and thin, his chin sharp with a peppery Vandyke, and his curly gray hair swept back around his high collar, Parkhurst drew gasps from his respectable congregation just one minute into his sermon. He told them bluntly why their city was rotten to the core. The pastor blamed the mayor, the district attorney, and the Tammany-controlled New York police force for allowing—and even profiting from—all manner of vice. A reporter for Joseph Pulitzer's *New York World* newspaper was seated among the stunned faithful. He was attending services that Sunday on

his editor's orders, acting on an anonymous tip. Now, the reporter scribbled fast to catch the fire and brimstone accusations in a small pocket
notebook. The story hit the front pages the next day.

As the city buzzed, Tammany circled its wagons. Nobody, certainly
not a starchy prig like Parkhurst, made public accusations like that about
the mayor and district attorney and got away with it. The reverend was
summoned before a hastily convened grand jury and ordered to show
proof that the city government used the police department to protect the
sex trade. Parkhurst had none, other than what he experienced living a few
blocks from the Tenderloin district, seeing with his own eyes and hearing
with his own ears, every single day, the lewd solicitations whispered from
the doorway shadows. Obviously rampant debauchery was condoned. You
only needed to stroll the blocks of the Nineteenth Precinct, between Fifth
and Seventh Avenues, from Twenty-fourth to Forty-second Streets, to see
that the Tenderloin was an open market—especially after sunset when the
city's new electric street lights cast a jaundiced glow over the nightly flesh
trade. The grand jury, however, dismissed the reverend for making allega-
tions without legal evidence.

Mortified but undaunted by the grand jury's snub, Parkhurst sought
the advice of his friend, David Whitney, the head of the Society for the
Prevention of Crime. Whitney told Parkhurst that if he had no specific
evidence of widespread vice and corruption, he should go out and get
some. Whitney suggested that the pastor tour the city's underbelly.
Whitney even had the perfect guide for the reverend's undercover
odyssey, a rugged and mustachioed private eye named Charlie Gardner,
who would serve as chaperone for $6 a night. For two weeks, Parkhurst,
Whitney, and Gardner posed as playboys, nightly roaming the city's
pleasure houses and saloons. In multicultural New York at the turn of the
last century, many brothels specialized in nationality or ethnicity—there
were German Freudenhaus, French boudoirs, and Chinese opium dens.
The trio sampled them all on their evening rounds—looking but not
touching, at least in Parkhurst's case. On the final night of their tour, and
much too close to home, the reverend saw enough. In a perfumed bor-
dello just three blocks from his church he watched, red-faced and scowl-
ing, while a bowler-hatted Gardner played leapfrog in a lacy boudoir

with three naked women. Dumbfounded, feeling foolish, and maybe shocked by his own illicit stirrings, Reverend Parkhurst had all the evidence he needed.

That Sunday and the next, Parkhurst's sermons fumed from the pulpit. The reverend described how, like Dante, he had descended "Down into the disgusting depths of this Tammany-debauched town." He demanded that authorities shake off their complacency. The congregation spilled out onto the church steps, straining for every word. The *World* reprinted Parkhurst's salacious catalog of horrors and saw its editions fly off the newsstands. The publicity assault continued for months, while Tammany Hall, feigning reform, counterpunched with one ineffectual grand jury after another. Cynical New Yorkers, jaded by decades of corruption, were outraged at last. The New York Chamber of Commerce, worried about the city's reputation—not to mention members' own wallets—demanded a state investigation. And early in 1894, the Lexow Committee (led by State Senator Clarence Lexow) was finally sworn in.

The committee held seventy-four sessions, called almost seven hundred witnesses, including the police commissioner, and amassed well over ten thousand pages of sworn testimony. The result was a scathing exposé of police corruption, telegraphed across the country by the *New York World*. Thirteen-year-old Fiorello LaGuardia, living out in the Arizona Territory with his military family, became obsessed with the story, racing to the country drugstore for every national edition, later claiming his hatred of corruption started then. Millions of readers learned how madams paid the police $35 to $50 every month to operate freely, and how a new precinct captain would receive a $500 gift from the local brothel, plus a $150 Christmas bonus. One madam even testified to having shelled out $35,000 a year to her local precinct. As the revelations echoed across the nation, the New York City police became synonymous with graft. Vaudeville comics had only to turn their backs, open their hands, and wiggle their fingers to send audiences howling with recognition.

One individual in particular seemed to embody the corrupt system: police inspector Alexander Williams. A powerfully built former ship's carpenter, with a thick handlebar mustache and close-cropped dark hair,

Williams was nicknamed "Clubber" for his expertise with a nightstick and the joy he took in using it to enforce the law. Asked by the Lexow Committee to explain a Connecticut country house, a yacht, and several large bank accounts on his policeman's salary, Clubber drew a roughened forefinger across the tips of his mustache and paused. Thrift, he told them, with a level gaze. Thrift, and wise investments in Japanese real estate.

Clubber Williams wasn't the least ashamed of his wealth. With what he'd paid out for advancement over the years, he felt he'd earned his payback. In fact, the Lexow Committee, more than any other exposé up to its time, laid wide open Tammany Hall's destructive system of patronage. Eighty-five percent of all appointments to the police force were Tammany recommendations. An ambitious young man needed only to fork over the requisite $300 admittance fee. To move up through the ranks took more cash. Patrolmen paid $2,500 for promotion to sergeant; $10,000 to $15,000 to advance to captain; and upwards of $20,000 to become an inspector. The only way to afford advancement, in other words, was to keep a wide-open palm. As Williams winked to his fellows when assigned to the profitable Nineteenth Precinct, "I've had nothing but chuck steaks for a long time. Now I'm going to get me a little of the tenderloin."

The Lexow Committee report was scalding. Seventy indictments were handed down on twenty captains, three inspectors, and numerous former officers, and commissioners. Tammany Hall's influence was rich, though. Despite a number of convictions, higher courts overturned many of them. Some indicted officers were even returned to duty. No action whatsoever was brought against Clubber Williams. But the old seaman must have sensed a change in the wind. He retired within the year and joined the insurance business, where he added millions more to his bank accounts.

As for Reverend Parkhurst, reformers were pleased with his hard work, despite the mixed results. He had dented Tammany Hall's armor—the Tammany mayor was defeated in the next election, and a feisty young blueblood, Theodore Roosevelt, was named to the police commission. Officially at least, police promotions were now based on merit, rather than graft. Many thankful crusaders wanted to raise an arch to Parkhurst's honor in Madison Square Park; the most grateful, though, proclaimed that a more fitting tribute would be to rename the city "Parkhurst."

Lexow wasn't the end of New York's ordeal, however. In fact, to some, it seemed to be just the beginning. Five years later, in 1899, the Mazet Commission was ordered by the state to dig into more charges of corruption in city government, this time centered on the bribes that greased the city machinery. Some indictments were handed down. But soon it appeared certain that Tammany would continue to resist change, and reform stalled.

Rookie patrolmen like John J. Ryan quickly learned the ropes in the post-Lexow police department. A promotion required hard work, not just cash. But there was never a lack of temptation in New York City. The city's criminal activity had grown increasingly complex and violent, especially after 1920 when Prohibition became the law and crime exploded nationwide. The line between cops and robbers, good guys and bad—hardly ever clear—had blurred altogether, like a chalk outline in the rain. Honest cops of the Ryan variety trod warily. The policeman's job was to uphold the law, no matter how that law was received—and that was the problem.

In 1920, ratification of the Eighteenth Amendment outlawed alcohol. But rather than abolishing liquor consumption, Prohibition merely drove it underground. Rarely had a constitutional amendment been so flouted. Bootleg liquor and beer were sold from speakeasies hidden behind mom-and-pop storefronts and darkened basement doors with grilled peepholes and secret passwords. A drink was so desirable, so in vogue, that ordinary citizens concocted private stashes in bedroom and bathroom stills. The thirst made tipsy accomplices of millions.

By 1925, about the time Whitey Riordan was stealing his first candy bar, profits from the steady stream of illegal liquor coursing through the country generated a subterranean economy worth at least $40 million annually. Criminal syndicates, among the most famous of them Al Capone's in Chicago and Dutch Schultz's in New York, orchestrated the manufacture and widespread distribution of alcohol, steering smuggling routes that crisscrossed America, under the paid protection of political bosses. The profits not only bought influence but supported the garish lifestyles of brawling street toughs. Midwestern politicians, attending the wedding of Al Capone's sister, watched the tuxedoed gangster wheel out a nine-foot-tall cake for the beaming bride. In New York City, a gambling racket that brought in $35,000 a day paid for Dutch Schultz's $300 suits—complete with powder-blue vest and spats. "Lucky" Luciano, by then the head of the Unione Siciliane—America's early Mafia—and running his bootlegging and prostitution empires from a well-protected, high-rise suite at the East Side Barbizon Plaza, bragged about paying $10,000 to $20,000 a week to New York police headquarters. By comparison, federal agents assigned to enforce the Eighteenth Amendment did so on little more than $2,000 a year. Given the raucous disregard in which the law was held, and the obscene sums changing hands, the temptation of graft was overwhelming for many policemen, especially as the economic good times of the 1920s soured.

By the early '30s, the hard times seemed never ending. Four area hospitals reported ninety-five deaths by starvation in 1931, as the Great Depression deepened and breadlines shuffled along the sidewalks. In 1932, New York's worst year of the catastrophe, nearly sixteen hundred people killed themselves—the most suicides in more than three decades. It was hard to stay honest in such dispiriting times, when the only people riding around in luxury were the gamblers and the crooks, and the obvious choice seemed between the ledge and the gun.

Whitey Riordan and Patches Waters, among thousands of others kicking over corner fruit stands in the 1920s and '30s, saw crime as the way out, gangster riches as the instant wealth that would fumigate sour tenement smells. They weren't the only ones. A criminal fury swept the whole country, both cities and plains, flaring up in Prohibition's dry years and licking out through the dustbowls of the Great Depression. While immigrant urban kingpins and their every-vice empires catered to mass appetites, homegrown rural bandits like John Dillinger, "Baby Face" Nelson, and Bonnie and Clyde machine-gunned their way from Ohio to Arizona, Wisconsin to Oklahoma, looking out for their own. Newspaper pages and newsreel footage of the mayhem excited the public's imagination. Hollywood picked up the cue, and the gangster's golden age was reflected on movie screens, but less in glorification than as tragic morality play in which violent means inevitably led to violent death. The studios even made it official—Hollywood's 1933 Production Code barred the filming of any screenplay based on John Dillinger, lest audiences get the wrong idea.

But despite Hollywood's best intentions, something about the flickering images in a darkened theater invited moviegoers to identify with the outlaws, anyway—the many young adults, trying to crawl out from under poverty's thumb; the ragtag city kids, the lowest of the low, with little more to look forward to than the back of a father's hand or the beat cop's club. They might not have 25¢ for admission, but they could sneak into the Forty-second Street picture palaces, hunker down in the popcorn-scented dark, and watch Edward G. Robinson and James Cagney shoot it out in tailored, three-piece suits. Never mind that the bad guy always died bullet-riddled in the street—Whitey and the others likely saw the rich potential shining in Cagney's sneer, and lots of them would reach for a gun.

One sultry August night in 1930, a missing persons report sparked the last, and biggest, shake-up in Tammany's New York. A state supreme court judge, Joseph Force Crater—last seen waving from the back of a darkened taxicab on West Forty-fifth Street—disappeared without a trace. When the resulting investigation uncovered a $22,000 bank deposit, a transaction that coincided with Crater's taking the bench, the officials expanded their case to probe Tammany's buying and selling of judgeships in New York City. As part of the investigation, a state supreme court jurist, the aristocratic Samuel Seabury, was commissioned that same month to examine the city's lower criminal court, the magistrates court in Foley Square.

The ugly headlines—detailing yet another police-sponsored blackmailing sex scheme, in addition to all the judicial corruption—also splashed badly on New York's playboy mayor, the Tammany-installed James J. Walker. First elected in 1926, and the laughing face of high-living, pre-Crash New York, the two-term Mayor Walker was still going strong in the depths of the early Depression. Nicknamed "Beau," this was the willowy dandy who in his youth had penned the Tin Pan Alley ditty "Will You Love Me in December as You Do in May?" before sauntering into law school. The same mayor who sported neat three-piece suits in pastel shades, a silver flask of the finest bootleg in a side pocket, while out-of-work New Yorkers frayed on the sidewalks. Tales of judges for hire, and a sex scandal on his watch, seemed to tip many New Yorkers' patience for Walker's grinning high jinks.

Not surprisingly, there were plenty. Besides a secret safe-deposit box, with checks worth more than a quarter of a million dollars from a businessman hoping for city contracts, Seabury's investigators found more. Fanning out across the country, they discovered that the frivolous Walker was the front man for a cabal of Tammany politicians and out-of-state businessmen looking for quick millions in public money. Known as the Equitable Coach Company, the profiteers hatched a $20-million scheme to control New York City's municipal bus service, which was being phased in to replace the old trolley cars dismantled at the end of the 1920s. The trifling mayor may not have known all the particulars—he wasn't crafty or mean-spirited so much as stubbornly fun-loving. But even he must have suspected the legality of a slush fund that financed his extended European tours. Judge Seabury had all he needed.

On a bright May morning in 1932, thousands of New Yorkers cheered their scoundrel mayor as he mounted the courthouse steps in Foley Square. Tammany loyalty still ran deep. The patrician Seabury, his brass-handled cane clicking alongside as he climbed through the same crowd, ignored the hisses spat his way. Mayor Walker took the witness stand decked all in blue ("Little Boy Blue is about to blow his horn—or his top!" Walker cracked to his valet the morning of his testimony). Seabury scoffed at an aide's warning not to look the mayor directly in the eye while questioning him because Walker was such a charmer that his arched stare would confound the thoughtful judge. But Seabury took no chances and stood to the side of the witness stand just in case. In a two-day exchange that the *New York Times* headlined "A Prize Fight," the adversaries tangled before a packed courtroom. But despite Beau James's brio, by the end of Seabury's relentless examination, it was clear that the mayor's career was at an end. He had become an embarrassing liability to the state governor, Franklin Roosevelt, who was preparing for the Democratic presidential nomination. While the governor needed the Tammany machine, with his weakened legs in a brace he needed a strong national face even more, without the blemish of a Walker administration. Mayor Jimmy Walker hung on through the summer, but he must have known his time had come. In early September, as the summer heat began to fade, New York City's last Tammany mayor waved the white flag and resigned.

In 1934, the diminutive Mayor Fiorello LaGuardia gusted into office declaring, "What I'm going to do is, I'm going to grab every tinhorn gambler in the city of New York by the scruff of the neck and throw him over into New Jersey!" The dynamic reformer had the office at last, and he wasted no time. He appointed the upright Lewis J. Valentine as police commissioner, with explicit instructions to do whatever it took to put an end to gangster rule. Valentine, long exiled to the outer precincts for zealously investigating dirty cops, was finally returned to favor and seized the assignment with both fists. Incensed by the prim appearance of one suspected murderer in the lineup before him, Valentine told his men, "Blood should be smeared all over that man's velvet collar." The gloves, in other words, were off. John J. Ryan, in sympathetic company, was newly minted as deputy inspector that same year. Officially, at least, a new day had dawned.

But weary New Yorkers likely would believe that when they saw it. For certain kids, exiting the movie house instead of the school door, squinting in the afternoon light, and wondering what next, the storms of corruption beating about the city government, year after year, justified their own petty crimes. Why should they try so hard when the cops collaring you, the judge staring you down—the very mayor himself—were literally a bunch of crooks and pimps?

Whitey Riordan may not have known all the details of the Walker scandals, but he had two clear eyes. He passed a newsstand every day on his way to nowhere, with enough of the classroom in him so that a glance at the headlines told him all he needed to know. The old mayor's a crook? More power to him. The new mayor's going to clean up the city? Sure he is.

Meanwhile, there's a cash register at the A&P on Ninth Avenue or a wallet in the pocket of the swell on the corner. Whitey figured he'd take them.

━━━━━

CHAPTER THREE

HELL'S CHILDREN

O N TUESDAY, MAY 16, 1939, the day after the Harlem Con Ed robbery, the front pages of New York City's daily papers broadcast the heist
as one of the biggest holdups of the year. "6 THUGS GET $35,000 IN CON ED
RAID," the tabloid *Daily News* trumpeted with customary overstatement,
while the more conservative *Herald Tribune* put the estimated take at
$10,000. But the *Tribune* still put the story front page, second column—
right between Nazi aggression in Poland and the fiery standoff in Harlan,
Kentucky, pitting striking coal miners against National Guardsmen.
Even the *New York Times* weighed in with a breathless front-page double-
boxed headline: "5 GUNMEN . . . SUBDUE 100 . . . INVADE EDISON BRANCH
AND ESCAPE WITH LOOT IN 3 MINUTES—WOMAN TELLER FAINTS."
Whether or not the police had leaked their suspicions, the reporters had all
come to the same conclusion—the Shopping Bag Gang had struck again.

In the coming days, the best that newsmen could gather was that
"clews [are] scant in Edison hold-up." The suspects had vanished. Investigators didn't need a crystal ball to know where to start looking, though.
Following the lead of witness descriptions and matching them against
mug shots, police would come to focus on the mainstay criminal digs—
the Lower East Side, for one, and definitely the Middle West Side
neighborhood of Hell's Kitchen. As any street cop could tell you, there
were more crooks per square inch in Hell's Kitchen than anywhere else in
the city.

After a job, the bandits would have known to lay low. Lulu was probably safe enough back in New Jersey with his wife; but he also kept an apartment on West 107th Street for such occasions. Willie Athalias would have shacked up with his girlfriend on 155th Street, a dime-a-dance gal named Mae Ruggles, who had been hiding Willie from the police off and on for the past few years. Rusty and Mac had connections upstate. Patches likely continued the routine of his pinball rounds—collecting his nickels so nobody would notice an absence. And Whitey went back to work on the docks, stevedoring on Pier 90 at the end of Fiftieth Street, just down the block from where he grew up. With all the cops asking questions on the waterfront, he was safest surrounded by friends, best hidden in plain sight. If anyone knew how to stay camouflaged in Hell's Kitchen, it was Whitey Riordan. Hell's Kitchen was home turf. Its traditions—both good and bad—of clan loyalty and criminal aspirations were as familiar to him as the saint's medallion he wore on a chain around his neck, or the blue steel of the .38 in his hand.

Whitey was the third child of Irish immigrants, born in February 1915. His parents, John Riordan and Elizabeth Conty, had both arrived in New York in 1888—not necessarily together—at the crest of the nineteenth century's immigrant wave. When he first settled in Hell's Kitchen, John Riordan was a young man in his twenties; Elizabeth was a child of eleven. Both of their mothers' names were O'Connor, but it's unknown if John and Elizabeth were in any way related, as first or second cousins, perhaps. The evidence is suggestive only—besides arriving the same year into large families, both the Riordan and the O'Connor clans have origins in Ireland's County Cork. The newcomers were likely welcomed to their strange, bewildering city by the extended families who preceded them, and who were themselves helped by the Tammany machine.

Despite the eighteen-year age difference, once the couple married—sometime around 1908—John and Elizabeth created a fertile union. They produced five children: Margaret, John, Mary, Patrick Joseph, and Andrew. Whitey's first distinction, or lack thereof, was that his siblings were given the significant family names—Margaret and Andrew, namesakes of paternal grandparents; Mary and John, namesakes of maternal grandparents. It seems as if from birth, the generic name "Patrick Joseph" isolated Whitey from his lineage and destined him to navigate a course of his own.

Large Irish Catholic families were almost cliché—many children were like wealth to the poor, an expression of grace. But tragedy was ever present in slums like Hell's Kitchen. Mary Riordan died in 1916, possibly as a newborn—no other date but the year of her death is etched on the family headstone. The child's passing expressed an all-too-common event. Throughout the first decades of the twentieth century, Hell's Kitchen held fast to its reputation as New York City's worst ghetto, with record-breaking mortality rates. In fact, even as late as 1939—the year of the Con Ed heist—*The WPA Guide to New York City* described the neighborhood as still containing "the largest group of underprivileged families in the city" and stated that, according to city health center statistics, Hell's Kitchen had "the highest general mortality rate in the city, and ranks first in pneumonia and cancer, second in tuberculosis, and third in infant mortality." For families like the Riordans, every year in which a child grew older there was a year on which the luck of the Irish smiled.

Hell's Kitchen held other dangers besides disease. Since the 1800s the West Side had spawned some of the most notorious criminals in the city's history. By the time the Riordans arrived, the roughly thirty-block area of Hell's Kitchen had already cemented its well-deserved reputation as a lair of hoodlums. Brutal living conditions in the mid-nineteenth century had disintegrated many immigrant families, filling the streets with abandoned children. Inhabiting tenement basements and coal cellars, thousands of homeless boys and girls scavenging through the mud took root as the neighborhood's first gangs, with names like the Gophers—so called for their hidden basement nests—and the cocaine-fueled Hudson Dusters. These substitute families roamed the region at will in the mid-to-late 1800s, robbing and murdering citizens, pillaging businesses, and fighting one another for supremacy.

The Gophers, variously led by a rogues' gallery of thugs with aliases like Stumpy Malarkey and Goo Goo Knox, were the largest and most powerful of the Hell's Kitchen gangs. Their most colorful leader, the tubercular "One-Lung" Curran, ruled the gang with a distinctly individual nerve. One-Lung's claim to fame was blackjacking a patrolman, stealing his blue-wool uniform overcoat, and giving it to his girlfriend, who custom-tailored it into a fetching wrap and caused a sensation. The fashion proved so popular among the neighborhood molls that Gophers up and down the blocks ambushed cops for their coats. The fad didn't end until policemen began to patrol the streets in nightstick-swinging packs.

The Gophers even had a fearsome women's auxiliary, nicknamed the Battle Row Ladies' Social and Athletic Club and bossed by the bat-wielding Battle Annie. Following in the hobnailed boot steps of her predecessors, unholy terrors like Hell Cat Maggie and Sadie the Goat, Battle Annie preferred the pointed stick to the delicate word while prowling her territory along Thirty-ninth Street, between Tenth and Eleventh Avenues. She gave tutorials in street fighting and ran a profitable sideline hiring out burly women to agitate and fight on both sides of labor disputes.

The constant supply of goods shuttling daily through the area's rail lines, freight yards, and waterfront assured the gangs steady plunder. But the wild success of even the most incidental of the Hell's Kitchen gangs proved to be the criminals' undoing. After decades of near anarchic lawlessness manipulated by Tammany politicians who hired the thugs to ensure the vote, the railroads and other exasperated corporate interests finally took matters into their own hands. If lawful due process was compromised, they reasoned, they would organize their own justice system. In the early 1900s, the railroads created an informal, ad hoc security force made up of many former policemen eager to right old wrongs.

Freed from the restraints imposed by corrupt superiors and emboldened by the railroads' full support, the vigilantes fought back with a vengeance. As one cheerful combatant boasted, the gangsters were clubbed "from hell to breakfast." When the gangs responded with guns, the security guards, well trained in firearms, aimed back with precision, sending the crooks to hospitals and morgues. Those not killed or wounded were rounded up and sent to Sing Sing. Their stranglehold on the neighborhood, and especially on the New York Central Railroad, was broken. And although the legendary street gangs were not completely eliminated—

were in fact scattered, only to resurrect in a more organized form during Prohibition, run by bootleggers like Owney Madden and Dutch Schultz— their nineteenth-century heyday was only a memory by 1910.

Hell's Kitchen hadn't always been so violent. In fact, from colonial times, when the Dutch and English competed over Manhattan Island, up until the early 1800s, New Yorkers considered the Middle West Side a paradise. Gurgling streams bordered lush fields that rippled north from present-day West Fourteenth Street all the way to 125th. The Dutch named the rolling meadows Bloemendael, "Vale of Flowers," and the grasslands became the playground of well-to-do coaching parties that rattled along the quiet lanes, spreading picnic baskets brookside.

Anglicized to Bloomingdale by the eighteenth century, the pastures were divided into private farms as the city grew northward and demand for produce increased. Some families, of course, were more successful than others in reaping a living from the land, and the economic transition then underway from agriculture to industry put added pressures on the farmers. And there was always ready money in the new city when a farm foreclosure threatened.

By 1800, a German immigrant named John Jacob Astor, a former butcher's helper, was making a fortune in Canadian furs. Memorialized in a Gilbert Stuart portrait, Astor's coal bright eyes, bloodless lips, and tapered chin are the picture of avarice, and he proved as shrewd a manipulator as he looked. Cleverly avoiding the British tariffs in place, and cutting out the middlemen, Astor made personal buying expeditions to Montreal and then sold his furs direct to the manufacturers. In one deal for Chinese tea and spices, he traded over thirty thousand sealskins and more than a thousand beaver pelts. He then made a calculation that would change the landscape of New York's West Side. With a keen eye on the future, Astor rolled the profits from the Chinese deal, about $184,000, into his true calling—real estate. He avoided investment in existing structures, instead plowing the fortune into building lots sandwiched between Broadway and the Hudson, which he then leased to eager developers. Astor had perfectly sized up the financial promise of the spreading city's demand for cheap housing.

In 1803, when one of the largest tracts foreclosed—the West Side's lovely, and aptly named, Eden Farm—Astor smelled a beautiful opportunity. The "landlord of New York," as the furrier was becoming known, grabbed the parcel for $25,000, a high price for the time but a pittance to a man of Astor's means. In time, it would cash out as a remarkable bargain.

Within sixty years, another millionaire, shipping entrepreneur Commodore Cornelius Vanderbilt, cut his own designs on the neighborhood. Vanderbilt made his first fortune at eighteen, ferrying supplies to American garrisons around New York in the War of 1812, and he compounded that wealth by setting a price and shuttling panicked refugees from the 1832 cholera epidemic across Long Island Sound by steamboat. Now, he shifted his focus, investing heavily in the newfangled railroads fuming across the Manhattan countryside. The commodore would have little faith in the city's future subway systems—open water and spacious land were his blank canvas. But he saw sure potential in the above-ground iron horses.

In the 1850s, he extended a branch of the rail line between East Albany and New York City down Manhattan's west side, creating the Hudson River Railroad. The access caused a new building boom on the subdivided fields of old Bloomingdale. Astor was gone two years by then—the richest man in America when he died in 1848, with a $20-million fortune—but he surely would have been right in there with his surveyor's chain. The old German's lots expanded further, becoming row after row of squalid three-, four-, and five-story brick tenements, cheaply constructed by bottom-line developers. The buildings congested the blocks between Eighth and Tenth Avenues, from the West Twenties to the West Fifties. By the late 1800s, Astor's and Vanderbilt's commercial pursuits had transformed the pastoral beauty of Eden Farm into Hell's Kitchen.

The origins of the neighborhood's diabolical name are as disputed as the area's boundaries. One popular legend says the nickname was coined by two "battle weary" patrolmen during a bloody nineteenth-century riot at West Thirty-ninth Street and Tenth Avenue. ("This place is hell itself," the younger man told his partner. "Hell's a mild climate," his mate replied. "This is Hell's Kitchen.") Another account claims that the moniker came from a bandits' hideout that stood on a rocky outcrop at the same intersection. Still another insists the name is taken from a similarly rough section in London. Whatever the source, a more suitable name for this ever-widening and dangerous place could scarcely have been imagined.

As the nineteenth century chugged along, screeching steel wheels displaced the cows lowing in pastures; limekilns, distilleries, and soap factories were strewn haphazardly beside the railroad tracks, like cinders kicked up in the locomotives' wake; and docks tacked northward up from the Battery, tightly stitching the neighborhood to the North River, as the Hudson was then known. Hell's Kitchen didn't just grow through the 1800s, it metastasized. And like a malignancy, its definitions were often unclear. Opinions clashed, often violently, on exactly where the boundaries were. And while you may have defended with fists and boots your interpretation of the borders, there was no denying your senses.

By the turn of the century, a long-time resident might have closed his eyes and found his way around the crowded streets merely by following his nose—from the urban stockyards just beyond the region's northernmost fringes at West Sixtieth Street, to the stinking abattoirs on Forty-second Street and south; from the greasepaint and powder of the glittering theater district across the eastern boundary, all the way west to the effluent North River. A blind wanderer might have been blown off course by the many breweries and brickyards, gashouses and glue factories spread throughout the neighborhood, each with its own specific malodor. But he would still generally know where he was—Hell's Kitchen brewed its own distinct miasma.

The area was marked by a medley of noise as well. The street-level freight train that rumbled up and down Eleventh Avenue was the most notorious of the clattering rail lines girding the district. To avoid accidents en route, a horseman preceded the train, shouting and waving a red flag. Nevertheless, he often failed to prevent screaming collisions with pedestrians and horse-drawn wagons; the many accidents earned the thoroughfare the nickname "Death Avenue." Even into the 1920s, neighing, clanking horse carts were hard to avoid. They clopped everywhere, carrying supplies to market, produce from the factories, and polyglot crews to and from work sites—and like the Eleventh Avenue freight train's iconic cowboy, they linked this modern industrial city to its rustic past.

Besides the deadly freight, there was the less dangerous but equally earsplitting Ninth Avenue Elevated, transporting passengers at a safe remove from the perils below. Opened in 1871, the steam-powered El train thundered three stories above the dismal streets, showering side-walk pedestrians with soot and burning cinders, and rattling flush against the tenement facades in some places. It wasn't the lack of privacy that infuriated the apartment residents so much as the hot oil spraying out as the trains rattled past. The fares were affordable—10¢ a ride, the tickets threaded with silk to prevent counterfeiting—and Hell's Kitchen resi-dents would cram the Forty-second Street station, as crowded in the late nineteenth century as it is today.

Adding to the discomfort and the din were the many industries attracted to the area's low rents and cheap labor. Foundries and sawmills, stonecutters and construction companies, all were edged and angled against the tenement rows. And like phantoms from the area's vanquished rural past, stray goats wandered through the cobbled streets, wreaking havoc with merchants and greengrocers. The smoke and flames of the mercan-tile powers unleashed by Astor, Vanderbilt, and others consumed every square inch of Hell's Kitchen by the turn of the twentieth century.

But the Irish called it home.

———————

Escaping the disastrous Potato Famine blighting the Emerald Isle, the Irish had dominated Hell's Kitchen since the 1840s. They'd been coming to America for decades, of course, fighting it out in the 1820s with the homegrown Know-Nothings in the Five Points neighborhood down-town. But the Famine sent them across the ocean in droves, rural peas-ants afoot in a clanging city. They settled on the West Side, crowding into the tenements tilting block after block, and took whatever jobs they could find in the factories and on the docks. Within decades, the cramped, tubercular slums housed some three hundred fifty thousand inhabitants.

Living conditions were appalling, and charities and churches made periodic calls for reform. The demands led to the creation of the first municipal Board of Health after the Civil War. But the meager regulations imposed on the slum landlords—such as requiring a water closet or an outhouse for every twenty residents, and transoms for unventilated rooms—did little to alleviate the epidemics of cholera and smallpox that repeatedly devastated the neighborhood. In fact, poverty and overcrowding were so entrenched that Hell's Kitchen residents saw little improvement in their living conditions over the next fifty years. For example, in 1914, one year before Whitey Riordan's birth, a sociological study underwritten by the charitable Russell Sage Foundation described the district's stubborn poverty as "a spider's web." The inquiry found: "[I]n street after street are the same crowded and unsanitary tenements; the same untended groups of children playing; the same rough men gathered round the stores and saloons on the avenue; the same sluggish women grouped on the steps of the tenements in the cross streets . . . square, dull, monotonous ugliness, much dirt, and a great deal of apathy." Nineteenth-century louts like One-Lung Curran would have felt quite at home.

But the study couldn't account for the equally tenacious immigrant will to survive. Over the years, the Hell's Kitchen Irish gained control of an important local economic segment—the waterfront. Pressed along the riverside, their large numbers had come to dominate the neighborhood docks, an insular world thick with pitch and the shipping industry's steady thump and whir of moving cargo. Through close-knit—and closed-mouthed—factions, Irishmen linked by blood and fealty controlled particular docks up and down the North River, and ruled them like private fiefdoms. Local gang wars of power and attrition broke out regularly, but the ferment remained within the greater family. The piers in all their turmoil became a tradition and a way of life for many in Hell's Kitchen. When Patrick Joseph "Whitey" Riordan beat the odds and survived to childhood, he entered a world whose cobbled streets and neatly bricked alleys twisted and turned but always led back to the waterfront.

———————

Eighty years after serving as one of the Riordan family's first tenement homes, a building on Tenth Avenue boasts a trendy, ground-floor bistro

that sets out white tables for its sidewalk café. Lunch for two runs about
30 bucks, what Whitey's father John made in a lucky week. The narrow
apartment upstairs was probably typical for Hell's Kitchen: three or four
rooms maximum, kitchen, dining and sitting room combined, two bedrooms at most. Now, the *New York Times* real estate listings boast, "Hell's
Kitchen 1 Bedrooms—Full Service For Under A Million." Times have
changed.

In pre–World War I Hell's Kitchen, the tenement walls—plaster,
wood, brick—would have barely shielded the family from the noisy,
smoking city beyond. The whole house rang with banging doors, shouts,
and crying children. It was a tumultuous beginning but typical of the
thousands of other Hell's Kitchen Irish—not only the Riordans but also
the Clintons, the Leahys, the McCabes, the Beadles, and the St. Johns.
Families whose children palled around and fought one another on the
streets, whose parents knew the neighborhood's other denizens by sight
as well as by reputation.

On his death certificate, Whitey's father John is listed simply as a
"laborer." Like other immigrants, John Riordan would have been part of
the army of workers who scratched out a living in the neighborhood's factory bays and railroad yards and especially on the docks. Dock work was
particularly fickle, though, dependent not only on local, national, and foreign economies, but on the weather and tides, too. Add on the lopsided
ratio of a large workforce and capricious need, and longshoring was a pre-
carious business. But if it was what you knew, it was what you did.

Men looking for work made the shape-up on the pier every morning
at 7:55. They jostled anxiously in a semicircle with hundreds of other
longshoremen from around the city while the boss stevedore chose the
twenty-man loading crews. The shape-up, a hiring system unchanged
since Melville's time, guaranteed a vast labor pool, at least two men for
each job, which benefited the shipping companies and the contract hirers
at the expense of the workers. Crews loaded and unloaded cargo tonnages
by hand—everything from Oregon apples to barrels of oil to scrap iron.
With hand hooks, longshoremen hefted sacks of coffee and sugar;
winches lifted cotton bales on whirring iron cables; and chained slings
carried pallets of refrigerated goods and pig iron out of the ships' holds

and swung them onto the docks. During the First World War, the pay had jumped to 75¢ an hour for this heavy duty, up from 35¢ just a few years before. You could make a living on the docks, but you needed to get in good with the hiring boss if you wanted steady work. Otherwise, with all the variables, you could barely feed a growing family.

Neighborhood housewives, like Whitey's mother, Elizabeth, had to be shrewd to raise their children on the fluctuating wages their husbands brought home. A quart bottle of milk cost $2\frac{1}{2}$¢. For a few cents a pound, an enterprising housewife could keep her family fed on nutrient-rich organ meats—beef hearts, lamb kidneys, calves' liver, eyes, and brains— that butchers might otherwise discard. On Saturday nights—as their husbands hit the saloons—Hell's Kitchen housewives would head to Paddy's Market, a gathering of pushcarts under the Ninth Avenue El between Thirty-ninth and Forty-second Streets. There, local Irish women haggled and sparred with Italian and Jewish peddlers from the Lower East Side, perhaps scoring enough bargain fruits and vegetables to last until the following week. Never mind that the produce was mostly days' old castoffs from wealthier neighborhood markets, and that the dishware and household merchandise were all factory rejects, or that the very name "Paddy" was a derogatory term for poor Irish. To survive as a poor woman in New York, you had to have a thick skin. As one contemporary remarked, "No wonder we were tough in those days." It was a mother's lot in life—she kept the kids fed and washed, and the apartment scrubbed, regardless of the slanting floors or the newspaper-patched windowpanes. Even the critical Sage report claimed that the average Hell's Kitchen mother "meets her responsibilities with a matchless heroism."

For the children of Hell's Kitchen, the only playgrounds were back alleys and vacant lots. A middle child like Whitey, shouting to be heard above the commotion of a large family, might find escape in the streets from a tired father's slashing hand. Outside with his brothers John and Andrew, neighbors Johnny Clinton, Eddie and Spot Leahy, Danny Kettles, and others, Whitey Riordan and his friends sought release, pushing against the stultifying anonymity, the concrete apathy that blanketed the neighborhood. By the mid-1920s, the people of Hell's Kitchen had internalized the explosive violence that marked the old days of the Gophers and Battle Annie, the riots and the casual mayhem—but a heavy atmosphere remained. Like the residue from an ancient flood, bleakness settled over the neighborhood, the dim sediment of its roiling, lawless past.

Kids found escape from the boredom in the many surface dangers. A popular game, for instance, was to dare the Eleventh Avenue Death Train. Up until the rail's dismantling in the mid-'30s, when the street-level tracks were lowered underground, one true measure of a neighborhood boy's or girl's courage was to race along up to speed and then leap onto a passing freight car. The train may not have been tearing down the avenue, but to grab the iron rungs on a swaying railcar bucking five feet above the cobblestones on squealing metal wheels and then hoist yourself aboard demonstrated an adrenaline strength and prowess that earned instant respect.

In summertime, the waterfront provided wet relief from the steaming streets. Any August day, the splintery pilings along Twelfth Avenue were mobbed with half-naked children diving into the North River. A street kid wouldn't cringe at the rats scurrying around the rotted posts and stones—rats were everywhere, after all. He wouldn't blink at the sewer and storm drains leaking the slum's filth and the factories' corrosion, either; and he sure wouldn't think twice about the refuse from the Sanitation Department's dump at West Fifty-fourth Street and Twelfth Avenue polluting the pea-green water, already stained pink by runoff from the slaughterhouses. But a kid might give a second thought to swimming the river's width. It took peak physical condition, and a steely nerve, to leave the familiar New York shoreline behind and swim all the way to New Jersey, for the stowaway return trip aboard the ferry. "You swam with the tide," one old-timer remembered, "but you were real tired when you got there."

These afternoons built trust, and Hell's Kitchen kids forged bonds that lasted a lifetime. You came to know on whom you could rely—the arm swinging down to pull you aboard, or wrapping around you as you gasped yards from shore. Facing the everyday terrors, eagerly seeking them out to overcome them, created an unspoken language of common experience. Life in Hell's Kitchen bred its own honor code—and the willingness to take risks, to grab fear with two hands, even hold it close, because your friends were watching your back.

And what was true for childhood pranks became especially useful in crime. A closed-mouth loyalty was essential when it wasn't the trains or the river you were outwitting but the police and the world at large. In Hell's Kitchen, you didn't squeal on a friend, no matter what—not if you wanted to keep living in the neighborhood.

Of the boyhood group surrounding Whitey, not every one became a career criminal. But enough passed through rituals of adolescent thieving to become familiar with both its attractions and its costs. And some who started out as shoplifters did indeed find a lasting role in various rackets—at least once they were old enough to spend full-time on the docks. Crime was the next step up, not just bucking the neighborhood's confines but flouting the very rules on which the better-dressed society beyond Hell's Kitchen depended.

Committing crime lent its own special aura. Lots of kids dared the Death Train or the North River. But criminal acts demanded a special enthusiasm, a particular abandon that not every kid braved. If you were willing to break the law, though, you gained a brilliance that contrasted with the neighborhood's drab surroundings—your exploits were storied around the blocks and sometimes beyond. Being seen as someone big enough to take on the well-heeled world elevated you above the crowd.

Whitey could have used the boost. The Riordans weren't much to talk about, after all. Like thousands of other Hell's Kitchen families, they worked hard for the little they got. Reputations like theirs were a dime a dozen—forgotten in an instant. The real name in the neighborhood, on the lips of everybody around Tenth Avenue and West Fiftieth Street and in the surrounding blocks, was Clinton. Whitey's boyhood pal, Johnny Clinton, came from an illustrious and long line of gunmen and crooks.

Thickset and strong as a middleweight, with close-set eyes shielded by a heavy brow, Johnny Clinton had ambitions to box. He, Whitey, and the gang would have sometimes hung around the newly built Madison Square Garden on Eighth Avenue at West Fiftieth Street, on the eastern fringes of their turf. Twelve-dollar ringside seats were far beyond the means of neighborhood kids; but leaning against the brick walls and crowding the exits on Eighth and Ninth Avenues, you might catch sight—or even get the autograph—of favorite stars such as the Irish boxing greats and rivals, the urbane and literate Gene Tunney and the power-hitting heavyweight champ Jack Dempsey. Johnny Clinton's appeal, though, came less from his knowledge of boxing than from the ambient glow of his infamous folks.

Johnny's father Jack Clinton and his "uncle" Johnny Sheehan parlayed a bootlegging partnership into a dangerous and successful truck thieving operation. In the early 1920s, with bootlegging a multi-million-dollar-a-year enterprise, competing gangs earned tidy sums—and lasting enmity—hijacking one another's contraband. For protection, Clinton and Sheehan threw in with some bigger names, particularly "Legs" (Jack, to his face) Diamond. Legs was a Philadelphia transplant and a former Gopher; his Hotsy Totsy Club on Broadway and Fifty-fourth was always packed with gunmen, girlfriends, and hangers-on listening to a jazz band and drinking the finest bootleg. Diamond had gotten his start dealing heroin and gunslinging for Arnold Rothstein, the Jewish mobster reputed to have fixed the 1919 World Series. After Rothstein's murder, Legs moved on to hijacking and bootlegging. But his continuing feuds with, and repeated shootings by, rival bootleggers, especially his great nemesis Dutch Schultz, made for a risky cash flow for the Clinton gang.

Clinton and Sheehan capitalized on the "Coolidge Prosperity" of the 1920s. Automobiles, radios, electric refrigerators, and other gadgets rolling off assembly lines became the measure of success in a booming economy. Clinton and Sheehan stole trucks full of merchandise from the docks and local factories, fenced the property, and financed a small but profitable underworld living. Dodging bullets the whole time, the Clintons expanded to include occasional armed holdups in their repertoire, and they also had moved into the rackets, running a numbers operation out of their apartment on Ninth Avenue. The Clintons were successful in a hard-pressed neighborhood. And while many families looked down on the source of their relative wealth, the elder Clintons weren't stamping *their* feet in the shape-up on cold winter mornings. And some impressionable boys, noting the link between Johnny Clinton's newer, well-fitting clothes and his family's reputation, must have found the desire to emulate the outlaw clan irresistible.

On November 9, 1927, Whitey received his first conviction. He was twelve years old. Records are sealed for petty crimes committed by minors, but all subsequent documents state that Whitey's misdeed was thievery. New York City's Child Court, the precursor to today's Family Court, which heard the cases of offenders under sixteen, reduced Whitey's larceny charge to juvenile delinquency, put him on probation, and released him to his family. But his trouble complicated an emerging problem at home. After forty years of sweating through the grimiest, most backbreaking work, Whitey's father had finally sickened. The nature of his illness—apparently hemochromatosis, a metabolic disorder brought on by overexposure to iron-based pigments—suggests any number of manual jobs, from keelhauling on the docks to work in construction, perhaps as a painter or a plasterer. In any case, it seems that over the years, on job after job, John Riordan had slowly absorbed minute particles of metal that bronzed his skin from the inside and poisoned him at last.

As the scope of the disaster became clear—the primary breadwinner mortally ill—the Riordan family pressures increased. Whitey's older brother John, eighteen by then, had been working the docks for a couple of years. He now made every shape-up. But Whitey was still too young to do more than run an occasional errand on the docks. He made deliveries for a local market, the nickel and dime tips jingling in his pockets, enough for candy, or a picture show if he saved. But for some reason the thirteen-year-old couldn't stick with the straight and narrow for very long. Johnny Clinton's nicer clothes seemed a constant taunt perhaps, or the temptation to mimic Dutch's and Legs's tabloid exploits became overpowering. Whatever the case, within a year, Whitey had broken his probation, and the City of New York was as good as its word.

He was remanded to the Bronx, sentenced to three months at the New York Catholic Protectory, where for the past seventy years almost every child crook and vagabond ended up.

CHAPTER FOUR

WELFARE BOY

IN THE PARKCHESTER SECTION OF THE BRONX, where Union-port Road and Metropolitan Avenue intersect, a traffic circle lined with stores and garden apartments lies atop the buried heart of the old Catholic Protectory. For decades, the Protectory was a well-known refuge of last resort for thousands of hopeless or homeless adolescents, and a safe way station for ghetto kids whose only alternative was the streets. But it has been razed from the city's collective memory.

In 1938 Mayor LaGuardia signed off on plans for the "largest integral housing project . . . in the United States" on the former asylum's one hundred acres, erasing the spooky, seventy-five-year-old Gothic buildings and wide shaded lawns from the city's consciousness. The mayor budgeted an astronomical sum to acquire the additional acreage and to plan and construct the necessary homes and schools, churches and shops needed for "a completely balanced community": about $50 million—well over half a *billion* in twenty-first-century dollars—all underwritten by the Metropolitan Life Insurance Company. The Catholic Protectory, with fewer and fewer wards admitted each year by the late thirties—the victim of its own success, perhaps—and with a more tranquil, rehabilitative campus in rural Westchester County, jumped at the chance for that kind of money.

When Whitey Riordan was sentenced to the Bronx facility in 1928, the Protectory's *Sixty-sixth Annual Report to the Legislature of the State of New York* included a "Bird's Eye View" artist's rendition. The drawing shows a foreboding but neatly groomed settlement with imposing stone buildings and expansive fields. To a casual observer it could be a once prestigious Victorian university, perhaps, just weeks away from the wrecking ball. But in reality, the Catholic Protectory served a population that was much younger and far more troubled.

The Catholic Church had been active in the city's slums for generations. In Hell's Kitchen beginning in 1858, five new parishes opened up within twelve blocks of one another. The many churches were one of the social mainstays that Irish immigrants brought from the old country, the other one being the local pub. On Ninth Avenue, at the north edge of Hell's Kitchen, St. Paul the Apostle Church created a Temperance Society in the 1870s to counter the drunkenness spilling from the neighborhood's five hundred saloons. The effort became the largest abstinence program of any parish in the nation, even though most working poor in the neighborhood ignored it. Another church-inspired charity, the St. Vincent de Paul Society, tended to the spiritual and material needs of the poor, handing out thousands of dollars to hundreds of families by the turn of the twentieth century. The Catholic Protectory was a similar response to the misery sprawled over the streets, but it stood alone as an institution.

The Protectory was established by the archbishop of New York and commissioned to the Brothers of Christian Schools in 1863, when street kids in Hell's Kitchen were first blooming into cutthroat gangs and children in the Tenderloin were being bought and sold for sex. Its mandate was to offer asylum to the city's most destitute and unwanted children. Written into its charter, though, was the agreement that the Protectory would also house wards remanded by the city's overburdened courts and Correction Department. These delinquent kids, the "idle, truant and vicious" children as the Protectory literature described them, quickly came to dominate the population. When Whitey arrived, he was one of about nine hundred juvenile delinquents muscling through a total population of nearly sixteen hundred.

The sexes were firmly segregated, of course, to quell the passions of what the Christian Brothers called "Flaming Youth." Separate buildings with locked doors and windows faced one another across long stretches of grass. However, boys and girls were inadvertently brought together en masse one night in 1872 by a fire that blazed through the girls' dormitory. According to the Protectory, everyone got out safely, with the boys risking their lives in "noble conduct," braving the flames and rescuing the school's valuable sewing machines. But other than that, woe to any kid overcome by hormones who tried to breach the gap. In keeping with contemporary notions of childhood corrections, punishments likely included lashings and solitary confinement.

Whether the children were criminal, orphaned, or destitute, the Christian Brothers' solution to every social problem seemed to be "constant occupation." Every activity was rigidly structured and supervised. Besides learning academics and music, kids were kept busy perfecting crafts like printing, tailoring, chair-caning, and other "mechanic arts," as the Brothers called them. The cobblers' shop turned out five thousand pairs of shoes a week, for instance, in a strict and unwavering routine that showed little change over sixty years.

At six o'clock each morning, a cassocked Brother stood in the dormitory doorway and clanged a brass handbell. Whitey would have stumbled from his bed, immediately turned around to make it up, and then washed up and dressed in a white shirt and tie for seven o'clock breakfast. His placement in workshop classes would have depended on his aptitude— according to later state documents, he might have been assigned to the print shop. There was no skipping school; the Brothers watched a child's every move with the "great aim," as they saw it, "to mold their hearts to the practice of virtue."

The strict regimentation wasn't easy. Old newspapers are salted with one- and two-paragraph items about dubious events at the Catholic home, escapes or fires. Two years before Whitey arrived, the *New York Times* reported how fourteen-year-old Max Hahn tied his bed sheets together one forlorn September night, hung them out the window, and started down. The makeshift rope broke, and poor Max fell four stories. He landed in a courtyard and lay there for the rest of the night, alive but unconscious, with a fractured skull. A watchman found him around six in the morning. That was Max's second escape attempt in two weeks. In 1934, again according to the *Times*, eighteen boys "infected with Spring fever" broke out with a stolen passkey. Nine police cars and two emergency trucks spread throughout the surrounding neighborhood and started rounding them up. All but two were captured by nightfall. In a statement, one Brother Michael said he couldn't blame the kids "for wanting to go home to see their parents." But he denied that they were "prisoners" and attributed the break to "a boyish prank." Clearly, the Protectory's exacting routine was no easy cross to bear.

Underpinning the entire structure, of course, was a rock-solid belief in the reformative power of faith. But teaching catechism to children whose basic necessities were so completely neglected couldn't have been an easy job. The frustration is suggested in a passage from the 1928 *Annual Report*. Brother Alban, director of the Boys' Department, fairly clenches his fountain pen describing the "appalling" task of teaching the Sacraments to "boys of fifteen and sixteen who do not know how to bless themselves." Coming from an Irish Catholic family, though, perhaps Whitey escaped the lash on that score.

Two months into Whitey's sentence, the relentless daily round was interrupted. On November 9, 1928, a year to the day after his conviction, the boy was summoned to Director Alban's office. To Whitey's surprise, his nineteen-year-old brother John was standing beside Brother Alban's mahogany desk. The director motioned Whitey to a chair and in a kindly voice told him that his father had died. After whispered condolences, Whitey was immediately released to John's custody for the long, rattling subway ride back to Hell's Kitchen and the wake and funeral. Then after his father's burial in Calvary Cemetery, Queens, under a late autumn sky, Whitey was returned to the Protectory to complete the remaining month of his court-ordered sentence.

———————

For a time after his release, Whitey stayed out of trouble. Perhaps some of the Protectory's lessons in discipline stuck with him. Maybe he felt guilty about his father's death—Whitey's inability to keep his hands off things that didn't belong to him surely added to his father's stress. Possibly he even tried to steer clear of the guys around the corner—no sense tempting fate, those late nights on the street with nothing to do, and then somebody's bright idea. There was no question that with his father gone, the Riordan family would have to pull together. So Whitey tried to stay in school, most likely P.S. 111, the public school around the corner on West Fifty-third Street. But it all must have been too much—the grief, the guilt, his family's need. Whitey quit school in the seventh grade. It was 1928. He was thirteen.

The Riordans lived on Tenth Avenue, as they had for much of the decade, between Fifty-second and Fifty-third Streets. Back then, the avenue was lined with butcher shops. Stout Germans in straw boaters and bloody aprons swept clotted sawdust into the street at the end of every day. If you lived on the floors above, you had to be careful to wipe your feet before entering the apartment at night. Whitey sometimes ran errands for the butchers, for the other storekeepers in the neighborhood, and for workers on the docks. John was the main breadwinner for the family of five, though, bringing home as much as $40, sometimes $50 a week from the waterfront—equivalent to $400 or $500 today—the prosperity flooding the country finally sloshing against the West Side piers. After a postwar shipping slowdown early in the decade, when the First World War boom busted, foreign trade was robust again and American goods were being shipped around the world. Even in Hell's Kitchen, Fords and Chryslers far outnumbered horse carts, and tenement rooftops bristled with new radio antennas.

But too soon it all collapsed. The 1929 stock market crash reverberated around the world and promised changing times. When the dust cleared, deep fault lines in the economy were exposed, promising a wider depression. Within a year, national unemployment had rocketed to 6 million. In New York City, newly opened soup kitchens did a brisk business. The economic devastation, on view from any window, was detailed every day in the press. Even the show-business daily *Variety* gave the disaster a banner headline, but with a characteristic twist: "WALL ST. LAYS AN EGG."

In 1931 Manhattan, as news of the deepening depression competed with tales of official corruption, the shock waves spread across Hell's Kitchen. The bare-knuckle jobs that defined the area—construction, railroading, dock work—were disappearing. One of the city's largest unemployment offices opened on West Forty-ninth Street. Except for the few thrifty, far-sighted merchants who had saved their dollars instead of buying stocks, most small business owners up and down the block shuttered their markets and lunch-counters, putting clerks, waitresses, and cooks out of work. Families bundled in drab coats—their best wear long since pawned for cash—lined up outside soup kitchens set up in the basements of St. Paul the Apostle, St. Raphael's on West Forty-first and Tenth, and dozens of other churches and charities across the city. Even the neighborhood Democratic clubs, well financed by Tammany graft, were hardpressed to answer the overwhelming need huddling on the sidewalk before them.

Twenty-one-year-old John Riordan, his family depending on him, gathered each morning for the shape-up. Shuffling his boots in the cold wind that whipped off the North River, he and hundreds like him often waited in vain. The average longshoreman was lucky to work twenty-four hours out of the week. More than a third of longshoremen were on relief or in breadlines in the 1930s, and even steadily employed dockworkers considered themselves lucky to bring home $15 a week. The boom times were gone.

———————

About 12:30 on the morning of May 9, 1931, Patrolman William Shehan heard the tinkle of breaking glass while walking his Ninth Avenue beat. Policemen on foot patrol carried no radios in those days—in case of emergencies, they blew whistles and clattered nightsticks on the pavement. But this was clearly no case for general alarm; breaking glass was a nightly occurrence in Hell's Kitchen and meant little unless there was a body lying in the middle of it.

Shehan drew his flashlight and approached an A&P store on the ground floor of a five-story walk-up between Fiftieth and Fifty-first Streets. The front door glass was shattered. Officer Shehan stepped across the threshold, careful not to crunch the shards glittering on the floor in the light of the streetlamp. He unclipped his revolver at a rustling sound from the rear of the store and trained his light past the darkened shelves, near the cash register opposite the door.

Behind the counter, a husky blond youth in an old sweatshirt turned in the flashlight's glare and stopped. The patrolman ordered the kid to raise his hands. When the boy complied, he dropped his loot—ten tins of cigarettes, valued at 29¢ apiece.

Whitey probably knew it was a stupid thing to do as soon as the policeman's beam shined in his face. But on the spur of the moment, the caper had made sense. Money was tight. People were selling apples and pencils on Fifth Avenue—why not cigarettes on Tenth?

He was indicted in the Court of General Sessions for third-degree burglary, petit larceny, and receiving. His head bowed before the hearing judge, a blond forelock falling in his eyes, Whitey pleaded not guilty—and his public defender succeeded in getting the charge reduced. He then pleaded guilty to the lesser charge of unlawful entry and was released on 10 percent of a thousand dollars' bail until sentencing. His mother must have been livid.

Elizabeth Riordan had grown resilient with all she'd had to deal with through the years, especially the death of little Mary. But Elizabeth, thirty-eight when Whitey was born, was now in her mid-fifties, and life wasn't getting softer as she aged. Within the past year, she'd had to move the whole family around the corner to a smaller, cheaper apartment on West Fifty-second Street. And now her middle boy was in trouble again.

The $100 for bail was rent and food money. Even if Elizabeth and her daughter Margaret were able to supplement John's income with one of the few jobs available to Hell's Kitchen women—such as laundry work, cleaning at one of the city's big hotels, or working on the line at a neighborhood twine factory—Whitey's legal problems threatened to sink them. Before turning to the loan sharks circling the docks, though, Elizabeth would have likely applied elsewhere for help.

It wasn't uncommon for neighborhood Democratic clubs to quash particular indictments, but the Riordans didn't have that kind of pull. Elizabeth may have asked the parish priest for a handout, explaining the trouble her boy was giving her. But whatever the case, Elizabeth secured the $100 for bail, and Whitey was released to her custody.

He probably felt ashamed, but the family would have found it hard to blame him completely. There was a different code in Hell's Kitchen, and though you might not follow it to the letter, you understood the text. The Clinton-Sheehan gang from the next block over had supported wives and children all through the 1920s by hijacking trucks. The Beadles farther down on Tenth Avenue—David and his brothers Frank and Dickie— had taken over the lucrative loading operation on Piers 84 and 86, after Davie proved himself by shooting three notorious gangsters, the Lawler brothers, in an Eleventh Avenue saloon. The famous Seabury Commission was investigating the very district attorney, C. T. Crain, whose name was scrawled crookedly across the bottom of Whitey's indictment. To kids like Whitey, it must have seemed there was only one way to get ahead in the world. If you could get away with it, all the facts seemed to ask, why not turn to crime?

But that was Whitey's problem—he couldn't get away with it. A few months later, on a warm September midnight, Whitey and a pal, Danny Kettles, staked out the corner on Tenth and Fifty-first, one block from the Riordan apartment. When a clerk named Fred Kirby came up the street, the boys stepped out of a doorway. Whitey threw a forearm around Kirby's neck and dragged him along the sidewalk until the man went limp. Officer Daniel Keough, turning the corner, found Whitey and Kettles kneeling on the pavement and going through Kirby's pocket, for a grand total of $6.46. For committing the robbery while on bail, Whitey was sentenced to twenty months at Elmira Reformatory, on a charge of grand larceny second degree.

With this sentence, sixteen-year-old Whitey waved so-long to childhood. Beginning in Elmira, Whitey would circle through a turnstile of incarceration and release for the rest of his life.

Like the Catholic Protectory, Elmira Reformatory, a state-of-the-art facility, held out the hope of rehabilitation. Its strict military regimen was complete with dress uniforms and parade drill, trade and educational classes. By the time Whitey got there, organized recreation, including team sports like baseball, was part of the routine. Many of these programs were devised in part by a certain former Elmira guard and current warden of Sing Sing prison, Lewis E. Lawes. Warden Lawes was earning a national reputation in the early 1930s with his bestselling books and popular radio show. This would not be the last time the paths of the famous warden and the young inmate would cross.

Elmira's educational and sports programs apparently had a negligible effect on Whitey. More important to his development was the education he received *after* his release from the upstate prison. Upon his parole and return to the city in June 1933, Whitey was arraigned on the outstanding A&P burglary and sentenced to three months at the New York County Penitentiary on Welfare Island, which the *Herald Tribune* that year called "the worst prison in the world."

————————

In the middle of the East River, the island—now called Roosevelt Island—today supports sturdy, red-brick buildings on tree-lined streets, with welcoming shops and restaurants. Once a dreaded destination, it was reborn in the mid-1960s as a planned community. Now city dwellers covet an address on Roosevelt Island for the stunning, sought-after skyline views offered by comfortable, rent-stabilized apartments. Riding home to the island on the city's only aerial tramway, Manhattan's lights glittering on the East River fifteen stories below, residents might forget that not too long ago one of the city's greatest concentrations of human misery was housed there. They need only look south to be reminded. There at the island's end, across the water from the glass face of the United Nations, spotlights still illuminate the crumbling facade of the city's old smallpox hospital.

Throughout its early years, in fact, Roosevelt Island seemed the perfect home for outcasts. In colonial times, it was known as Varcken ("Hog") Island, for all the pig farms the Dutch slopped there. By 1673, British army captain John Manning had retired to the mile-and-a-half long island in disgrace after surrendering Manhattan to the Dutch and having a sword ceremonially broken over his head at City Hall. Early in the eighteenth century, with the city firmly back in English hands, a Mr. Robert Blackwell married Captain Manning's stepdaughter, gaining possession of the island (renamed Blackwell's Island) as well as of the bride.

During the nineteenth century, as the city's hospitals and asylums teemed with the sick and poor, New York City built a cluster of government facilities on Blackwell's Island to handle the overflow. Public charity hospitals, an insane asylum, a workhouse, and a penitentiary crowded the narrow landscape. Recognizing the island's isolating potential, the city situated its only smallpox hospital at Blackwell's southernmost tip during the Civil War, perhaps hoping that it would slip off into the currents.

In the subsequent century, a different misery prevailed there. In the early 1900s, when Tammany reigned and government services were a cash business, a public scandal erupted over conditions at the Blackwell's Island prison. Charges of overcrowding, drug peddling, and favoritism led the aldermen to whitewash the place with a new name, one more in keeping with the island's purported mission: Welfare Island. But once the glare of publicity dimmed, the old abuses resurfaced. Indeed, the aldermen's paint job was shoddy work, quickly peeling to reveal the rot beneath.

Back from Elmira in the summer of '33 and awaiting transfer at the Tombs, a jail in lower Manhattan, Whitey Riordan probably heard from other inmates that Welfare Island—known as "the Pen"—was hard time. Harder than the Tombs? That was difficult to imagine. The Tombs, with its blunt, brownstone corners and sharp pitched roof, looked more like the remains of a medieval castle than a modern city's jail. The accused held in the Tombs could read the pleadings of former inmates scratched into the walls of their rock cells, before shuffling in chains across the aptly named "Bridge of Sighs" to the criminal courts building next door, to be either sprung or doomed. But confinement in the Tombs was nothing, the other inmates would have warned Whitey, in comparison with time spent in the Pen—the Pen was a jungle. Whitey could only hope that the skills he'd honed on the streets, and perfected behind Elmira's walls, would sustain him: not the sign-painting he'd been taught upstate but the tingling sensation in the back of his neck, the silent alarm that triggered his instincts when something bad was coming.

After a ferry from the East Seventy-eight Street dock brought him to the Pen's grim facade, Whitey would have encountered the smell. It hit a visitor like a mallet. The summer heat was early, and seventeen hundred men, almost three hundred over capacity, sweltered in the century-old, rough stone structure. Eight hundred cells built for single inmates were jammed with two or three men each, the metal cellblock tiers stacked back to back in the center of the long, narrow, four-story building. The block walls sweated with island damp, and the grated iron cell doors were flaking and rusted. Toilets were rudimentary, little more than a slop bucket.

But the real shock was the noise. Overlaying the usual shouts and curses came cries and tears, the incessant clanging of iron doors and gates, and the ringing of boots on metal stairs. And above it all, like the needling soundtrack from a fever dream, floated the crackling strains of hundreds of radios. At Elmira, radios were played low for individual relaxation. But here at the Pen, intense volume seemed the rule. Echoing from the cells day and night, Dodger games and *Amos 'n' Andy* competed loudly with "Star Dust" and "Stormy Weather."

Florid and overweight, the prison warden, Joseph A. McCann, was hardly a stern disciplinarian. In fact, he and his subordinate, Deputy Warden Daniel F. Sheehan, had effectively sold control of the Peniten-tiary to rival inmate gangs. Both McCann and Sheehan, who sported comfortable summer-weight tweeds rather than the regulation blue wool uniforms, were terrified of the political machine controlling city services, and specifically of the powerful Harlem boss, James J. Hines, Dutch Schultz's Tammany protector. The real bosses to reckon with at the Pen were two flamboyant inmate gangsters with firm Tammany connec-tions—Joie Rao and Ed Cleary.

Cooperative rivals, Rao and Cleary each commanded a 500-man army of inmates. Both bosses were fond of comfort and had set them-selves up accordingly—Rao in the Penitentiary infirmary, Cleary at the Correction Hospital. The legitimately ill—cancerous, tubercular, and syphilitic convicts—were consigned to the jail's pervading squalor. The Penitentiary and the Correction Hospital were the island's two prison facilities, hemmed in among over thirty buildings run by the city's Department of Hospitals. Despite the island's overwhelming number of hospital department employees—five thousand, nearly half of them women—privileged convicts had the run of the place. They seem to have kept their interests focused, preferring to manage the prison facilities as well-connected criminal syndicates, and apparently left the women employees alone. Rao ran the Italian inmates, Cleary the Irish, and together they marketed everything from smuggled dope and pilfered food to protection and sex. They also did a healthy trade in new inmates' clothing, all in an atmosphere of roiling corruption rivaling anything in Tammany's history.

Joie Rao, tall, with dark, pomaded hair, and a former prizefighter's graceful bearing, was a lieutenant in Dutch Schultz's Harlem mob. Rao had ridden shotgun with Vincent "Mad Dog" Coll on Schultz's beer-running routes between New York and New Jersey. Later, Rao moved up to drug peddling and then to gambling, once ducking a broad-daylight assassination attempt by the traitorous Coll that killed a child. When Rao was arrested for extortion and conspiracy in 1932, he was operating Schultz's lucrative slot machine racket in Harlem and had developed a taste for fine living.

At the Pen, Rao and his inner circle were literally above it all, ensconced in the infirmary on the top floor of the Pen's Administration Building, in quarters known as "Politician's Row" because of all the convicted Tammany officials who passed their sentences there in relative ease. According to reports, of the fifty men living in the Penitentiary hospital ward, only six were actually ill.

Rao had luxurious tastes and kept them well satisfied. He preferred to lounge about in a maroon robe, listening through earphones to radio broadcasts of popular music and opera. In a chest at the foot of his bed he kept caches of perfumed talc, lilac toilet water, and fine soaps, nestled among stacks of elegant dark blue boxer shorts. Valets from among his inmate staff polished his shoes and pressed his suits—no heavy prison gray uniforms for Joie. In fact, Rao seemed to have it better in jail than on the streets; at least no one was shooting at him inside.

Pushing a bent metal spoon through the mess hall slop in those first few days, Whitey must have quickly seen the cellblock-level effects of mob rule. The inedible junk on the table before him was proof enough. The kitchen pantry was raided constantly by the Italian and Irish gangs, who stole the best food to cook in their headquarters and eat on fine smuggled-in china, and by their convict customers, who bartered stolen food for goods and services. What was left over was boiled into a thin stew and served to the general population. Eating elbow to elbow, the twelve hundred regular inmates hunched over the scarred wooden tables never saw the bosses or gangsters in the mess hall. Often, when the tension became too much to bear, mealtimes would erupt with fistfights and howls and tin plates trailing streams of gruel would be hurled around the mess hall.

Very occasionally, Whitey might catch a glimpse of Rao walking on the grounds outside. He was usually attended by his well-fed minions, his movements fluid, on his way to the private, fenced-in garden he'd had constructed. Tan and scrubbed, he'd relax on the pilfered city benches that were angled on a patch of bright green lawn, enjoying the blooms or watching his pet milk goat nuzzle among the tomato rows—all he needed to complete the tableau was a crony playing the lute.

Ed Cleary, the Irish mob boss, was a study in contrasts. A streetwise tough who specialized in assault and armed robbery, Cleary wasn't as notorious or as dandified as Rao. His rap sheet is a failed thief's itinerary of frequent trips to Elmira and Sing Sing; Rao's record shows nine dismissed felonies in as many years—from robbery to homicide—suggesting a lot of luck and probably bribe money behind him. Nevertheless, Cleary rose to power on Welfare Island through cunning and ruthlessness. Big and sloppy, beady-eyed, and with a red pitted nose, he swaggered around his own domain with an expensive cigar or cigarette clenched in his teeth.

Cleary lived in ease at the Correction Hospital. Above a corner bed, the choicest in the room, and beneath the sun streaming through the south-facing window, Cleary kept a dagger stuck in the wall within reach. Really a mess hall spoon filed to a point, the weapon suggested that Cleary was less sanguine about his situation than Rao was. For further protection, he kept a German shepherd puppy named Screw-Hater chained under the bed. Screw-Hater had been smuggled in to help Cleary scare off any guards bold enough to interfere; but in truth, the attack puppy cowered whenever Cleary himself staggered near.

Just as Rao had his garden, Cleary also had a private retreat, a small room off the main ward, done up with soft mattresses and pale green walls. There he could relax with drinks—he preferred pint bottles of whiskey to the cigarette tins of heroin that he marketed to the island's addicts. But occasionally Cleary, too, enjoyed smoking a pellet or two of "schmeck."

Cleary's footlocker offered further contrasts to Rao's tastes. Where the Italian mobster fancied intimate indulgences like lotions and perfumes, Cleary filled his locker with culinary treats: half-gallon cans of peaches, tomatoes, and spinach. An ornate grandfather clock, its pendulum long gone, served as an overflow pantry where Cleary stowed more pilfered food—baskets of fresh cranberries, jars of pickled herring, and cans of condensed milk. The Irish boss kept a full complement of silverware, too, including knives and forks, even meat cleavers. And to complete his menu, he often mixed a potent concoction of homebrew, which he fermented in a gallon can stored on a rafter above his bed, out of the damaging sun.

Both mob bosses raised pigeons, an old tenement custom. Cleary kept a pigeon cote on the roof of the hospital; Rao's birdhouse was built on the grounds, against a storehouse with water views. Between the two of them, there were more than two hundred birds, cooing in homemade wire cages. More than just a nostalgic hobby, the homing pigeons—specifically trained to return home—served useful purposes. With the help of outside confederates, Cleary and Rao used the birds to supplement their drug smuggling operations, ferrying small bundles of cash and contraband, as well as messages, back and forth across the East River.

The birds weren't the primary means of this commerce, though. Narcotics were regularly smuggled into the Pen. They were taped to the bottom of a visitor's foot or hidden inside a bodily orifice. Visitors wore drug-soaked handkerchiefs tied around necks. Narcotics were concealed under postage stamps on letters. Or perhaps simplest of all, drugs were bundled and dropped off the Fifty-ninth Street Bridge, which towered almost directly above the Pen, right into a gangster's waiting hands.

Evidently Whitey Riordan was not a user, but the drug traffic was nothing new to a Hell's Kitchen kid like him. Opium had been smoked in New York since the last century, and morphine had been a favorite of skin-poppers for generations. Aspirin-maker Bayer had legally sold heroin as cough medicine around the turn of the twentieth century, and

by 1915, the year Whitey was born, the white powder was a smash underground hit—about a third of all drug addicts chose heroin. But facing
dopers on the streets was one thing—they were unpredictable and utterly
dangerous, and you tried to avoid them. Being locked up with them was
a whole other story.

On Welfare Island, they were impossible to ignore. Scores of addicts
roamed the wards like zombies, runny-nosed and shivering, half-clothed
in rags with blankets wrapped around their shoulders—any useful clothing long since bartered for dope. Moaning in agony without their dose,
they were so desperate that if they had no syringe they'd slice open a vein
and pour drugs directly in the wound.

But perhaps even worse than the junkers, at least for an eighteen-
year-old street kid, were the homosexuals and transvestites. You couldn't
help but run into them in prison. At Elmira, they were a segregated
minority and were kept under strict control, required to wear state-issue
like everyone else, lest they lead the heterosexual inmates astray. But at
the Pen they mingled with the general population, many wearing full
makeup, wigs, and lingerie. Belying their dainty affectations, however,
these were tough, violent men. A new kid fresh from the streets, a good-
looking blond, would certainly catch their eye. Whitey scouted around
for protection among likely allies.

He was West Side Irish, which automatically placed him under
Cleary's ethnic umbrella. Maybe Whitey made it into Cleary's army,
maybe not. A young thief of no distinction—$2.90 worth of cigarettes
from the A&P—it's impossible to tell. But Hell's Kitchen was a small
world, the docks even more so. Whitey could drop familiar names from
the neighborhood, the Clintons, the Beadles, and the St. Johns. In any
case, he evidently found the connections he needed to stay in one piece.

With twelve hundred desperate men dominated by two small, ruth-
less minorities, smaller associations were cemented among a population
divided, like the city itself, by ethnicity, language, and customs, and then
cut again by substantial subgroups such as the homosexuals and drug
addicts. The Pen swirled with tiny cliques orbiting one another and fend-
ing for themselves. Whitey and his newfound pals, guarding their own,
participated in the plunder.

They traded for beefsteaks and chops, which they fried on rigged grills in their cells, using books from the prison library for fuel. The cells were cluttered hovels, crammed with makeshift and electrical stoves (depending on your status), foodstuffs, pots and frying pans, magazines like *New Yorker* and *True Story*, and piles of clothing. The men perched where they could, plates balanced on their knees. It was likely at these informal dinners that Whitey and his pals recounted events of the day.

The story went around, for instance, about the time Joie Rao got a thirst for lemonade one summer afternoon. No less than Warden McCann searched high and low for fresh lemons, huffing and puffing his bulk up and down the kitchen stairs so his favorite inmate could wet his whistle. But the favors were reciprocal. Rao made sure vases of fresh flowers, cut from his own garden, adorned McCann's office when the warden returned from vacation or sick leave. It was even mentioned that Rao had a say in paroles. One time the warden handed him a list of upcoming Christmas-time releases for his approval. Rao took one look and stormed out, upset that some of his friends wouldn't get out in time for the holiday. McCann heaved to his feet and chased after him, terrified that word might get back to Dutch Schultz and from him to Tammany boss Hines that the warden wasn't doing right by Rao.

To Whitey, all his experience made it plain that authority was firmly rigged. The political and criminal justice system was made of men and women looking out for themselves, just like the crooks and everybody else. Tammany boss Jimmy Hines was a prime example. And with models like him, and Joie Rao, and Warden McCann, what motivation was there to go straight? What was straight, anyway? The real world, whether inside or outside the walls, was what you made it.

———

Four months after Whitey Riordan's release from the New York County Penitentiary, Rao's and Cleary's cozy setup came to an abrupt end. On a freezing January morning in 1934, Austin H. MacCormick, Mayor LaGuardia's newly appointed commissioner of corrections, conducted a surprise raid on Welfare Island with five stunned reporters in tow. Bespectacled and reed-thin, with the earnest manner of a young college professor, the commissioner had offered to lead the reporters on a tour of the city's brand-new prison facility on Rikers Island, scheduled to open within the year.

This was no routine public relations jaunt, however. MacCormick, trim in a gray wool suit with matching fedora and spats, and flanked by his burly entourage, led them not to Rikers but instead to Welfare Island to storm into what he called "a gangster's paradise." A newspaperman from the *Sun* thought Warden McCann "seemed greatly relieved" watching MacCormick and his troops regain control of the jail. As flashbulbs popped, detectives and officers emptied the cellblocks of all contraband in a methodical, daylong procedure, throwing the loot and rubbish onto the ground-floor hallway outside the cells, known as the flats. Within minutes the debris was piled knee-deep.

Ed Cleary was manhandled out of his hospital lair and slapped into solitary confinement. Ever the showoff, Cleary took a burning cigarette from his lips and ceremoniously offered it to his new neighbor as the gate clanged shut.

Joie Rao, interrupted by a deputy while shaving before his bathroom mirror, calmly told the policeman, "I'll go along in the second wave."

"Oh no you don't, Joie," the officer said, brandishing a Billy club. "You'll come right now."

Rao smiled and shrugged, put down his razor, and went along to solitary without another word.

The drug addicts were rounded up and taken to the island hospitals for treatment. The transvestites, their heavy makeup and lacy attire alarming to the staid young commissioner, were segregated in a south wing of the prison. By evening, order had been restored.

The Welfare Island raid, sensationalized by the newspapers, seized the public's imagination in the dull winter of '34. Mayor LaGuardia complained that the revelations were "a typical illustration of what this city government has inherited from its predecessors." One of the U.S. attorneys for New York considered a federal investigation. Five years later, Warner Brothers produced a movie about the raid. But maybe too much time had passed by 1939. The *New York Times* found *Blackwell's Island*, starring John Garfield, "laughable," with inmates in "striped silk pajamas, ordering the keepers around like lackeys." There was definitely a comic aspect to the film version of heavyweight Warden McCann's red-faced search for lemons fresh enough for Joie Rao. But funny or not, the Welfare Island raid revealed the serious depths to which city corrections had sunk under Tammany. It also hastened the opening of the new penitentiary a year later on Rikers Island, isolated in the northeast stretch of the East River, between the Bronx and Queens. For over a century, the growing city had piled garbage and cinders there, as well as the excavated dirt from ongoing subway construction. The continuous dumping led to sprawling rat infestations and to subterranean fires that burned for decades. Even today, after a rain, a moldy stench that brings to mind an old sneaker pervades the island's atmosphere, although a hardy feral cat population keeps the rats in check.

The newly constructed prison trumpeted an advance in corrections in 1935. Commissioner MacCormick saw the Rikers facility as a "repair shop." Through innovative workshops and programs based on the latest theories of reform, the commissioner was determined that Rikers Island would truly achieve inmate rehabilitation. But until the new prison opened, convicts would have to put up with the decrepit conditions on Welfare Island—albeit now under strict city control.

Whitey Riordan, however, saw little evidence of MacCormick's fine theories. In between short stints of freedom, during which he worked the docks, Whitey built up his rap sheet. He was cemented in the ways of his Hell's Kitchen streets, and his next three years were a gray blur—on April 8, 1934, material witness to homicide, discharged; on July 30, 1934, disorderly conduct conviction, sentenced back to the Pen on Welfare Island; on September 15, 1934, returned to the Pen once more for nearly two years for parole violation (he was among the first inmates ferried over to Rikers when the Pen closed for good); and on August 11, 1936, four days after his release from Rikers, he was returned to Elmira Reformatory for another parole violation. When Whitey got out in August 1937 for his longest period of freedom since childhood (a whole eleven months), he was eager to put into practice all he'd learned over the past ten years. Whitey was ready to organize. At home in Hell's Kitchen, and keen to get moving again, he decided to look up some old friends from the docks.

CHAPTER FIVE

THE PISTOL LOCAL

O N PAROLE, IT WAS ONLY LOGICAL that Whitey Riordan would look for work on the docks. Besides crime, that was what he knew. He'd been running dockside errands since he was a kid—coffee gofer, perhaps, moving up to messenger—and began longshoring at eighteen in between prison stretches. Now, at age twenty-two and with solid lockup time behind him, Whitey was a real asset. Young men like him, seasoned ex-cons with reputations for keeping their mouths shut, were indispensable to the International Longshoremen's Association. At that time, the union was infamously corrupt, a well-documented front for organized crime. The ILA controlled the city's piers through a variety of labor rackets. Keeping the regular dockworkers in line sometimes took force—intimidating tough longshoremen into accepting criminally unfair working conditions wasn't always easy. The union needed hardened bullies to maintain control, men comfortable with violent solutions. Whitey Riordan, veteran of half a dozen prison sentences, seemed a natural.

If you were criminally inclined in 1937, and you wanted a piece of the action on the North River docks in Hell's Kitchen, the man to see was Richard "The Bandit" Gregory. A West Side native, twenty-seven-year-old Gregory was the union delegate for ILA Local 824—known to the police and reporters as the "Pistol Local" for all the murders committed in its district. Married, with a three-year-old daughter, the Bandit arranged the union membership necessary to work the docks north of Forty-second Street. Regular workers had to pay a stiff $150 for the membership "book," which was stamped each time a longshoreman paid his dues. The ex-cons needed for labor control, though, were men of influence, old friends from the neighborhood, say, or the trusted friend of a trusted friend. They were hired for their rough character, and a good word was usually all they needed to get the best waterfront positions.

Besides Bandit Gregory, the main boss was another local fellow, David "The Beetle" Beadle. A heavy-set thug from the 600 block of Tenth Avenue, two blocks south of Whitey's old tenement, Davie Beadle controlled the loading and unloading on Piers 84 and 86, right where the aircraft carrier USS *Intrepid* years later would berth for museum visitors. The Beetle had gained notoriety in April 1930 by shooting a band of neighborhood outlaws, the Lawlor brothers, in their own speakeasy on Eleventh Avenue. Killing one, wounding two others, the twenty-two-year-old beat the rap despite barroom witnesses and a policeman alerted by the fusillade. The Hell's Kitchen code was firm: nobody ratted to police, even when your brother was bleeding on the floor.

By 1937, Beadle had blasted out his own West Side niche, rising to dock boss with a string of assault and robbery charges floating behind him. A fastidious dresser, his expensive suits adorned with gold and diamond jewelry, Davie didn't take his success lightly. He swallowed pills by the handful for a touchy heart condition. The thirty-year-old knew that someone could come gunning for him at any time. Maintaining control while bossing a crew, negotiating loading and unloading terms with the shipping companies, and overseeing million-dollar rackets eventually took a physical toll. Despite the pressure, though, dock boss was an enviable position.

The North River piers were the coveted heart of New York Harbor, part of a $7-billion-a-year empire and America's largest, most vital waterfront. Contemporary WPA maps of the North River show an almost unbroken fringe of piers lining Manhattan's cobblestone edges from the Battery to the Upper West Side. Ocean liners from Europe competed for dock space with local steam ferries, cargo freighters, and tugboats. The entire 755-mile-long city harbor—including the East River and Brooklyn waterfronts—held 200 deepwater ports, each ready to accommodate two liners at a time. There were also nearly 2,000 smaller

piers, the largest, most profitable of which were leased to worldwide shipping lines run by such companies as the Eastern Steamship Line and the
Cunard White Star Line. Since 1900, New York had grown to become
the world's busiest port city.

Commandeered by the International Longshoremen's Association,
this vast waterfront was divided into ethnic territories reflecting the composition of adjoining neighborhoods. Lower Manhattan, the East Side,
and into Brooklyn were dominated by the Italians; the West Side piers,
partitioned into Greenwich Village, Chelsea, and Hell's Kitchen, were
ruled by the Irish. Mirroring the ethnic divisions on Welfare Island, these
distinct fiefdoms manipulated lucrative systems of criminal rackets, all
the while keeping their union books up-to-date.

Piracy made good copy, inspiring articles in *Harper's Magazine* and
Collier's Weekly in the 1940s and '50s. According to Malcolm Johnson,
whose *New York Sun* exposé of corruption on the docks won the Pulitzer
Prize in 1950, New York Harbor had been a "waterfront jungle" for
decades. Bad enough that the mobs charged add-on loading fees to the
truckers hauling ship cargo off to market; those costs, estimated at millions of dollars a year, were passed on to consumers. But exploitation of
the workers was the worst crime. Longshoremen desperate to be picked
out of the shape-up would agree to kick back to the union a percentage
of their salaries. The mobs also sponsored gambling, everything from
organized dice games to bookmaking. Longshoremen who didn't play
didn't work. Almost every day a hat was passed around because so-and-
so's family needed money. Dock men reached deep and dropped in their
change, knowing full well that so-and-so's family would see just a piece of
the total collection. Payrolls were padded with ghost workers, drugs were
smuggled within legitimate loads, and cargo was pilfered—all in well-
run payoff and kickback relays that benefited the union dock bosses and
their crews.

Walking west toward the river in 1937, Whitey Riordan was hoping
for his share. He knew Davie Beadle; the Beetle had put him and his
brother John to work before. Even Whitey's old pal Johnny Clinton, the
boxer, who knew next to nothing about longshoring, was getting his union

book stamped at Pier 88 at West Forty-eighth Street. Clinton's real specialty, though, was a loan-sharking operation run with Frankie McCabe, another of Whitey's neighborhood friends. The pair loaned money at high weekly interest rates—anywhere from 10¢ to 25¢ on the dollar, a bruising payback for longshoremen hitting the skids due to injury or illness. Saddled with kids who needed feeding, or webbed with gambling debts they had to pay back or else, regular dockworkers made easy marks.

Whitey found his own specialty, though, once he shook hands with Bandit Gregory. Officially, Whitey was a hiring stevedore, a prize job choosing the work crews out of the shape-up. As the mobsters' front man, the hiring stevedore gave the gangsters complete say over who loaded or unloaded the ships. Filling the ranks with handpicked minions solidified mob control of the docks. Unofficially, however, Whitey Riordan was Davie Beadle's union enforcer, what they called a strong-arm.

———————

There are any number of reasons why the port of New York was infested with criminal rackets. As Daniel Bell puts it in *The End of Ideology*, "Central to any understanding of crime is the political setup of a city." Tammany Hall's legendary corruption—a sludge of paid political influence, business interests, and bare-fisted tactics—had long been fed with dockside profits. According to the *New York World*, in 1905, one Tammany leader fattened up his construction company by channeling its way $30 million worth of Dock Department contracts. Besides the politicians, though, there were the gangsters.

After Prohibition's repeal in 1934, organized crime began pushing into the labor rackets. Dutch Schultz, for instance, squeezed the restaurant unions, forcing business owners to join his association and making waiters and cooks pay union dues. Another reason for waterfront corruption was the harbor's porous frontier and loose-knit establishment. Unlike the steel or automobile industry, for example, the waterfront wasn't stabilized by a few large companies capable of fixing price structures; it was run by local operators too small and unsteady to fend off violent mobsters. Still another reason for crime's hold on the docks was the waterfront's domination by immigrant groups. For some newcomers, long marginalized by established social elites and suspicious of anyone outside their own ethnic clan, crime often proved "one of the queer ladders of social mobility in American life," an immigrant's entrée to the American dream. But whatever the reasons, Davie Beadle and Bandit Gregory, Whitey Riordan, and Johnny Clinton didn't take as their role models the hardworking longshoremen held down by the system. Whitey and the others fought and schemed in the street-level, brass-knuckle tradition of celebrity crime bosses like Dutch Schultz and, on the docks, the infamous Paul Kelly, garbage-scow hand, gang boss, and nightclub owner, who became one of the ILA's original founders.

As a union boss, Paul Kelly had an impeccable, if restless, pedigree. Born Paolo Vaccarelli in 1871, he started out on the East River garbage barges, organizing the hands into the Scow Trimmers' Union. Drawn to fame by hook or by crook, the dark, slight Italian adopted his Irish moniker to Americanize an early career as a bantamweight boxer. But even the ring couldn't satisfy Kelly's taste for violence. He also headed the infamous Five Points gang, Lower East Side contemporaries of the Hell's Kitchen Gophers. By 1901, with hundreds of gangsters at his command, Paul Kelly was one of Tammany Hall's favorite enforcers.

Around 1912, still leading his old Scow Trimmers' Union, Kelly was feeling pressed by the growing competition between two precursors to the ILA—the Longshoreman's Union Protective Association, the organization of New York dockworkers run by Richard "Big Dick" Butler, a jovial Tammany Irishman; and the ambitious T. V. O'Connor's Licensed Tugmen's Protective Association of the Great Lakes, the Midwest's tugboat union that also had controlling interests over the Pacific and Gulf coast docks and even into Puerto Rico. Rather than be taken over by force, Kelly threw in with Butler and O'Connor, reinventing himself as a union player and keeping control of his third. He'd made a wise move. The massive union, known as the International Longshoremen's Association, soon controlled all longshoring work in the country.

In New York City, Kelly and Butler threaded their Tammany associations into a blanket agreement between the city, the shipping companies, and the ILA that consolidated and strengthened their mutual power even as it weakened the longshoremen. Collective-bargaining goals were agreed to by mutual consent, without workforce strikes, and usually to the benefit of the power brokers. Despite statistics weighted against workers—a 1 in 500 chance of being killed on the job; a 1 in 40 shot at lifelong disability—the best incentives the men could hope for were measly increases in hourly pay. Union goons silenced any talk of wildcat walkouts to improve conditions. When Whitey Riordan signed on with Bandit Gregory and Davie Beadle in 1937, he joined an outlaw army that defended criminal interests and kept the honest working men under firm control.

———————

Davie Beadle and Bandit Gregory liked Whitey's prison credentials and things went well at first. Clearly, the money was huge. Goods and services worth anywhere from $65 million to $100 million were being swindled from New York Harbor by the waterfront rackets every year. The New York Police Department's Waterfront Squad knew about the Beadle mob but could do little unless there was bloodshed over the loot. The profitable collusion of city government, the shipping companies, and a mobbed-up union kept the police at arm's length. For Whitey Riordan, Bandit Gregory's right-hand man, it was perfect. He was no longer a petty thicf. He had graduated from Elmira Reformatory into the big time.

Besides the money, he and Bandit had a lot in common. They shared about the same number of arrests—Whitey's eleven to Bandit's even dozen—although Whitey led Bandit in convictions. Still, Whitey had things to learn. Bandit was much more violent, for one thing. His record, based less on larceny than Whitey's, was studded with felonious assaults, even three homicides—including the fatal sidewalk beating of an out-of-town engineer. But the murder charges never stuck.

Like most of Whitey's efforts, however, his strong-arm career didn't last long. The work was messy, and not everybody shut up like they were supposed to. One night in April 1938, for instance, Whitey and Bandit accosted a man asking too many questions. While Whitey held him, Bandit flicked open his knife and cut off the man's nose. Despite the West

Side code, that sort of mayhem was a difficult thing to keep quiet. Whitey and Bandit were arrested and charged with felonious assault and maiming.

The trial lasted ten days. John Riordan, Whitey's older brother, attended nearly every day, along with Johnny Clinton. They might have been genuinely moved to support a brother and a friend charged with such a gruesome crime. Or they might have had another motive. All during jury selection, the two burly longshoremen sat in the courtroom, probably right behind the defense table. During breaks in the trial, John and Clinton stood around in the courthouse hallway, breaking off conversation to watch jury members pass by. The jury got the message. In the end, Whitey and Bandit were acquitted of assault. Whitey was hit with parole violation, though, for associating with a known criminal, and was sent back to Elmira Reformatory for three months. John Riordan's and Johnny Clinton's cold stares could do nothing about that.

When Whitey was released in October 1938 and came back to work on Pier 88 at the French Lines, the twenty-three-year-old seemed different. Hard for the family to put their finger on the change. For Whitey, maybe it was the sharp autumn air slicing down the North River, or the colder light on the water. Maybe he couldn't get the assault out of his head—the man's pleas; his struggling against Whitey's grip on his hair as Bandit wielded the knife; all the blood. Maybe Whitey had found his limit and he wasn't as tough as he thought he was. But there were other hints that a change was called for.

Things at home had turned for the worse. His brother John, the family's stalwart provider during the toughest times after their father died, had found his own share of trouble. In April 1936, after a long night of drinking, John and a local longshoreman named Warren Reddy had tried to hold up a Broadway-area nightclub at six in the morning. As John waved a pistol and threatened to shoot, Reddy rifled the cash register for a grand total of $12. As they were backing out of the club like characters from a Cagney picture, two off-duty policemen entered and grabbed them. John spent a year and a half in Elmira and came out an altered man—not exactly reformed, just much more careful. Even baby brother Andrew was in and out of custody on various theft charges. But Whitey had to wonder—who were they all kidding? This wasn't the movies. They'd never be as big as the Clintons. And how did his mother stand it? There must be a better way—if not necessarily legit, then at least something with more return for the risk. Back on the docks in the fall of 1938, squeezing juice from the rackets, and biding his time, Whitey met the man who would soon catapult him onto the front page of every paper in the city: John "Patches" Waters, a hard-drinking, twenty-eight-year-old ex-con who seemed to have it all figured out.

Plain and simple, John Waters had a knack for making money. Severe acne in his youth had earned him the nickname Patches; his homeliness hadn't slowed him down, though. He was slightly built, with receding dark hair—Whitey's blond brawn was his picture negative. But the two men had plenty in common. Their families hailed from the same area of Hell's Kitchen, around West Fiftieth Street, before the Waters clan headed out to Queens. Whitey and Patches also shared an early preference for street crime, their first major offenses almost carbon copies of each other. Sixteen-year-old Whitey had dragged a man to the sidewalk on Fifty-first and Tenth for a six-dollar take. Patches was seventeen when he and three other teens had accosted a young man on a corner a block west, one spring night in 1927. Patches and his boys also got six bucks, plus a set of three keys valued at a quarter apiece. They were caught, and Patches was sent to Elmira Reformatory, as Whitey would be three years later. Grown up now, the kid stuff all behind them, the two men felt an immediate bond working the docks in the autumn of '38.

For Whitey, meeting Patches was decisive. Older by more than five years, Patches seemed to have all the answers, without talking loud about it. He worked his own schemes and kept to himself, unlike most mobsters palling around in Whitey's circle. He was strange sometimes, his pale eyes staring off across your shoulder as he spoke, as if including something beyond you in the conversation. But that gave him an air of mystery, as if he were in the know on something, and if you stuck around, you might just find out what. Over beers after work at the Hudson Hofbrau on Twelfth Avenue, Patches opened up to Whitey, watching the freighters

glimmer on the dark river from a table by the window, a cigarette burning between his yellow fingers. There were all manner of schemes that
made you money, Patches would explain to his new pal while buying the
drinks from a bankroll that covered his whole palm. He wasn't flashy
about the money, Whitey must have noticed. On the contrary, it seemed
a matter-of-fact thing with him, something anybody might be able to
manage if things worked out just right.

Patches mentioned the pinball racket he and a buddy had going, for
instance. Since Mayor LaGuardia had taken a sledgehammer to the slots,
the syndicates had gone into pinball machines. It was legitimate—lease
however many machines you thought you could handle to bars and candy
stores, make $35 to $50 a machine per week. Anyway, he might have
shrugged, nobody had cracked down yet. To Whitey, it must have
sounded cleaner than cutting off noses.

Whitey continued on with Beetle and Bandit, though. The rackets
were a very good business, not something you walked away from. But
Whitey was intrigued by Patches, who it seemed didn't truck too much
with the big shots yet still made out okay. On another evening, in
November, Patches wondered out loud if Whitey wanted to meet some
pals of his, good guys with solid views on things. Sure the rackets were
foolproof, Patches could have told him; but everybody needed a little
something on the side.

Judging from newspaper reports, court documents, and police transcripts,
it appears that the Shopping Bag Gang had been around for a while in
one form or another. An early version first hit the streets in 1935, three
years before Patches and Whitey sat together in the Hudson Hofbrau
spinning tales of quick money. In the middle of the Great Depression,
the gang was just another anonymous stickup mob with visions of glory.
For the most part, they had avoided New York City's narrow streets,
choosing their knockovers from within the peaceful hamlets surrounding
the busy metropolis. Like so many of the era's would-be Dillingers, they
targeted small-town suburban banks—and a week before Christmas
1935 their first short-lived spree culminated in the lower Hudson River
Valley.

Just east of Dobbs Ferry, and north of Yonkers in Westchester County, the town of Ardsley nestles comfortably among sculpted, land-scaped estates and lush-green country clubs. Even seventy years ago, the small town quietly gleamed. Benefiting from the 1920s boom in subur-ban housing, grand farmhouses in the Colonial style hedged against mock-Tudor cottages along quiet neighborhood streets draped with chestnut and elm trees. Twenty miles north of New York City, commut-ing Wall Street bankers drank weekend martinis with midtown insurance men and their wives. The gentility suited the affluent tastes of go-getting city executives. But about eleven o'clock on a Tuesday morning in December 1935, the tranquillity was disturbed when a late-model sedan rolled to the curb outside the First National Bank of Ardsley on Main Street. Despite the approaching holidays, the sidewalks were still; only a few matrons braved the gray cold to browse the quaint decorated store-fronts for a perfect last-minute gift. As the automobile idled at the curb, five young men climbed out, pulled up their overcoat collars, settled their fedoras close on their brows, and entered the bank.

A very few customers were doing business with the tellers, while the bank president, Harvey Slaybaugh, spoke softly on the telephone. The five men immediately took up positions—one by the door, one at Mr. Slaybaugh's desk, and the others heading for the tellers' cage—while the gang leader, a tall man with an olive complexion and a loud voice, announced a holdup. The robbery team worked fast, herding the startled employees and customers into Slaybaugh's office and emptying the tellers' cash drawers into brown paper bags. A gunman with a pitted face and empty blue eyes pressed a revolver to a young teller's jaw and com-pelled Mr. Slaybaugh to open the vault. In less than five minutes, the bandits relieved the bank of nearly $8,400 in cash and over a thousand dollars in stock certificates. As the alarmed village police raced to the bank, the robbers abandoned their car a couple of miles away in Yonkers and disappeared south into Manhattan.

The Ardsley job, which frightened the sleepy village nearly half to death, capped a successful string of bank robberies stretching from sub-urban New Jersey through lower New York State all the way north and east to leafy Connecticut. The FBI was tracking the robberies state by state, but the Ardsley police would not be outdone. They were humiliated and furious—the town's well-heeled residents had entrusted them with upholding a sedate and dignified reputation—and the police were determined to solve the case before the G-men stole their thunder. They doggedly questioned every witness, over and over, until the assailants' descriptions jelled. In short order, two arrests were made. The suspects, James Fay and John Flood, held their tongues about the names of their accomplices despite police fists, but three "John Doe" warrants were issued with federal charges attached. William "Willie the Greek" Athalis, also known as "Speed," the gang leader—a twenty-three-year-old first-generation Greek American and unemployed cabinetmaker's helper (with a year of high school, the most highly educated of the gang)—had finally brainstormed himself onto the FBI's wanted list. He and his fugitive partners, John "Patches" Waters and Edward Kiernan, aka "Eugene King," were on the run.

Patches and Kiernan were longtime partners in crime, dating back to the dormitory they shared at Elmira Reformatory when they were teenagers and to a subsequent stretch in Sing Sing. And like most of their ventures, the Ardsley job ended in a courtroom. Within the month, Kiernan, his thinning red hair combed back wetly and his doughy face resigned, and Patches, a thousand-yard stare in his blue eyes contradicting the blood in his cheeks, stood before a judge and heard the robbery charges dismissed. Their captured confederates Fay and Flood, already in custody, refused to bargain and testify against them, and the witnesses' memories, so firm just a few weeks ago, had begun to dissolve. The robbery charges didn't stick, but Patches and Kiernan had violated their parole by keeping each other's company. Stylish before the bench in their John David suits, the two were hustled back to Sing Sing at the end of January 1936.

The early gang was scattered, but William Athalis had a better run. He apparently headed south to the Florida sunshine for a year, rented a cheap though not dingy room in Miami, and spent a lot of time behind sunglasses at Hialeah Racetrack. When he felt the heat on him had cooled a bit, he came back north. But he couldn't go home to Queens and the cramped apartment he'd shared with his parents and five younger sisters all his young life. Most likely, the police still showed up there from time to time, only to leave frustrated by his Greek-speaking parents. Athalis, though, wasn't called Speed for nothing. In addition to the alacrity he brought to bank jobs, the nickname suggested a quickness of mind and also put a fine point on his lifestyle. Willie liked spending money in nightclubs where bands blew dance tunes deep into the hours and women sparkled in the dark.

In the heady days following Prohibition's repeal, well-tipped New York cabdrivers would steer their customers to dim places where a man could enjoy a drink and a foxtrot with the resident girls—called taxi-dancers—for a reasonable price. But Mae Ruggles, a platinum blond dancer at a downtown club, didn't need a coin to dance with Willie Athalis. As soon as he'd shown up sometime early in February '37, Mae was attracted to his curly dark hair, his hooded eyes looking as if he'd just awakened. During long nights at the bar with cigarette smoke painting the air, Mae would shake off the droopy salesman at her elbow when she saw Willie come in the place.

But Willie needed a favor, needed to advance their relationship in a hurry. They'd been together enough times; trusting Mae seemed like a safe option. And he wasn't bothered by her work. As they sashayed across the tiny dance floor, Mae smiled into his sleepy eyes and said, sure, he could stay at her apartment east of Broadway at 156th Street.

The plan worked to both their advantages: Willie got a quiet, out-of-the-way hideout, in the arms of a gorgeous doll no less; and Mae was paid handsomely for her accommodations. Willie still had a bankroll, and he wasn't stingy with it. As the weeks folded into months, Mae might have even wondered if she was in love. But Speed couldn't sit still for too long, no matter how soft the cushions. Soon enough, he was back looking for action.

————————

Instinct should have told Willie to stay clear of a guy at the bar called "Lulu." Word was that he was a cop, for one thing. For another, Thomas "Lulu" Gentles had a way about him. He was handsome with his sculpted mouth and dimpled chin—but he had a swagger that verged toward menace when he drank. Willie had been making book, selling wagers on the horses, since coming back north—nothing heavy, but supplemental, so he wouldn't go broke all at once. Lulu was a steady customer, a bettor who favored long odds. And when his horses didn't win, banker Willie didn't have to pay out. It was a good arrangement, and Willie came to like Lulu. So when Lulu suggested teaming for a caper he'd been working on, very low-key but with great potential—a bookmaker, Milton Kessler, took action from a car parked on a quiet West Side block—Willie said he was interested. He was still too warm to walk into banks; the Ardsley robbery had been only fourteen months ago. But maybe Lulu was on to something. Kessler sounded like an easy knockover. And if Lulu really was a cop, what could be safer?

Late on a winter afternoon, on Thirty-first Street west of Ninth Avenue, between the General Post Office and the railroad yards, Willie, Lulu, and his buddy Maurice Rue approached an automobile parked at the curb. Rush hour was grinding into gear on Ninth Avenue behind them. Two figures, Kessler and another man, were sitting in the auto's front seat. Lulu pulled a wallet from his greatcoat pocket and rapped on the driver's side window with his knuckles. The window cracked open, Lulu flipped the billford wide, and a silver badge caught the streetlight.

"Police. Open the door."

Kessler was an older man, his face as rumpled as his overcoat. When he unlocked the door, Maurice came around and shoved in behind the steering wheel. Kessler took a sharp breath and slid over against his partner. Lulu and Willie climbed into the backseat, and Maurice eased the car away from the curb.

"Give us the slips," Willie said. The betting slips were as valuable as cash if sold to the right people.

"Stop the car," Kessler said. He'd been through this before and knew the routine. "Let's talk this over."

Lulu and Willie told him to shut up.

Maurice was steering south on Tenth Avenue, looking from the side view to the rear view mirror all of a sudden. "Someone's behind us. Got a police plate."

Lulu craned to look out the rear windshield. "They got us, step on it." He rolled down the passenger window, reached into his greatcoat pocket, and tossed out a .38 revolver. Willie threw out his pistol, too. The car behind them raced abreast and veered them to the curb. Officers leaped out, guns drawn, and forced them out of the car and to the ground. The Ardsley bank job was sure to come out, Willie must have worried as he spread himself across the ice-cold sidewalk.

But Speed thought quickly. He told the court he was a waiter from Miami, was new to town, had known Lulu only a couple of weeks. Taking a chance, he jettisoned his identities, William Athalis and Speed, and heard himself sentenced as Mr. John Levy of Florida to six months at Rikers Island for conspiracy, oppression, and impersonating an officer. Responsible for thousands of arrests every day in the city, and with a penitentiary population approaching two thousand, the New York City justice system was unwittingly protecting the newly minted John Levy from federal agents investigating the Ardsley bank robbery.

When the six months were up, Athalis emerged from Rikers Island eager to make up for lost time. He'd made it through half a year in the penitentiary without the Ardsley caper coming to the surface. Surely, luck was in his favor. And the farther the bank job retreated into the past, the easier it would be to stay ahead of it. Despite the Kessler fiasco, Willie apparently held no ill will toward Lulu; in fact, during their time together at Rikers, it seems he'd grown even fonder of him. Friendships tested in the pressure cooker of a city jail either evaporated or toughened like leather. The men came to depend on each other no matter how grim or dangerous their surroundings.

But Lulu was no criminal mastermind. Shakedowns were small potatoes, sticking up some old chump—what was Lulu thinking? Willie was determined that the Kessler job would be the last time he'd listen to Lulu about something as important as a heist. They were on the outside now, free and clear—and as far as the jobs went, Willie would put them together for himself.

First of all, banks were out. Very lucrative, but they brought too much heat. He'd stick to armed robbery. But he'd target cash businesses, establishments with transactions and payrolls, jobs that alerted the flat feet of overworked city cops but not the feds with their government funds. Otherwise, it would be the same formula he'd developed years ago, the model they'd used for the Ardsley job—five-man teams plus a driver, with everybody knowing their positions, fast in and fast out. He'd make inquiries and assemble a new gang. From the comfort of Mae's frilly Harlem bedroom, Willie took his time to plan things right.

Apparently Lulu, kept out of operational planning, proved to be a talented recruiter. He knew of a guy named Mac Hanley, who lived down the block from Lulu in West New York, New Jersey, and had a pal named Rusty Mello, both of them experienced and reliable stickup men. Lulu even had a lead on the perfect gun drop, an old friend in the Gashouse District on the Lower East Side, a numbers taker named Little Joe. To Willie's surprise, Lulu seemed his own red, white, and blue "I Want You" poster.

Willie, meanwhile, found out that Patches was out of Sing Sing and back at work on the West Side docks; but Kiernan was still inside, transferred to Auburn State Prison. Patches brought in an old friend of Kiernan's instead—William Wade, aka "Billy Dalton," a skinny, reddish truck loader from the docks and a fast and steady driver. The new gang was all set: Willie and Lulu, Mac and Rusty, Patches and Wade. And like a harbinger of things to come, their initial job in October '38 was a rousing success. Hitting the Lever Brothers Soap Company warehouse in Brooklyn, holding fourteen truckers and employees at bay, the gang escaped with over $4,500. But some crooks are more reliable than others. When Wade got locked up on a burglary charge, Patches suggested a new guy to Willie—a blond kid Patches had met on the docks, a stand-up guy from Hell's Kitchen called Whitey.

By early 1939, Willie Athalis liked the direction this crew was taking. The boys came from all walks, bringing individual talents and connections that contributed to the welfare of the whole. They were working out like America's own enterprising immigrant dream, with a criminal twist. Still on ice at the Tombs, getaway driver Billy Wade, an Irishman, found them a gem burglar, Jacob "Jake the Butch" Maislich, a Jew, who had a great eye for casing targets—the Con Ed job on Audubon Avenue in December had brought them $12,000. Patches and

Whitey also had vision and perspective, and Willie was only too pleased to have their connection to the upper echelons of the West Side Irish waterfront. That was a closed world to a Greek like Willie—but when you got on the inside, there was beaucoup money to be made, as Whitey and Patches would prove.

———————

A few months later, on February 23, 1939, fifty-five-year-old Joseph Picaso kissed his wife goodbye and left his St. James Place home in Brooklyn just before eight o'clock in the morning. He tightened his grip on a brown leather valise containing over $6,000 in cash and walked toward the IND subway line at the corner of Fulton Street. As supervising dock teller for the Cunard White Star Line, Picaso intended taking the cash—passenger receipts from the *Queen Mary*, which had berthed at the North River's Pier 90 the previous afternoon—to the Customs House vault in Lower Manhattan. But he and the tellers hadn't finished tallying the duties until almost six o'clock; a trip to the Customs House would have added an hour to an already long day. Of course, bringing the money home was a direct violation of dock rules; but Picaso had done it before on other evenings when he'd been pressed for time, and no one had been any the wiser. With over thirty years' experience, he knew what a man could get away with.

As he approached the corner, he caught sight of a tan automobile idling up to the curb beside him. Someone needing directions, he figured. When he turned to look, the doors flew open and three men jumped out. They were around him in seconds, revolvers held low and pointed at his midsection, hands grabbing at his briefcase. A fist slammed into his face and knocked off his glasses.

"Give us the bag," one said, "give us the dough."

Picaso, not a large man, had neglected to bring his assigned pistol home with him the previous night. But he dug his heels into the grass beside the sidewalk as the robbers pushed him toward the sedan's open rear door. He swung out with his left fist, lost his balance, and felt the valise slip from his grasp. The car doors slammed. He fumbled across the concrete for his glasses as the car sped around the corner and disappeared.

He got to his feet, trembling, and brushed himself off. The street was quiet, a few cars passing by, a couple walking farther down on St. James. No one was rushing to his aid. He smoothed his hair, then took out a handkerchief and passed it over his forehead. He couldn't go home. His wife would want to know everything, and he didn't have the time—he really had to speak to his supervisors first, try to explain what happened. Then he'd call the police. There was a telephone booth at the candy store on Fulton; Picaso hurried to call the pier.

According to the *New York Times*, the robbery marked the first in city history of government money being stolen from a customs inspector. The police and federal agents all agreed that the robbers must have had inside information, but a shaken Picaso would identify the thieves only as "young men of Latin appearance." He was in enough trouble with his bosses; he wasn't about to anger an Irish mob as well.

A couple of hours later, with the $6,100 transferred to a blue canvas gym bag, Whitey Riordan met Bandit Gregory at the Hudson Hofbrau on Twelfth Avenue. Bandit held the bag under the table, counted out a percentage for the gang, and handed Whitey his share. Barely twenty-four, Whitey must have felt at the top of his game.

A contract job like the Picaso holdup, in addition to the gang's independent work, seemed the perfect merger to Whitey, a natural union. This was how you ran a professional organization: a profitable freelance operation that was versatile enough to hire out for tailor-made mob assignments.

Everybody was happy.

CHAPTER SIX

"5 ARRESTS SMASH MOB"

June 15, 1939

A MONTH TO THE DAY after the Harlem Con Ed holdup, Little Joe Salvatore had to take his mother to the doctor's office. After that, he hoped to head over to the poolroom, probably by one o'clock. His mother wasn't sick, thankfully; it was just a routine checkup. His aunt and his cousin Alice, though, *marone*. They seemed to get flattened by every little ache and pain—Alice with her leg in a cast from a fall, and her nervous disposition. Ever since his father had died a few years ago, Little Joe had kept a close eye on the family, calling them every day, running errands. He was the only man of the house, so he was at their constant beck and call. But they were family, and that wasn't something Little Joe took lightly.

He drove up Second Avenue. Only the middle of June, barely ten o'clock, and it was already as sticky as August. He passed the poolroom at Thirty-fourth Street, the sun flashing off the plate glass, a couple of guys smoking cigarettes in the awning's shadow. It looked like business as usual. Too bad. Joe had a three-month suspended sentence for a numbers arrest the previous week, so he was laying low. Periodically, the police cracked down on runners like Joe, who collected bets from players, so when he stopped by the poolroom lately it really was to shoot a game or to listen to the Yankees on the radio.

But his other venture—the briefcase in the closet he could tell no one about—was still in full swing. Just the day before yesterday, none other than Willie the Greek had stopped by the apartment. Little Joe hadn't seen any of the boys since they'd taken up his whole afternoon in May. Willie seemed distracted, almost on edge, looking around the apartment as if he'd forgotten something. He asked Joe for the shirt and "lumber jacket" that Willie had left behind the time he'd changed clothes after a job.

When he was leaving, his stuff wrapped in a bag under his arm, Willie seemed lighter, even relieved. He had invited Joe out to Coney Island on Thursday, today, to enjoy the ocean breezes. Willie was taking his girl-friend Mae; Joe and his wife could make it a foursome. Joe wasn't sure. Ever since the subway expansion in 1920, Coney Island was like Mecca for New York's grittier classes. Gilded Age restaurants like Stauch's and Henderson's were replaced by scores of hotdog stands and custard coun-ters. On a hot June day the beach would be thronged cheek to cheek, the boardwalk ringing with packed shooting galleries and freak shows. Joe liked Willie well enough, but he was glad for the excuse of his mother's doctor's appointment. And that was that. Willie was out the door. He hadn't taken the guns, though. They were still tucked away in Little Joe's bedroom closet, still the unmentioned something that Joe and his wife Rose Angela dragged along between them.

Little Joe parked down the block from his family's apartment at 411 East Eighty-second Street. The headlines on the newsstand at the cor-ner of First Avenue were terrible, as usual. This time it was a French submarine, the *Phenix,* sunk in the South China Sea, with more than sixty men lost. The idea of being buried alive under all that water, seeing it coming . . . a baseball fan like Joe would automatically snap open the sports pages. The Indians' Al Milnar was facing off against Yankees rookie Atley Donald in the third game of their series. It looked like a good game, and Little Joe was surely eager to get down to the pool hall and listen to it.

Up in the apartment, he hugged his mother. His good Italian aunt probably had the sauce going, the heat notwithstanding, the apartment steaming with the aroma of bubbling spices enough to make a man's stomach growl. Cousin Alice would have been irritable with the heat, her leg plastered stiff before her, her forehead sweaty. Later, in a letter to authorities, she would write how much they all depended on their Joe, Alice in particular, "more now than ever."

It was nearly noon when Joe and his mother returned from the doctor's, and almost one o'clock by the time they'd eaten. Joe said he had to leave, kissed them all, told them he'd talk to them tomorrow. They gave him guff about eating and running, but they weren't serious—they expected to see him again in a day or two, as usual. When he closed the door behind him, though, he had no idea that it would be months before he laid eyes on the family again.

Across the river in Brooklyn, Acting Captain Frank C. Bals, 10th Detective Division, 70th Precinct, Brooklyn, nodded once or twice as his detectives, Walter Laurie and Frank Griffiths, briefed him in the squad room, the air stale with sweat and cigarettes. The detectives, ties loosened and jackets slung on the backs of their chairs, had a tip about the Shopping Bag Gang. As lead investigator on the Brooklyn angle of the inquiry, initiated after the Lever Brothers warehouse holdup the previous October, Captain Bals had been overseeing the shoe-leather detective work of twenty-five officers for the past seven months. There had been little to show for it, so this tip was good news.

A policeman since 1916, Bals had earned two commendations and two "excellent police work" citations, mostly for ferreting out syndicates and racketeers infesting the labor unions. Corruption ran in the streets, and Bals found it wasn't always easy to keep his expensive shoes and tailored suits clean in the Brooklyn swamps. Time after time, the captain had seen the clean-government reformers' waves crest over the department, crash into the district attorney's office, and then ebb away. For Captain Bals, dodging the splash-back, the Shopping Bag tip was most welcome, even though it seemed to come from the middle of the bog.

A veteran policeman, Bals knew the value of criminal informants. The Brooklyn racketeers and gambling syndicates entrenched throughout the borough were thick with information. Abe "Kid Twist" Reles, for one, right-hand man to Brooklyn waterfront boss and Murder Inc. kingpin Albert Anastasia, ran a vast and lucrative policy operation. According to the *New York Times,* proceeds from one arm of the gambling organization, about a million dollars worth of loan-sharking profits, were used to buy protection from the Brooklyn precinct houses.

Cop and crook partnerships, corrupt though they were, offered the exchange of information, as well as money. One detective, resistant to the temptation yet aware of the lure, noted, "The borderline between me and them was very thin." Policy controllers, conveying money and information from collectors like Little Joe Salvatore to the underworld bank, where the numbers were tabulated and winnings determined, apparently circled in a limited world.

Detectives Laurie and Griffiths told Captain Bals that there was word going around of a collector on the East Side, working out of a poolroom on East Thirty-fourth Street and Second Avenue, who seemed to know something about the robberies. Informants knew that this collector, who was called Little Joe, hung around the pool hall most afternoons. Detective Laurie read from an arrest report filed with the 60th Squad, 13th Precinct, on the East Side. Little Joe had been picked up the week before on a policy charge, his address listed as East Twenty-fifth Street, just west of Second Avenue. Captain Bals suggested that they take a ride.

———————

At about the same time, Willie the Greek and his girlfriend Mae, sun-kissed and lazy, were packing up their blanket and leaving the Coney Island beach. For nearly two years, their living arrangement had worked out beautifully. Willie couldn't have been more fortunate. Mae had turned out to be more than a hideaway. She'd remained Willie's rock-solid alibi, even as she bluffed her way through telephone calls from FBI agents still chasing Willie for the Ardsley bank robbery. Deliberately throwing the feds off his trail, risking her own freedom—that had to be love.

The aroma of fried oysters drifted up from a shack down the boardwalk. It was past lunchtime, time to go. They headed back to the car.

———————

Captain Bals and Detectives Laurie and Griffiths drove across the Brooklyn Bridge and up the East Side. They had arranged to pick up

Detective McCarthy, the 13th Precinct's arresting officer for Little Joe's policy charge. The sedan passed the poolroom, and McCarthy pointed a thick finger in front of Bals's face. That one there, the little fellow, looks like a poor man's Max Baer. They pulled to the curb one block north on Second Avenue. Bals unclipped his holster, shook out of it, and handed it to Laurie. No one had to mention that only cops wore jackets in this weather. The heat helped sag his careful appearance, and with his suit coat draped over one arm, Captain Bals looked like a tired player determined to win.

Little Joe stood on the sidewalk in the awning's shade and watched the stranger approach.

"Come here, Joe," the man said out of the side of his mouth. "I got some information for you."

Joe cocked his head, a "Who me?" look on his face.

He walked up the block with Captain Bals beside him. Joe was racking his brain, wondering how the man knew him, taking liberties with that heavy palm on his shoulder. Joe was sure he'd never seen the guy before.

Away from the men outside the pool hall, as the two came abreast of the policemen's sedan, Bals showed Joe his shield.

As though the detective had just fanned out five of a kind, Little Joe swallowed and understood the situation in a flash. He hadn't taken a number all week. The only other thing in his life was a briefcase of guns, which he'd never wanted in his bedroom closet in the first place. He peered at the policeman's badge, a captain's bright gold, and pictured Willie the Greek nervously stopping by the apartment the other day to pick up some clothes—no trace of *him* around that briefcase. Little Joe shook his head. He might have been a "drop," but he was no fall guy. So he scrunched up his face and asked, "What's it about? Willie?"

The detectives hustled Joe into the car and pulled away from the curb. Stuffed in the backseat between Detectives Bals and McCarthy, the car rank with sweat, Little Joe felt his heart drumming. He didn't deserve this; he was a numbers runner, for Christ's sake. He'd never hurt anybody. And what if his mother needed to see the doctor again? When Captain Bals started asking questions, Joe cleared his throat and answered every one.

At the apartment, Little Joe pointed out the bedroom closet to the detectives. Griffith got on his knees and dug out a heavy paper bag, two steel vests, and the blue briefcase. Laurie piled it all on the bed while Bals and McCarthy questioned Little Joe. He was thankful that Rose Angela was out.

The detectives loaded the evidence into the car and took Joe to the Parkville Station in Brooklyn. Detectives Laurie and Griffiths continued on to Coney Island. Little Joe apologized that he couldn't be more specific, but he thought the policemen might find Willie the Greek cruising Surf Avenue. By late afternoon, spotting a car that matched Joe's description, the detectives had arrested Willie and Mae. And after hours of questioning, the names and likely whereabouts of the others became clear.

────────

Whitey Riordan, Patches Waters, and Billy Wade—wanted in connection with the December Con Ed robbery on Audubon Avenue—were rounded up and brought down to the stationhouse. Everyone else— Lulu, Mac, and Rusty—had vanished. In a lineup, witnesses from both Con Ed holdups positively identified Whitey and Patches as the gunmen who had robbed the cashiers, and Willie the Greek as the armed man who had given the orders. Witnesses from the October Lever Brothers job in Brooklyn also pointed to Willie and Patches. Police were triumphant—they had finally cracked the case. The Shopping Bag Gang had pulled their last job.

Herman Stichman, a New York City assistant district attorney, offered to reduce Joe's bail from $5,000 to $100 in return for his cooperation and testimony. Joe agreed and began to talk in great detail, his family running through his mind the whole time. By November, though, with the holidays just around the corner, Joe was still at the dreadful Tombs, writing letters to the assistant D.A. Little Joe carefully explained how he'd "gladly stay until you found it convenient to let me go, but I would consider it a great favor if you will kindly let me off in my reduced bail so as to give me the pleasure in being home with my folks for the holidays." But Christmas came and went.

Willie was whisked away by the FBI and interrogated about the Ardsley bank job. They couldn't make it stick after all those years, but Willie did receive from fifteen to thirty for armed robbery on the Con Ed cases. He was sent to Sing Sing before being transferred even farther upstate. Mae Ruggles was arraigned for "harboring and concealing" him during his fugitive years. In court, the flashy taxi-dancer made quite an appearance at the hearing, the whole scene relished by a *Journal and American* reporter. The platinum blond was dressed to the nines, click-clacking down the courthouse halls with a "tricky little hat perched jauntily" on her head. Overcome by emotion, she pressed a hanky to her upturned nose and made "the marble corridors echo with her wails." Newsmen and spectators gathered around the darling blond with the crying jag, but it was hard to tell whether her tears were flowing for herself or for Willie.

The feds were furious with Mae Ruggles. They'd been planning a trap for Willie the Greek, with Mae as the bait. But apparently, she wouldn't betray her man like that. It took the New York Police to deliver Willie up to them, finally. But Mae's tears and innocent act seemed to work. Instead of immediately being locked up, she was released on $500 bail for a grand jury hearing. Eventually, charges were dropped.

Rusty Mello and Mac Hanley were captured in the fall of 1940, after burgling the post office safe in Wappingers Falls, New York. They were freed on that charge, despite blood evidence from a cut finger that left a trail from the cracked safe to Mac's automobile. But they were immediately transferred to Albany to face indictment on a bar and grill holdup, for which they received from fifteen to thirty years apiece in Clinton prison. They were never charged with the Shopping Bag crimes. The New York district attorney cited lack of evidence, to wit, the fading memories of witnesses.

Lulu Gentles, the ex-policeman and Little Joe's old acquaintance, was caught in October 1940 after forging a signature on the vehicle registration for a new car. Sporting a mop of silvering curly hair and a trim Dillingeresque mustache, Lulu evidently had hidden in the open for more than a year. He divided his time between the apartment he kept with his wife in West New York, New Jersey, and a room he rented on West 108th Street under the name Lawrence Murray. He'd apparently moved on from shaking down bookies to extorting homosexuals, figuring they'd be the last to call the police. His carefully handwritten recipes for "Green Peppers and Tomato Slices" and "Boiled Veal or Beef" proved to be his undoing. The prosecution used them as handwriting samples to establish forgery on the car registration. However, luck was ultimately with Lulu. The district attorney decided that the robbery witnesses wouldn't be able to identify him any better than they'd identified Mac and Rusty, and Lulu was released after sixty days at Rikers Island.

Billy Wade, the suspected getaway driver for the Con Ed Audubon job, was also released for lack of evidence. An associate of Jake the Butch, the jewel thief who had cased both Con Ed offices and then stood back, Billy Wade couldn't be connected to the robberies without corroborating testimony. But Whitey and Patches were tight-lipped longshoremen—they refused to rat and denied knowing anything at all about the robberies, Wade, or anyone else involved. William Wade, it would prove in the months to come, was tremendously grateful.

Admitting nothing, Whitey and Patches nevertheless pleaded guilty to the lesser charge of robbery in the second degree, and they received from fifteen to thirty years at Sing Sing. Their holdup careers were over for now, their crew scattered to the winds. Over $40,000 taken in a seven-month-long roller coaster ride, the equivalent of more than half a million dollars today—all for nothing. Bundled off to Sing Sing, cuffed with Whitey in the back of the prison paddy wagon, Patches began to think about Little Joe.

Sitting there in the sweltering Brooklyn station house with a cold Pepsi-Cola in his sweaty palm, Little Joe had watched as Whitey, Willie, and Patches were paraded before him in handcuffs. Assistant D.A. Stichman asked if Joe knew them; Joe nodded sure, and said by what name. He'd committed the ultimate West Side sin—ratting them all out, even his old pal Lulu. And in return, the robbery charges against Joe were dropped. He took a one-year sentence on a gun rap; that was all. Patches could only steam.

Whitey, for his part, was humiliated. His dreams of organizing his life, and finally making it big, had crumbled. There he was, chained in the back of a stinking prison transport, bumping along upstate. The only big time he faced now was years in Sing Sing. Still, if he could have glimpsed the future, he might have felt luckier. Had Whitey remained free, within the year he could easily have met the same fate as his former partners, dock boss Davie Beadle and union delegate Bandit Gregory. By Christmas 1939, Beadle had been gunned down outside a bar on Tenth Avenue, minutes after washing down his heart medicine with a glass of water. A year later, Bandit would be shot dead inside the Hudson Hofbrau, the old gang hangout, his union card clutched between his fingers. Seen in hindsight, Sing Sing held out yet another chance for Whitey.

Like his partner beside him, Patches Waters probably wasn't thinking of redemption, either. Staring through the bars on the prison transport windows, he was likely wondering how to make it up to Little Joe. Or maybe he'd already begun to cook up a new scheme, from force of habit—something bolder and riskier than anything he'd come up with before. The paddy wagon turned a corner. Outside, the North River widened, and the Palisades opposite became steeper and more wooded. The transport entered the small village of Ossining and turned onto a narrow street that twisted past ramshackle houses perched above the gray water.

As Sing Sing's towered, limestone walls rose into view through the trees, it would only have been natual for Patches to wonder: how might a guy break out of one of the biggest, toughest, and most infamous prisons in the country?

PART TWO

SING SING

Convicts are great dreamers.
—FYODOR DOSTOYEVSKY
The House of the Dead

CHAPTER SEVEN

THE PRISON THAT LAWES BUILT

FROM HIS OFFICE ON THE SECOND FLOOR of the Administration Building, Sing Sing warden Lewis E. Lawes could stand at the wide arched windows and see west into the lower prison. Through the steel bars, Lawes had a perfect view of the recreation field in the prison's old section, down at the Hudson River's mossy edge. There, on any given summer weekend, prison inmates challenged visiting teams from the local area to lively games of baseball. If business kept him from his seat behind home plate—in prison, a weekend was a workday, too—the warden was almost certain to steal a few minutes from his desk to catch a game. The batters would swing hard under the watchful eyes of the guard assigned to 10 Post—the tower behind home plate—and of the spectators in the always-crowded bleachers that stretched along the first and third base lines. Prison inmates were passionate about their team, the Sing Sing Orioles, and their noisy cheers rose on the warm river breeze drifting through the office window's open transom—pure music to the warden's ears.

Of all the changes the warden had accomplished in his twenty years at Sing Sing—the list was long, he liked to boast—Lawes Field was one of his proudest achievements. One of Lawes's predecessors, Warden Thomas McCormick, had instituted baseball as an official recreation back in 1914. But Lawes had the vision to build on that initiative, landscaping a scrub lot at the river's edge to a professional-grade ball field. He even went so far as to invite major league teams, such as the New York Giants and the Yankees, to take on the inmates. No less a star than Babe Ruth had pointed his bat at the Administration Building one Sunday afternoon, launching a ball way over the twenty-foot-high wall, where it bounced across the New York Central railroad tracks bisecting the new and old prison grounds. According to a recent Lawes biography, one lucky Ossining boy in attendance at the game hustled down the embankment and grabbed the home-run ball. Later, the kid got the Babe to autograph the treasure, and Ruth then handed it to his great rival Lou Gehrig, who also signed the ball for the awestruck lad. (Decades later, a member of the local historical society reported that the boy, by then a man in his eighties, had lost the ball and from time to time would drop into the museum to ask—apparently still hoping against hope—whether word of the souvenir's whereabouts had surfaced.)

These games, which filled column inches in the local newspaper as well as bleachers and sidelines, not only gave the notorious prison a public relations face-lift but also exemplified one of Warden Lawes's favorite maxims: "prisoners should be encouraged to spend their leisure in healthful recreation." But, Lawes was quick to add, only those inmates who earned the privilege. Rehabilitation was a two-way street: if a man followed the strict prison code, only then would he enjoy increased freedoms.

On one August weekend in 1940, however, Lawes could spend little time rooting for the home team. The prison's annual budget report was due in Albany in only a few weeks. Returning to work, Lawes would settle back at his desk, the cheers outside rising higher and then fading as the runners rounded the bases. He may not have noticed it every day, but the carved wooden escritoire, like much of Sing Sing's office furniture, was a work of art. Ornate, delicately filigreed by the inmates assigned to the woodworking shop, the desk was a manifestation of the warden's belief that prisoner rehabilitation could be achieved only by "turning these prisons into plants where human impulses and the desire for normal living can be recharged with vigor and encouragement." Almost anywhere you looked in Sing Sing during Lawes's tenure, you saw other examples of this progressive thought at work: not just in the popular baseball team or the convict-crafted furniture, but also in the new school (with mandatory attendance for all inmates with skills under a sixth grade level), the football team (the Black Sheep), the prison band, and—perhaps most famous—the lavish rose garden landscaped by Charles Chapin, a former editor of the *New York Evening World* who was serving a life sentence for killing his wife. Despite occasional criticisms that Lawes was coddling the inmates, no one could deny that New York's third oldest prison represented the latest in prison reform.

As much as he might like to be down at the ballgame with "the boys," as he called them, the budget report was waiting. A regular at Manhattan nightclubs—smoky places like the Cotton Club and the Silver Slipper, popular with celebrities and gangsters alike—Lewis Lawes and his wife usually had Saturday evening plans, and it was already midafternoon. The warden was responsible for a nearly $30-million institution, whose smoking workshops produced the manufacturing output of a midsize factory town. Each year Lawes signed off on more than $3 million in annual expenditures, including security and salaries, maintenance and supplies. But more than just tallying dry numbers, Lawes fashioned annual reports that were evidence of his expert stewardship, which he believed was second to none. In the warden's humble opinion, his far-sighted administration had made Sing Sing a world-class example of what a modern prison could be. The cheering ball games were bright cases in point.

But a change was simmering that August, down there in the bleachers at Lawes Field. Something was coming, a plan circling in whispers and quick glances between two new arrivals and a veteran convict. The three were "yeggs," prison slang for stickup artists, and their actions in the months ahead would alter the course of the famous warden's career and stain his carefully planned-for legacy. Lawes once wrote about inmate fans watching a game, reporting that "there was not a shady or ominous thought in all that crowd of men."

That summer, his boast could not have been further off-base.

———

When Lewis Lawes arrived in Ossining in January 1920, he found a small, decrepit prison straight out of the nineteenth century. No wonder the state had trouble finding anyone willing to run the place. To the progressive-minded Lawes, even worse than the physical decay were the archaic, brutal methods of punishment used on a population of twelve hundred men. To top it off, despite a burgeoning roster of inmates, New York's most infamous prison complex was still crammed onto a plot of land not much larger than the original fourteen-and-one-half-acre site.

Nearly a century before, after frequent rioting and persistent overcrowding at New York's first and second prisons—Newgate in Greenwich Village, and Auburn upstate—the state legislature authorized the construction of a third prison to contain the increasing flow of convicts from New York City. The state commissioned the warden of Auburn, Captain Elam Lynds, and his handpicked team of burly convict quarrymen to cut Sing Sing out of the dolomite hills of an abandoned silver mine thirty miles north of Manhattan. The native inhabitants from the region's Mohegan, Chippewa, and Delaware tribes had called the area Sint-Sinck, Ossinee, and Asin-Es-Ink, meaning, respectively, "stone on stone," "stones," and "a stony place." The small rocky village nearby came to be called Mount Pleasant, but Captain Lynds's sweating inmates would have appreciated the natives' more literal perspective. Bivouacked in temporary barracks, the smoke from slapped-together cookhouses and banging iron forges thick in their noses, the convicts raised their own cellblock in a silence enforced by the steady rise and fall of the captain's lash. The workers were unchained, the better to freely swing their pickaxes and sledgehammers, but they were always within the sights of surrounding rifles.

By 1828, the thousand-cell prison block on the Hudson was complete. Newgate prison was shuttered, and its inmates were transferred up the river. While Sing Sing waited for its new arrivals, the cellblock's first inmates were its builders—one hundred seventy men locked behind heavy iron-grill doors in individual cells of rough-hewn limestone, barely seven feet deep, three feet wide, and six and one-half feet tall. Built only inches above the water level, the block's every cell was damp and cold. The prison's stark environment in the early years often led convicts to risk the guns and race for the water or the hills. Yet despite near-daily escape attempts, the state legislature took almost fifty years to approve the funds for an enclosing wall around the prison. The bureaucrats, it seemed, had full confidence in Lynds's legacy of merciless discipline—so severe, it was rumored that Lynds preferred to hire prison keepers who couldn't count, so that the constant confusion would provide added excuses for whippings. As New York's inmate population continued to grow throughout the nineteenth century, the new state prison underwent almost constant expansion within its confined site. The old cellblock's roof was raised twice, and a fifth and then a sixth tier were pounded on. In short time, the original fourteen and one-half acres, hard by the waterfront, was densely packed with a kitchen, a hospital, and a chapel.

Almost immediately, Sing Sing earned a foul reputation. Dysentery, cholera, and smallpox ravaged the men. Food rations were meager—only two eggs per inmate were allowed for the whole year—but only the bravest souls grumbled. Complaints brought nothing good. Methods of prisoner control developed at Auburn were instituted at Sing Sing, including the lockstep, which forced inmates to march in single-file lines, sometimes shackled at the ankle. New prisoners had their heads shaved and were issued striped uniforms. The stripes were a form of scarlet letter, in effect forcing the convicts to wear their criminal records quite literally on their sleeves. According to one historian, single, double, or triple stripes branded inmates, respectively, as first-, second-, or third-time offenders. Four stripes signaled that a convict was considered incorrigible and earned him the nickname "zebra."

Discipline continued to be a dark affair, relying on such instruments as the cat-o'-nine-tails (nine strands of leather dangling from a hard wood bat), cold shower baths, and the dreaded yoke—two forty-pound iron bars strapped to a rebellious inmate's outstretched arms and fastened at the neck. One unfortunate prisoner, chastised for "poor work," was bound to the yoke and was so disabled by the ordeal that he was laid up in his cell for two weeks. Finally returned to the workshop, and no more certain of his factory skills than before, he chopped off the fingers of one hand rather than face another round with the crippling device. Brutality like that, over time, took its toll on convicts and guards alike.

Finding capable administrators for such harsh policy was no easy task. Sing Sing's first hundred years saw forty-two wardens come and go, mostly political appointees with no particular experience or skill. Not surprisingly, they served short terms, working an average of scarcely over two years. In December 1919, faced with yet another vacancy in the warden's office, Governor Alfred E. Smith decided to recruit the promising young superintendent of New Hampton prison farm, Lewis E. Lawes. The governor summoned thirty-six-year-old Lawes from upstate to the Biltmore Hotel in New York City and turned on the Irish charm. Cigars were offered, and Lawes expectantly settled back in the governor's suite. The old Tammany leader, smiling through the smoke, got right to the point. "How about going up to Sing Sing and take charge?" Governor Smith asked in his Lower East Side growl. The offer wasn't a complete surprise—Lawes had heard about the job opening. In fact, as he tells the story in one of his many memoirs, he had no intention of accepting the position. The salary was no better than at New Hampton, and the job far worse. Plus, he'd have to answer to state politicians whose only concern was for their own careers. Lawes politely declined. "It's a tough spot, I don't blame you for being scared," the governor shrugged, tapping off an ash. "It'll take a big man to go up *there* and stay." Lawes's cheeks blazed. He saw through the governor's game, but the challenge still hit home. As Lawes wrote, "though I asked for a week to think it over, I knew then that I would be the new Warden of Sing Sing."

Upon his official arrival, the prison staff met their new boss with polite coolness. They weren't intentionally aloof; they simply didn't expect much. Their attitude was best summed up in the standard joke: "The quickest way out of Sing Sing is to come in as warden." But it was no laughing matter. Lawes's predecessor, a former judge and tax appraiser, had literally shriveled under Sing Sing's rigors. In twenty-six harrowing weeks, the poor man lost forty pounds. But Lewis E. Lawes was a career jailer. Sing Sing didn't scare him.

The son of an Elmira Reformatory guard, Lawes was raised within earshot of that facility's blaring martial bands. Following in his father's boot steps, the future warden cut his teeth at a series of New York institutions. From Clinton prison—nicknamed the "Siberia of America" for its remote location in the northern Adirondack town of Dannemora—on to Auburn prison, and then back home to Elmira and a job at the Reformatory, Lawes steadily racked up cellblock experience. In 1912, he took a leave of absence from his position to attend the New York School of Social Work, a satellite of Columbia University. His ability to blend hands-on prison experience with the latest social theory of rehabilitation made a strong impression on his professors; the six-week summer program seemed custom-made for the twenty-eight-year-old prison guard. As Lawes put it afterward: "I was . . . confirmed in my ideals." When his former professor Katherine B. Davis became New York City's commissioner of corrections, she hired Lawes to his first superintendent post at the city's reformatory on Hart's Island, the former Potter's Field in Long Island Sound. The future great reformer was on his way.

But for all his work behind the walls, enforcing the stiff consequences of breaking the law, Lawes was an unimposing physical presence. Not tall by cellblock standards and of medium build, his cinnamon hair receding above a high forehead, in his three-piece suits the new warden of Sing Sing looked more like a fussy banker than a tough guy. Lawes's eyes, though, gave him away. Steel blue, and hard as tungsten.

On his first day at Sing Sing, January 1, 1920, the warden crossed a prison yard blowing with litter and stacked with debris. Caps pulled low, the inmates grouped freely, slouching against a bitter wind off the river, cigarettes cupped to their lips. Some showed the exalted status of criminal aristocrats, multicolored silk shirts peeking out from under their thick, state-issue cotton jackets. The old original cellblock was still occupied, a grim relic among the more recent construction, its air fetid from the slop-bucket toilets, and oppressive with a sense of the one hundred thousand lives that had been wasted there over the decades. The many small windows cut into the foot-thick walls, and barely wider than a man's spread hands, seemed only to accentuate the old cellblock's overwhelming gloom and dankness. The whole prison's cramped, ragged appearance was dispiriting. No wonder the convicts shuffled in sullen packs. As Lawes would later write, he faced a "man-sized job."

And he lost no time getting down to business. The new warden's introductory speech to the inmates was scheduled for noon that first day.

Lawes had composed several drafts before arriving on the job, scratching out and inking in the right tone. But after a walk across the yard, the reformer abandoned his careful speech. He knew what he had to say.

At twelve o'clock sharp, more than a thousand men were escorted into the old mess hall. Despite the noon hour, the overhead bulbs were snapped on—the grimy, iron-mesh windows dimmed the winter daylight. Lawes stood at the head of the room and watched as the inmates took their seats. The room grew stuffy, the iron radiators hissing out the woolen smell of rusty water. As the scraping of chairs settled down, a guard gestured for the warden to step onto a small platform set up in the center of the large room. Lawes shook his head and fixed the audience with his hard blue gaze.

"I'd rather talk to you men on the level," he said, his voice high and clear. "I hope to stay there."

The inmates murmured, then fell silent as Lawes raised a palm.

"I'm willing to meet you half way, and give you all the breaks that your record entitles you to. There'll be no 'you be a good boy and I'll be a good warden' policy. What you get in privileges, you'll have to earn. But if your conduct justifies it, you'll get as much leeway as your status as prisoners of the state warrants."

Warden Lawes stopped. He didn't offer to take questions—this wasn't a discussion. It was an address that he wanted the men to absorb.

That's all, he told them.

The inmates were still. Then someone began to clap, and applause spread across the room. But not everyone joined in.

As Lawes knew well, time would tell.

————————

And for the most part, his twenty-year tenure at Sing Sing produced a record of success. As the inmate population swelled, Lawes won a state appropriation of $8 million to renovate and expand the prison's deteriorating physical plant. Year by year, new construction crossed the railroad tracks, steaming and clattering up the hillside, leveling outcroppings, and raising four new brick and steel cellblocks with flush toilets and radio jacks in each cell. The biggest of them, A-block, is still the largest free-standing cellblock in the world, measuring 176 yards long—nearly the length of two football fields—and accommodating 684 inmates in 88 cells on each of the four tiers, front and back. Its companion, B-block, is the world's second largest.

But Lawes's plan didn't stop there. He went on to include a large, new multipurpose chapel that not only served the prisoners' many faiths but also became the auditorium for weekly motion pictures and live variety shows. In addition, the prison soon contained a new mess hall, kitchen, and bakery, as well as a four-story, state-of-the-art hospital with two fully equipped operating rooms—more than seven hundred operations were performed there in 1929 alone—and a clinic. The smoke and toil continued through two decades, as Lawes's reputation grew and the state money kept flowing—enough funds to complete an industrial laundry, a clothing shop, a bathhouse with complete locker facilities, a school, a library with fifteen thousand volumes, and even a barbershop, its long row of comfortable chrome and stuffed leather chairs rivaling the finest establishment in New York.

As befitted his station as master builder, the warden ensconced himself in a new limestone Administration Building, situated on a bluff halfway up the hill along the prison's north wall, overseeing the expansive Hudson and serving as the whole prison's main entrance. Earth from the excavated hills was dumped along the riverbank, adding 33 acres to the prison's original 14.5, making Sing Sing more than five times bigger than Auburn prison. In fact, with the new sewer and water lines, freshly graded interior roads, increased industrial production from fully overhauled workshops, and its own fire department, Sing Sing prison soon rivaled the adjoining town of Ossining in self-sufficiency.

As proud as Lawes was of his accomplishments, however, he recognized that hammering Sing Sing into a model prison was only the brick and mortar expression of a problem-solving philosophy. Molding minds *before* they went astray, Lawes was convinced, was the surest way to prevent the problem—crime—in the first place. But once a man was incarcerated, rehabilitation became essential. "The gesture of trust," Lawes wrote, "will bring forth its return in honor and faith." In 1933, after a decade as warden, Lawes brought this viewpoint to a mass audience with the hugely successful publication of his prison memoir, *Twenty-Thousand Years in Sing Sing*. (The title refers to the accumulated prison sentences served during his tenure.) An erudite writer (though rumors persist that the imprisoned *New York Evening World* editor, Charles Chapin, ghost wrote the book), Lawes quotes Carlyle, Shaw, and Emerson to argue that a prison warden deals not only with the lives of the prisoners locked up under his command, but with their families' lives as well. What went on behind the walls, how a man changed there, the warden reasoned, rippled across the fabric of society when a prisoner was freed.

The warden argued that crime's root causes could be traced to every level of American culture: from the inequities in a criminal justice system that extended leniency primarily to those with money and left the poor to languish in jail; to inadequate schools and underfunded programs designed to keep kids off the streets; to newspaper stories that glorified the gangster lifestyle. All of society had a hand in the inmate's fate, and the molding institutions weren't doing their jobs. "Guidance rather than deterrence," the author chided, "is the answer to crime."

But as much as the memoir set forth Lawes's sense of urgency underscoring his work in corrections, the instant bestseller was also an effective piece of self-promotion. Lawes's expert, if sometimes patronizing, point of view struck a nerve with a public both exasperated and bewildered by the past decade's lawlessness. As a penologist and astute social critic, the warden seemed to have the answer everyone wanted, and he was determined to spread his message across the land. He wrote articles defining corrections and rehabilitation for magazines, encyclopedias, and research dictionaries. His acclaimed memoir, though, got the most mileage by far.

After the serialization of *Twenty-Thousand Years* in the *Daily News*, Warner Brothers in 1933 fictionalized the memoir in a motion picture directed by Michael Curtiz (of future *Casablanca* fame) and starring Spencer Tracy as a gangster and Bette Davis as his moll. Even though filmed on location behind the walls, with Lawes as technical adviser, the movie veered wildly from the book and received only tepid reviews. The outlandish story line—convict Tracy is allowed an unescorted visit to Davis, hospitalized after a car wreck, and takes the rap when she kills her lawyer—led the *New York Times* to sniff that "Truth is more interesting than fiction here." But Lawes probably didn't care. The picture boosted book sales, and the publisher printed another five thousand copies.

With typical foresight, Lawes saw even further potential for the material in the nation's radio craze. He found a sponsor—Sloan's Liniment—and adapted his memoir for broadcast. Every Sunday evening, Lawes would narrate fictional stories of crime and punishment from the NBC studios in Rockefeller Center—though some claim he also broadcast from an old radio console in a corner of Sing Sing's former Death House. In any event, *The Sloan Liniment Hour* found the moral in tales of juvenile delinquency and drew bags of fan mail from around the country.

Lawes amplified that success with three more books. One of them, *Invisible Stripes,* was also adapted for the screen. His appreciation of the dramatic possibilities offered by his job, and his acute ear for hard-boiled (if corny) dialogue, were also evident in *Chalked Out,* a Broadway crime drama that he co-authored. The play opened at the Morosco Theatre in 1937, after Lawes sent a blizzard of invitations to friends and associates in corrections and law enforcement, publishing, and show business. Despite the fanfare, though, *Chalked Out* closed within the week. (New York City Commissioner of Corrections Austin H. MacCormick's note of apology declining an invitation to the opening-night performance didn't arrive at the prison until after the play had closed. The Welfare Island raider weakly blamed the delay on the Easter holiday.)

Lawes was undeterred. Bitten by the show-business bug, he sold the copyright to *Chalked Out* to the Zeppo Marks Agency ("Marks" is an apparent misspelling—the comedian Zeppo Marx had become an agent by the late '30s.) The play found a much wider audience as a Warner Brothers movie, *You Can't Get Away with Murder,* and a leading vehicle for Humphrey Bogart. Lawes had developed a close relationship with the Hollywood studio over the years, and his timing was superb. His many dramas and steady stream of social commentary—the noble themes of which were quickly reduced to the platitude "Crime doesn't pay"—caught a cresting Hollywood wave that had been slowly building through the '30s.

Within that decade's ever-popular genre of crime movies, prison pictures were a sturdy subtype with strong appeal. Besides a national long-
ing to get away from it all, a string of well-publicized jailhouse riots and
escapes in 1930 helped fuel the interest of Depression-era audiences.
And like the equally popular cops and robbers films, prison movies pep-
pered the national lexicon with tough-guy slang, such as "stir" for *prison*
and "chow" for *food.* By decade's end, prison movie production surged.
Twenty-seven prison films were released from 1937 to 1939 (twelve in
1938 alone)—many more than had been made in any comparable
period—and that production explosion further ignited Lawes's fame.
With his showman's intuition, the warden allowed several of those films
to be shot at Sing Sing. Besides *Twenty-Thousand Years,* pictures such as
Angels with Dirty Faces (featuring James Cagney's still-chilling walk to
the electric chair) and *Castle on the Hudson* (a 1937 remake of *Twenty-
Thousand Years*) were filmed behind the increasingly famous walls. Like
the well-publicized ballgames between the Orioles, the Black Sheep, and
visiting teams, Hollywood's presence in Ossining gave the notorious
prison a PR lift. State law forbade payment to inmates who acted as
movie extras, so Warner Brothers agreed to build a regulation-size gymnasium for the warden's boys by way of thanks. Between Lawes's writings
and broadcasts, and Hollywood's razzmatazz, prison life had never been
so popular since Warden Lawes came to Sing Sing.

Perhaps even more curious than the warden's promotion of Sing Sing as
mass-consumption morality tale was his family's life behind the walls.
Today, notwithstanding three double-wide trailers located under the wall
in the northeast corner—the Family Reunion Unit for the most trusted
inmates—the idea of raising a family at Sing Sing is inconceivable, even
laughable. No officer presently on staff, one imagines, could be persuaded
to live within the walls with his or her family. But such was Lawes's rap-
port with the inmates seventy years ago that his wife and three daughters,
with a serving staff of convict trusties, no less, were secure in a four-story
mansion on the prison grounds—as safe as if they lived far across the
Hudson. Cherie, the baby of the family—and the spitting image of her

dad—seemed to have a redeeming affect on the men. As Lawes points out in his book *Twenty-Thousand Years,* Cherie was the only child ever born in Sing Sing (there's no reason to doubt the warden's recollection, although for many years in the nineteenth century the prison did enclose a women's cellblock). A photograph in the book shows the child standing before a group of smiling inmates celebrating a comrade's release. After a moment's thought, Lawes had granted the men's request that his daughter be their guest of honor. There was nothing strange about that. Among her first nannies, after all, was a convict trusty serving time for armed robbery. The burly babysitter proved as careful with the warden's toddler as if she were his own. Lawes showed even more amazing faith in the men when every morning he leaned his head back for a shave. The trusty barber drawing the straight-edge razor across the warden's neck had once been convicted for cutting a man's throat.

Lawes's wife Kathryn—his hometown sweetheart and constant companion since his early days guarding Elmira—shared her husband's trusting nature and tolerant point of view. In her role as the warden's wife, she went out of her way to blunt the sharp edges of convict life. She was beloved by the men for her missions of mercy behind the walls. Confidante and advocate, Kathryn would lend train fare to inmates' indigent families so they could make the trip up from the city to visit their loved ones. When Kathryn died in a freak accident on Halloween weekend in 1937—a fall from a hiking path beside the Bear Mountain Bridge—the inmates she'd befriended seemed almost as stunned and grief-stricken as the warden's family, shocked that her love of the Hudson River, for nature and wild places, could have led to such an awful end. According to one obituary, two hundred "old time" inmates, touched by "her deep mother love," were escorted through the gates and up the hill by hulking Principal Keeper John J. Sheehy to file past her body in the warden's mansion.

A little more than a year and a half later, at the bottom of an inside page in the *New York Times,* a brief three-paragraph item confirmed a rumor that had been floating for months through the worlds of publishing, show business, corrections, and law enforcement. Dated June 12, 1939, the article revealed that on April 19, in Arlington, Virginia, the widowed, fifty-five-year-old warden had married Miss Elise Chisolm,

35, of Jackson, Mississippi, a "general publicity representative for the Dwight Deere Weiman Theatre Productions" company. Warden Lawes told a prying reporter that he'd intended to keep the nuptials secret so as not to upstage the wedding of his daughter Kathleen at the end of June; he said that he and Elise planned a "formal announcement" afterward. A source at the prison, though, beat them to it. But perhaps sensitive to any raised eyebrows about the warden's brief, eighteen-month grieving period, or to the May-to-December aspect of their relationship, or even to the apparently mutual advantage of their shared show-business interests, the new Mr. and Mrs. Lawes took a meandering honeymoon through Europe that July. When they returned to Ossining in the dog days of summer, the whole matter was old news.

By August 1940, six months into Whitey Riordan's and Patches Waters's fifteen-year sentence, and with another inmate baseball season nearing its end, Warden Lewis Lawes was almost through his twentieth summer at Sing Sing. Nearly fifty-seven, he must have felt his best years were behind him, like any lifer in the cheering stands. What more could he do? He'd devoted his entire life to public service, certain he'd made a positive contribution to society. Under his watch, Sing Sing prison had been transformed from a squalid outpost to a first-rate correctional institution—a model for the world. After two decades, perhaps the warden was ready for a change. He almost certainly felt he had plenty more to say—there were more books to write, articles and fiction, drama and advice, if only he could find the time. At the moment, he was turning down more requests for magazine stories and radio appearances than he was accepting, the demands of the prison seeming to increase as the years went on.

One project had been on his mind for a while. He'd been working on a screenplay for about a year, his bio-picture, the story of his life work captured on celluloid. It didn't take much imagination to see Bogart in the lead role. Lawes still had his contacts at Warner Brothers. And if Elise with her connections and insight could be of even more help, what was wrong with that? With enough time—undisturbed days, the glorious life of a writer—he'd be able to bring *Lawes of Sing Sing* to the screen at last.

The thought must have made him laugh, though. Of the more than twenty-five hundred men behind the walls, Warden Lawes was very likely the only man in Sing Sing wishing he had *more* time.

———

IN THE BIG HOUSE

Months earlier, on the first mild day in April 1940, Whitey Riordan and his fellow inmates of 5 Building would have been itching to get outdoors for "yard-out" privileges. Tucked halfway up the hill, fenced between the five-story brick cellblock where Whitey had been living for the past two months and the V-shaped chapel, the cramped exercise yard allowed Whitey to get out of the jail's humid interiors and stretch a bit. It wasn't much of a park, but if you kept your head down, and let your eyes follow the dirt path worn smooth by shoe leather through the tufted, brittle islands of yellow grass, you might for a moment forget where you were.

Bring your eyes up, though, and immediately any illusions cracked apart. Beside the iron-barred cellblock and the thirty-foot wall, the sloped yard was full of men clad in state-issue grays—the thick cotton jackets, bristly, pin-striped "hickory" shirts, and shapeless trousers. There was little variation. Some personal items of clothing were permitted, as long as inmates didn't take advantage of the privilege. Years earlier, former *New York Evening World* editor Charles Chapin had been photographed reading on the warden's porch, comfortably dressed in a cardigan and bow tie. Things weren't that lax in 1940, but Whitey apparently was allowed to keep his lumber jacket, the battered suede coat he'd favored as a stevedore. It would be decades before a city jail like Rikers Island would need to ban red and yellow garments because they denoted affiliation with gangs such as the Crips and the Latin Kings. Generally, however, uniformity was the

rule, and the prevailing color in the Sing Sing yard was gray. On weekends, inmates had yard-out privileges all day long, and a nice afternoon
brought nearly every convict outside. The men tossed balls back and forth,
played chess and checkers, and took walks in pairs or alone, like Whitey.
Individuality was expressed in the men's faces, which you didn't stare at too
long unless you were friendly with the guy, and in the tilt at which they
wore their blunt, gray caps.

The moment a man arrived at Sing Sing, his old life seemed to disappear. No matter your exalted status on the streets—and at the time Sing
Sing housed such criminal luminaries as former Tammany boss Jimmy
Hines, fresh from his losing battle with D.A. Dewey; and Louis "Lepke"
Buchalter, a kingpin connected to the infamous Brooklyn mob known as
Murder Inc.—all men were received the same. When Whitey was
herded out of the paddy wagon in February (two days after his twenty-
fifth birthday) he was taken to the Administration Building with a group
of other new inmates, his old partner Patches Waters with him in line.
They were marched up a flight of stairs to the Bertillon Department, a
pale green room with dark-varnished molding, crammed with filing cab-
inets and desks and smelling of ink and paper. The department's identification system was originally based on a painstaking method of physical
measurement devised by French criminologist Alphonse Bertillon.
Called anthropometrics—officially adopted by France in 1888; fully dis-
credited by 1903—the system tried to detect criminal tendencies from
the width of a convict's right ear, the length of the left foot, and the
dimensions of nine other digits and appendages. The front view and profile mug shot were Bertillon innovations, as was fingerprint identification. By 1940, though, Sing Sing's Bertillon room had dispensed with the
slide rule, relying on photographs and fingerprint cards for prisoner identification.

The men were received at a large desk by the middle-aged chief
clerk, buttoned tight in a vest, sweat staining the armpits of his white
shirt as the room filled up with nervous prisoners. He asked each man a
series of questions—parents' names and places of birth, the inmate's
own nativity, the number of his siblings and the inmate's place among
them, his religious background, his education and highest grade level

achieved, his occupation and most recent job. Then the queries got more pointed: Do you drink? Do you smoke? Do you use drugs? What was the reason for your crime? The sullen answers were all written down in a huge book, in the chief clerk's careful hand, the black ink scrawling along the page as if slowly draining out each man's identity and transferring it to paper. After that, after the fingerprinting, after handing over whatever money was in his pockets and whatever valuables were on his person, each man was seated before a box camera fixed to a wooden stand. A number was pinned to his lapel, the same number stamped on the page in the book where his information was recorded, and then the flashbulb popped.

Joseph "Whitey" Riordan was now Sing Sing inmate number 97752.

There was nothing new in the general procedure; Whitey had been through it in other prisons. But perhaps he sensed something more mechanized in Sing Sing's regimentation. The assembly-line processing was so precisely thought out, the rote questions reflecting the tried-and-true guidelines of a well-established plan, that each new arrival seemed to enter a large, bland machine. Under Warden Lawes, Sing Sing prison had become a buzzing factory for the production of new and improved men.

After Bertillon, Whitey and the others were taken to the State Shop. A guard gestured at their street clothes. Take them off, he told them. Naked and holding their clothes bundled at their waists, the men lined up before another clerk at a counter, who took the clothing and registered it in another book. Passing before another guard, the inmates were told to bend over and spread their duffs for a flashlit inspection. The guard then pointed his club at the dank shower room. Scrubbed and dried, the men were issued their uniforms of prison gray. Haircuts followed—not the scalp-wounding shave cut of the prison's early days, but close enough on the sides and back. After that, they were marched to Sing Sing's old cellblock and entered into the Reception Company, where they remained sequestered from the general population for two weeks in the block's bottom tier. The ancient building had been refurbished with plumbing and better lighting, electricity having replaced gas in 1897. But the filmy, narrow windows in the thick encrusted walls made a man glad the lodging was temporary.

Over the course of the following two weeks, Whitey and the others met with the psychiatrists. The doctors asked embarrassing questions and took notes on clipboards whether you answered or not. The routine was similar to Elmira's, and Whitey would have had his answers ready. No, he didn't associate with dissolute women. No, he hadn't frequented houses of prostitution. No, he had no homosexual inclinations. The intimate questions were designed to discover sexual deviance, as penologists of the day saw it, or, as Warden Lawes generalized, to gain "a thorough understanding of [the inmates'] mentalities and outlook on life."

Homosexual rape behind bars is a brutal cliché, although actual statistics may be hard to determine (according to Joseph T. Hallinan in *Going Up the River,* the state of Texas doesn't even keep records of sexual assaults in its prisons). But back in the early twentieth century all manner of prison sexuality was a serious concern for straitlaced wardens committed to reform. During his famous raid on the Welfare Island Pen, New York City Corrections Commissioner Austin MacCormick had been appalled by the transvestites running freely among the outlaw inmate gangs. At Elmira Reformatory in the nineteenth century, even masturbation was punished. Any inmate caught in the act had a metal ring sewn like a clamp into his foreskin by the Reformatory doctor. But luckily for a young man like Whitey Riordan, Warden Lawes was far more practical. "Self-abuse," he once understated, "particularly among younger prisoners, is practiced more widely than prison administrators are frank to admit." At least at Sing Sing, invasive surgery was not the cure. But even if Lawes took a pragmatic view toward inmate masturbation, he was determined to keep homosexuality controlled, estimating (with somewhat archaic terminology) that at Sing Sing "seventy-five percent of all our cases of sex perversion in prison can be traced directly to [the] custom of putting two or more men in one cell." The policy of one man per cell remained in effect until the mid-1990s.

Fingerprinted, photographed, and cataloged, twenty-five-year-old Whitey shuffled through Sing Sing's processes and toward his own cell in the general population. The Correspondence Department provided him with paper and pencil and instructed him in the limitations on letter writing. He was allowed to write one letter per week, what the authorities called a "Sunday letter." Given the closeness of the Riordan family, he most likely wrote to his mother, using uplifting generalities and skipping the details. He was interviewed by the Assignment Board, civilian clerks and prison officials perusing his record and asking about the sign-painting he'd been taught at Elmira. He might have been assigned to the print shop or to the paint shop; perhaps because of his dock experience, he was put on general labor crews. Whatever the case, his old life was gone. When he was relocated to 5 Building after his two-week orientation in the old cellblock, he must have felt that he'd been in Sing Sing for years. But as he'd soon tell Patches, he was ready to do the time. Already something inside him had changed.

The old Whitey was scratched in the pages of a massive book, his effects wrapped in butcher paper and stored in the basement of the State Shop. The new Whitey who had emerged from the Reception Company had lower expectations, weighed down by a lifetime of resisting the system. Sing Sing cellblocks were grim, and the work routine was monotonous. But the prison food was fresh and plentiful, and in the evenings, if you were good, you could listen to a game or a variety show on the radio through the headphones you requested from the guard. On Sunday nights the prison broadcast Warden Lawes's show or maybe a serial like the *Green Hornet*. Whitey must have wondered what it would be like just to go along for once.

The wild ideas he'd cultivated all his life—of standing out and making a name for himself, of fame and riches—well, they were fun while they lasted. But they hadn't led anywhere but here. Undoubtedly, his mother was quick to point that out to him during the visits she made every few weeks; his sister, too. The past decade had been a roundelay of failed attempts to keep him out of lockup. They were disappointed by his situation, of course, but perhaps also a little grateful, maybe even relieved that Whitey couldn't get into any more trouble.

He'd been going to Mass in the chapel. The Catholic chaplain, Father Bernard Martin, was a young priest, tall and balding, and seemed like a nice guy—unlike the Christian Brothers at the Protectory, who believed an occasional lashing was good for the soul. Father Martin said some good things in his homilies, stuff that made a guy think, like: "I was in prison, and ye came unto me."

In those first months, the new Whitey seemed content to take one day inside prison at a time, like putting one foot in front of the other every time he walked the yard. That April, like every spring, held the scent of the earth coming back to life in the wind. There was promise in the future; that's where he had to look. Otherwise, how would a guy get through the nine long years until his parole hearing?

The prison methodology that now controlled Whitey's life was the culmination of nearly two hundred years of experimentation with, and debate about, criminal justice. Immediately after the American Revolution, men like Thomas Eddy, a Quaker philanthropist, and Benjamin Rush, a signer of the Declaration of Independence, argued for a truly American response to issues of crime and punishment. English justice, with its "barbarous usages, corrupt society, and monarchical principals," as Rush put it, treated people like property and showed contempt for liberty. Eddy, Rush, and others sought a methodology that would embody the new nation's larger, victorious struggle for freedom from the tyrannous British crown. Capital punishment in particular was seen as antithetical to democracy. Given America's more enlightened laws, the death penalty was considered not only barbaric, but impractical: juries often nullified verdicts altogether rather than condemn an incorrigible thief to the gallows. Incarceration thus became the preferred method of punishing criminals; and America's first prison system was born.

Deterring crime, then, not rehabilitating inmates (as Lawes would later advocate) was the early prison's motivating aim. As such, prison construction was pretty basic, essentially walls and bars. Newgate prison, on what is now West Tenth Street in Greenwich Village, New York State's first facility, lacked any organizing principle beyond whatever it took to lock up a mass of people. From indigent drunks and violent thieves, to serial rapists and repeat murderers, all inmates lived together in large stone rooms, eating and sleeping in wary groups. Unsurprisingly, results were calamitous: with no methodology beyond simple confinement, prisons were vicious, disorderly places pulsing with near constant assaults and killings, riots and escapes. The chaos on Welfare Island during Whitey Riordan's time didn't even come close to this early madness. Alarmed, authorities hurriedly sketched out a model of single cells to separate the convicts.

By the late 1820s, it was clear to Jacksonian Americans that democracy, despite forging a unique path for the nation in other respects, had not eliminated crime. Robberies and assaults, rapes and murders, were on the rise, especially in the expanding urban centers. Some thought that America's open society was the cause and that too much freedom was to blame. In response, reformers welded the concept of strict routine onto imprisonment. If a restless society tilted unsteady individuals into a life of crime, then the prison would resettle those individuals, reacquainting them with society's rules and restabilizing the culture. Programs were developed to ensure that the delinquent who entered the gated walls as a social deviant would leave as a model citizen, completely reformed. In short order, rehabilitation became the goal of incarceration, the term *penology* entered the lexicon, and the American prison system got down to business.

Ironically, these early reformers sketched the blueprint that Captain Elam Lynds later followed, with the aid of his whip, as he carved Sing Sing out of the limestone hills. The architects' plans for Sing Sing were carefully crafted so that offenders, once imprisoned, would be forced to confront their guilt and repent. The Boston Prison Discipline Society, a reform group of the early nineteenth century, put out a report claiming direct links between rehabilitation and prison design. Moral behavior could be instilled, they wrote, by isolating walls, gated corridors, and narrow tunnels, which would confine and direct inmates' movement. Architectural determinists even suggested that incorporating aspects of prison architecture into civilian structures could morally benefit families, schools, and society at large. After all, it was the failure of these institutions that had produced the delinquent in the first place.

The country's first prison systems reflected competing ideas about how to rehabilitate prisoners. Supporters of the Pennsylvania and the Auburn models vied with each other to achieve what they considered the perfect method of reform. Both groups agreed that while inmates weren't born evil, they hadn't been socialized. In practice, however, the two sets of ideas were mirror opposites of each other. Proponents of the Pennsylvania system favored inmate separation: each convict was confined to a solitary cell where—utterly alone—he ate, slept, and worked for his entire sentence. The isolation was so complete that new inmates wore hoods while they walked to their cells. While serving their sentences, they saw and interacted with a few prison employees but never with their fellow inmates. The Auburn method, in contrast, was a "congregate" system: convicts worked and ate together, though in the strictest silence, with not even a glance allowed among them. At night, each prisoner was locked alone in a single-occupancy cell. Proponents of each system fiercely defended their method as the wisest and best and assailed their opponents' procedure. But despite the advantages and disadvantages of both, simple economics won out in the end.

The Auburn system, then being tested on the banks of the Hudson River at Sing Sing, was just plain cheaper. States found it prohibitively expensive to house, feed, and work convicts in total isolation, as the Pennsylvania method required. To prove the point, states with congregate models pointed to the tidy profit they made from the inmates' labor. Of course publicly, the states claimed that rehabilitating inmates—not making a profit—was the system's main purpose. And the Auburn protocol showed how to do it without breaking state budgets.

From the 1820s to the 1850s, congregate penitentiaries spread across the country. Prison officials vigorously pursued inmate rehabilitation by regimenting prison routine and maintaining it through strict discipline and order. Convicts rose at the dawn bell; dressed in identical striped uniforms; and marched in lockstep, right arm extended and hand placed firmly on the shoulder before them, from cellblock to mess hall to workhouse, where they labored until the daylight failed—all in an atmosphere of compulsory silence.

The success of the Auburn system had some drawbacks, however. Congregate methods—with many individuals suffering the same miserable experience together—tempted inmates to break the rules of silence. Captain Lynds wasn't alone in his fondness for the lash, although Sing

Sing was especially notorious for relying on the cat-o'-nine-tails to enforce discipline. Whenever an inmate spoke out or otherwise stepped over the line, prison guards across the country immediately reached for the iron gag, or the time-honored ball and chain.

But order grew even more difficult to maintain—despite such harsh policy—after the Civil War, as external events overrode the wardens' best efforts at discipline. A post-war rise in crime, due in part to the great wave of impoverished immigrants arriving in the United States, created a serious new threat to reform efforts—prison overcrowding.

As prison populations exploded, order deteriorated and wardens and guards ratcheted up their tactics to halt the breakdown. Hanging mutinous inmates by the thumbs became routine. By the 1870s, the prisons were overrun with hardened outlaws—career robbers, impenitent rapists, black-hearted killers. Congestion and chaos trampled the Auburn system, and by the end of the nineteenth century, at least in practice, enlightened methods of rehabilitation had fled through the prison bars.

Prison reformers, however, were a stubbornly optimistic lot. By the time Whitey Riordan and Patches Waters entered Sing Sing in 1940, yet another new era in rehabilitation had dawned. Penologists of the day preferred practical responses to the problems teeming behind the walls, such as separating the most violent and rebellious inmates from the run-of-the-mill thieves and nonviolent offenders. Sing Sing—after twenty years of forward-thinking guidance by Lewis Lawes—was at the vanguard of a transformation in penology: the concept of the Big House, which applied the reformatory's more edifying penological theories to an exploding prison population. Tactics such as indeterminate sentencing and parole based on inmate cooperation—approaches initiated and perfected at smaller institutions like Elmira Reformatory—were now directed at huge convict populations. Administered by professionals instead of political appointees, Big Houses were literally giant cellblocks, four, five, and six tiers high, housing an average total of twenty-five hundred men—about twice the size of a place like Elmira—and overseen by a security staff of approximately 150. Inmates labored in large prison workshops, and Big Houses like Sing Sing, as well as the infamous San

Quentin in California and the less well-known but equally formidable Stateville in Illinois, hummed like automatic machines.

But like the penitentiary and the reformatory ideas, the Big House offered no quick fix. Prison populations continued to grow. The year 1939 saw record incarceration rates nationwide—Sing Sing's inmate count swelled to well over twenty-eight hundred. Strict routines were still imposed on inmates identically dressed in gray, and steel gates still locked them in while they slept. Despite the reformers' best intentions, once a man was surrounded by cement and steel, rehabilitation became a test of wills.

Penologists countered with ideas inspired by the twentieth century's advances in medicine and psychiatry. If scourges like tuberculosis could be treated successfully, reformers reasoned, perhaps criminal behavior could be examined under a medical light. They began using psychiatric and medical methods, and language, in their work. With their new vocabulary, reformers diagnosed offenders as being pathologically driven to disobey the law, and they prescribed specific remedies. To help prison staff determine a convict's proper treatment, newly arriving inmates were given complete physical and psychological workups. Reflecting Warden Lawes's commitment to inmate rehabilitation, penologists at Sing Sing viewed a repeat offender like Whitey Riordan as no different from a chronic hospital patient—every effort had to be made to cure and release him.

———

Patches Waters probably would have laughed to think of himself as a patient awaiting release from a hospital. After what he'd found out soon after his arrival at Sing Sing, it's clear he didn't plan on sticking around for the full cure. As Whitey would later testify, from the moment Patches passed through the cellblock gates—as inmate number 97750—he was determined that he'd never finish his sentence. The betrayal by Little Joe Salvatore, the sudden end of what had become the most profitable run in Patches's life, from his pinball business to the Shopping Bag Gang's exploits, not to mention being taken away from his steady girlfriend,

Gertrude Carlson—Patches's whole life had been upended just as he'd gotten it running smoothly. All these scores would need settling. And he set about it right away.

Like Whitey, Patches was assigned to a cell in 5 Building—dead center in the upper prison—one of the four cellblocks Warden Lawes had built during the expansion. Although Patches and Whitey weren't locked together, they both could hear the freight trains and commuter locals whistling below them on tracks running straight through the walls—the sound of freedom passing them by. Up until the 1970s, the New York Central made stops at the prison in a specially fortified tunnel to unload staff. Listening to the wheels night and day, more than one inmate must have dreamed of breaking out through the high-walled train lock. But no one ever did.

Patches would soon discover an easier way. Turning the matter over in his mind, he approached the task of breaking out of the nation's most famous prison as though it were like any other knockover job: he just needed the right combination of planning and personnel. And then came an extraordinary stroke of luck. Patches ran into inmate Charles McGale in 5 Building, and the picture snapped into focus. For Charlie McGale, Patches quickly learned, had something that every inmate wanted.

He had a way out.

McGale was an old pal whom Patches had known years ago from the docks—they'd even done short stretches together in the Big House back in the '30s, on unrelated charges. A short, black-haired, slightly built steamfitter, older than Patches by a decade and a half, McGale was locked on the same tier. He was a trusty, an inmate believed reliable enough by prison staff, after years of trustworthy behavior, to be given wide access to work projects in prison areas. But with only four years remaining on his current attempted armed robbery sentence, McGale had become what he called "buggy"—not crazy, though the term means that too, but nervous and prone to sudden panic attacks. He'd been behind bars eleven of the previous eighteen years, and this was his fourth stretch at Sing Sing. This time around, the thought of another day inside the walls sometimes caused his entire body to break out in sweat and his heart to pound. When he least expected it, walking along to dinner or just working quietly, he'd get a jittering attack of the bugs.

But McGale had a secret plan—an obsession he'd developed if only as a way to keep busy, to stay calm. For the past few years, he'd been scheming alone, vaguely, though, and never getting anywhere. When he spotted Patches on the 5 Building tier, he must have felt he'd found the man who could focus his idea. Patches not only had brains but nerve.

As McGale would recall later, they met in the 5 Building yard during recreation one early April day in 1940. Early spring on the Hudson can be bitter, with a slicing wind off the river, the overcast sky close upon you like another wall. The acoustics between the cellblock and the chapel are strange; the wind sometimes carried normal conversation, so McGale kept his voice low.

"I got an out here for you if you want it."

Patches didn't say anything at first. The answer he'd been looking for since he got in was suddenly right in front of him like a bolt from the clouds. Halfway up the hill, they stood above the lower prison, level with the steep Palisades on the opposite shore. From up there you could almost imagine reaching a hand across the stone gray water

McGale explained that there was a tunnel, a vault built for steam pipes and wire conduits that ran from a sub-basement in the prison hospital all the way down to the New York Central railroad tracks. All that separated the tunnel from the tracks was a rusted metal plate. A mechanic who worked in the old refrigeration plant, McGale had been down to the steam vault plenty of times on repair crews. The out couldn't be easier.

Patches nodded and found his voice. "All right."

"I can get things ready, I can make keys and I got the rope and I can get the plate out, chip the plate out." McGale, finally able to unload what he'd been holding for years, was skittish with the excitement. "I got everything if you want to look at it. I will show you."

"All right," Patches said again. Was Charlie out of his mind? It seemed too good to be true. Even before Patches had devised his own escape plan, here was his old friend Charlie McGale claiming he'd already done half the work.

"I got everything if you want to look at it," McGale repeated. "I will show you."

Soon after, McGale did just that. He took Patches down to the hospital basement and showed him the door that led to the steam vault. They didn't enter the tunnel at that time, apparently. But the unchallenged reconnoiter gave Patches a sense of the possibility. If they could get themselves admitted to the prison hospital, and if Charlie could cut keys for any lock, they could bust this place wide open.

They'd have to be smooth, though. Patches likely saw that Charlie McGale's nerves were shot. All the programs, all the care, and prison still did this to a man. There were years, maybe even lives on the line, and Patches wouldn't have wanted anyone going off half-cocked. This was too big. With guards everywhere and snitches all over, the men would take their time to do this right. But do it, they would. He wasn't sure how just then, but if Charlie could get them through the steam vault, Patches would take care of the rest—a car, guns, everything.

His old pal could count on that.

———————

Days after talking to McGale, Patches approached Whitey Riordan with the idea. It says something about Patches that almost as soon as he'd spoken to McGale, and laid eyes on the entry door in the hospital basement, he thought of his younger partner. On the one hand, their shared history as well as the testimony of acquaintances suggests that Patches truly cared for Whitey, the petty thief he'd taken from the docks and molded into a professional holdup man. But on the other hand, ever the calculating businessman, maybe Patches was just being practical. At the moment, the escape team consisted of little forty-five-year-old McGale and Patches himself, no Johnny Weissmuller. An unimpressive pair like that needed a young tough to watch their backs, a big kid known for his strong arm and his cool with a gun. Given the fact that Whitey was a guy whom Patches could trust made him the obvious choice. In any case, with McGale's plan circling around in his head, Patches looked for the very first opportunity to feel out the idea with Whitey.

The yard was where inmates could really talk. Crowded as it was with men walking, playing catch, or hunched over card games, and with guards watching nearly every move, the yard offered the closest thing to privacy. If you wanted to discuss something sensitive—a problem with the wife or the kids or a grievance with another inmate or guard—you needed someplace where you could keep your eye on your surroundings. And for something as delicate as a break, to actually conspire with someone, you wouldn't meet at the baseball games in Lawes Field or at the basketball games in the Warner Gym; you'd avoid whispering at the weekly picture show in the chapel or muttering at breakfast in the mess hall. As Whitey once put it, "There are too many ears around." No, for maximum privacy, short of adjoining cells, you needed the yard.

By the end of April, the weather had broken, and outside 5 Building the sunshine was warm on a man's jacketed back. You could smell spring in the river air. It was the kind of day that made you want to skip work, and get away from it all, because nice days never lasted. Patches must have felt something like that, because when he met Whitey he got right to the point.

"How would you like to make a break?"

What a question. Every con's dream. But ever since landing in his own cell, Whitey had been thinking. One mark of the change coming over him was that he didn't jump at the chance Patches was offering. Not so long ago, Whitey Riordan had been the go-to guy whenever anything dangerous came up. But this early in his sentence, and on a nice spring day, from fifteen to thirty years didn't seem like an impossibility. He was only twenty-five. If he did his time without incident, he figured to get out on parole in a third of the time. Sing Sing, with its famous warden who cared so much about his boys, was tough but still rated better than some places Whitey had seen, especially with all the amenities, such as ball games almost every weekend and lots of food. Not so bad at all, after you've slept downtown in the Tombs or spent time at the Pen on Welfare Island. Here was the new Whitey, taking his time with an answer.

Patches waited.

But Whitey had decided. "I am not interested. I want to do the time."

His old partner wanted more of an explanation, though. "I am twenty-five," Whitey continued. "I will do ten years and be out when I am only thirty-five. I don't want to have nothing to do with it."

And that was that.

Patches didn't push it. Whitey was young, and this was his first trip to Sing Sing. Any preparations toward a successful breakout would take time to complete, anyway. Patches likely figured to let the bars do their worst. Warden Lawes might be a fair guy with his picture on the cover of *Time* magazine (once, ten years before), but Sing Sing was no spa. Two hundred yards from where they stood, New York State still electrocuted whomever it had a mind to. Patches would check back with Whitey closer to the event. Six, eight, or ten months inside those walls could make a big difference in a man's perspective. In the meantime, there was work to do.

After all, only three men had ever broken out of Lawes's Sing Sing with any lasting success.

CHAPTER NINE

FROM SAINT PETER TO PATCHES

I T IS SAFE TO SAY that the thought of escape has crossed the mind of almost every person locked behind cellblock gates. From the very first prisons, even before Saint Peter and the Apostles slipped out of a Jerusalem cell—with an angel of the Lord as an alleged outside accomplice—escape has occupied minds numbed by routine or terrorized by brutality. Inmates have nothing but time to dream of ways out.

From the prison authorities' point of view, escape has almost always been the ultimate expression of disobedience. From about 2000 B.C.— the estimated date of the earliest known prison records—ancient Egyptians were perhaps the first to consider prison escape a serious crime, as much as it compounded an initial offense against the holy order of the universe. In the Middle Ages, English jailers faced severe penalties for any escapes on their watch, and fugitives were considered traitors to the monarch. But it hardly mattered to the many in chains. By planning escapes, they could keep hope beating—even under the worst conditions.

In the summer of 1929 in the United States, such hopes pulsed violently. That year, one of the bloodiest in U.S. prison history, a nationwide series of carefully planned breaks deteriorated into deadly crash outs. In seconds, cool procedure turned chaotic. Most prisons were still nineteenth-century relics, and the summer heat only intensified convict resentment. An uprising boiled through Leavenworth Penitentiary, the federal prison in Kansas, which thirty years before had experienced a mass escape of seventeen inmates from its construction site before the facility was even finished. At the Colorado State Prison in Canon City, seven guards and five inmates were killed when a failed breakout devolved into a riot, costing the state $500,000 worth of damage. In New York State, Clinton prison—where Warden Lawes had begun his career—saw thirteen hundred inmates run wild, smashing factory windows and setting fire to the workshops. Wall tower guards opened up with machine guns, killing at least three inmates and wounding many more. Governor Franklin D. Roosevelt, with his mind on a presidential run and concerned about the spectacle, requested help from the U.S. Army. When the rioting abated, he toured the smoking prison from his limousine, admitting that only more prison construction would relieve the overcrowding.

Auburn prison, New York State's oldest, battled two bloody insurrections in 1929. In July, a week after the Clinton riot, four inmates escaped, sparking widespread unrest that killed two more. Seventeen hundred convicts broke into the prison's arsenal and torched buildings, causing half a million dollars' damage. Two officers were shot, acid was thrown in the face of one, and another was severely beaten. Three firemen from the Auburn Fire Department were injured, as well. Four months later, using guns hidden since the July incident, inmates took the warden and six officers captive in the yard. When the principal keeper walked across for a showdown, he was shot and killed. Authorities promised to provide getaway cars and safe passage for the convicts and their hostages, but when the inmates took up the offer, they were tear-gassed. Turning their guns on the hostages ignited a volley from the walls. In the ensuing mayhem, eight inmates were killed, and nine people—including the seven hostages—were injured. Three men went to the electric chair for their part in the riot. The December 1929 Auburn uprising would hold a forty-two-year record for the worst prison revolt in state history. (That record was broken in September 1971, years after Warden Lawes's era, when the state prison at Attica exploded in the deadliest prison riot America has ever witnessed. Forty-three people were killed, including ten hostages. After the public outcry—charges of inmate coddling versus accusations of racist brutality—and the state investigation, politicians legislated to improve prison conditions and security. No more individual correction in back offices, with blackjacks pulled from a bottom desk drawer. As one retired Sing Sing lieutenant put it, "Everything changed after Attica.")

The rash of escape attempts rolled on, the high-stakes escapades given a glamorous sheen by two of the 1930s' most well-known outlaws, John Dillinger and Willie Sutton. The pair was almost as famous for breaking out of prisons as for breaking into banks. In fact, Dillinger's professional bank robbing career began as the first step in a year-long plan to bust confederates out of the Indiana State Penitentiary. In 1932, twenty-nine-year-old Dillinger was nearing the end of a stretch for armed robbery when a thief named Harry Pierpont, an older, well-respected inmate, approached him. Pierpont wanted to make a deal. If Dillinger would be the outside man on an escape plot after his upcoming release—specifically, raising bribe money and finding a way to smuggle some guns inside—Harry promised to enlist the young robber as the "wheelman," or getaway driver, in a string of holdups they'd pull once they were all free. The ambitious Dillinger agreed. With an address list of robbery targets supplied by Pierpont, Dillinger got right to work as soon as he hit the streets. Thirteen months later, right on schedule, a 200-pound box of thread arrived at a prison shirt factory; hidden inside were four automatic pistols. Pierpont and eight others were ready. Three days later, after taking the shirt factory superintendent and a prison captain as hostages, the convicts walked through the prison's main gates and into the record books. It was the biggest prison break in Indiana history.

After the escape, the gang showed their gratitude. Discovering that Dillinger had just been locked up in Indiana's Allen County Jail on unrelated charges, Pierpont and the others made plans to spring him. Just after supper, as their trusted accomplice played pinochle with the jail's other inmates, Pierpont and the gang stormed in, shot the sheriff dead, and crashed the young bandit out. Dillinger's most legendary escape, though, was in 1934—four months before his death in an ambush by the FBI at the Biograph Theater in Chicago. Locked up in the Crown Point County Jail, outside Gary, Indiana, the breakout artist single-handedly engineered his way out, learning the jail's layout as he went along, capturing hostages one by one with only a wooden gun.

Where Dillinger's modus operandi was escape via gun, fellow bank robber Willie Sutton had a penchant for ladders. The one time he tunneled out—from Eastern State Penitentiary in the heart of Philadelphia—Sutton popped his blond head up from the ground between the walls and the sidewalk outside and startled two passing patrolmen. The chase ended a few blocks away. (Apparently, tunnels were the method preferred by most inmates at Eastern State. During the 1930s, prison officials found thirty incomplete passages grooving around the yard.) No, ladders were Willie's favorite means. At Holmesburg prison in Pennsylvania, Sutton used a smuggled gun to capture two guards and a captain, tied two ladders together end-to-end, and propped them against the wall under the cover of a blinding snowstorm. He climbed over, hitchhiked home to New York City, and remained free for five years.

But perhaps his best-known escape was a 1932 break from Sing Sing, which Sutton called "the most horrible prison I have ever been in."

As arguably the country's most famous Big House, the Castle on the Hudson has seen more than its share of breakout plots. Warden Lawes's facility expansion through the 1920s had not only brought Sing Sing into the modern era but tightened overall prison security. Sections of the prison's wall were heightened and thickened; an iron picket fence along the river was welded taller and spiked; and random cell bars were replaced with hardened steel, supposedly immune to hacksaws. But the improvements were sufficient only until the next escape revealed more unforeseen flaws. And Willie Sutton was a master at manipulating the subtlest defect in any security system.

In the decades before the Attica riot, the night staff at a state prison like Sing Sing was probably fewer than fifty officers. With the inmates locked in their cells, officials reasoned, the most likely emergency would be medical, and a small force could handle it. Sutton had learned that a wall tower behind A-block was empty during the overnight shift. Locked on the fifth tier—the top floor—of B-block, Sutton would first have to get out of his cell to capitalize on the diminished nighttime staff. He worried that the Lawes-renovated cell bars might contain a "spinning rod," an interior bar within the steel casing that caught a cutting blade's teeth and rotated with the saw's motion. He soon stopped worrying, however. The small hacksaw blades he'd taken from a workshop cut the cell bars easily.

Once out on the tier, hearing the voices of three officers below him on the flats, Sutton crept, shoes in hand, past cells full of sleeping inmates and all the way down the metal stairs to the basement. He found the two ladders a trusty had promised would be there, tied them together as he would at Holmesburg, and carried them outside. Alert for any alarm, he leaned the ladders against the east wall near the darkened tower and climbed over. No whistles blew. No machine guns chattered. His wife picked him up in a car and drove him home to the city. After dyeing his hair, Sutton moved to Philadelphia and resumed his bank robbing career until he was caught a year later.

Willie Sutton was exceptionally lucky at Sing Sing. Actually, Warden Lawes had seen an overall drop in successful escapes during his command. Since 1920, his first year on the job, eighteen inmates had broken out, and only three of them remained missing (one fugitive's skeleton was found within the prison years later, still curled in his hidey-hole). It wasn't hard to see why escape was so difficult.

Even if an inmate was fortunate enough to get beyond the cellblock—past the locked gates and the barred doors, the checkpoints and the patrols—he still faced the gun towers. Eighteen dark green, pagoda-roofed towers perched atop the surrounding walls or stood free at the river's edge. After Sutton's brazen act, they were fully manned around the clock. Unlit at night, so officers' vision was keen when they used their binoculars, and equipped with powerful searchlights mounted on turrets, the towers held high-powered arsenals: a tear-gas gun, a shotgun, and a Thompson submachine gun. Guards on Posts 12 and 18, situated above the prison's delivery gates, were also armed with .45 Colt revolvers. The Tommy gun, the infamous heavy weapon of the 1920s and '30s, was distinguished by its characteristic ribbed barrel and 100-round drum magazine. It was capable of firing fifteen hundred .45 caliber rounds per minute—a full magazine in four seconds. The Thompson's deafening staccato burst could shred a man in the time it took to strike a match. In November 1930, several inmates had broken out of their cellblock and into the yard, only to face the thunderous roar of the guns. One inmate, Harry Gordon, spun from the deadly burst; the others threw up their hands and surrendered.

But nothing stopped prisoners from trying. As one veteran officer put it, "These crooks are always scheming something." One break in 1933 proved especially embarrassing for Warden Lawes, since it suggested that despite his best rehabilitative efforts, any inmate would try to flee if given half a chance. Twenty-one-year-old Harry Kagel Jr., convicted for sixty robberies, worked as Lawes's butler—one of the most trusted jobs in the institution but still no match for the lure of freedom. One early spring day, Kagel disappeared from his assignment in the warden's mansion. A week later he was recaptured in New York City, armed with a pistol and still neatly dressed in his escape attire—Warden Lawes's overcoat and brown fedora.

The year before, one blistering August afternoon, a quartet of inmates made it all the way to the Hudson. Assigned to a work crew tunneling wire conduits under the north wall to the new powerhouse then under construction, the men grabbed tools that had been left behind in the tunnel and battered through a makeshift partition. Crouching, they ran along a deep trench, evading the eyes of the tower guards. Once free of the wall, the men broke into a full-tilt sprint, stripping off and throwing their grays behind them.

A nearby merchant couldn't believe his eyes. Joe Meister, drowsing in the late afternoon sun outside his small store just north and within earshot of the wall, was used to swimmers cavorting on the river shore. At first, he thought the fugitives were athletes racing one another for the water. But when the men stopped at the shoreline, their fingers poised at the buttons of their one-piece long johns as if too modest to bare it all, and then dove in with their Skivvies on, Meister became suspicious. True sportsmen wouldn't be so shy. He called out to the tower guard on the north wall, who telephoned Principal Keeper John Sheehy. A car raced out of the prison and then along the shore road, abreast of the four heads bobbing in the sun-flashed currents. Sheehy and his officers commandeered a skiff from the nearby boat club, cast off, and quickly fished up the escapees. The ringleader, George Donaldson, was a career burglar serving fifteen years to life and a practiced breakout artist with three previous attempts to his name. He indignantly denied he had just escaped from Sing Sing and insisted he was "Mr. Hickey of Yonkers." Donaldson remained in a huff all the way back to prison, then wilted when confronted with his Bertillon mug shot.

When an escape revealed cracks in security during Warden Lawes's time, the warden was quick to cement them closed. After the Donaldson party's escape, Lawes fastened a steel plate to the service tunnel's exit from the powerhouse. He also repeated his request to the state for a prison cruiser to patrol the river, but the legislators in Albany didn't appropriate the necessary funds. Warden Lawes was a realist. He knew that someday another sharp-eyed inmate would spot another previously unnoticed flaw in Sing Sing's security and try to take advantage of it. But he had no way of knowing the extent to which his own reputation and legacy would be affected by one such flaw.

If he had known, he might have checked the rest of Sing Sing's tunnels and steel plates a little more closely.

————

The New York State Police would later determine that Patches Waters "commenced making arrangements" for his angle of Charlie McGale's escape plot sometime in late spring and into the summer of 1940. Patches was responsible for the outside plan, and his scheme had two main components. First, a waiting getaway car—which meant enlisting a trustworthy team of outside men to procure the car and then to stow it. Second, communication—a good plan needed to be completely understood by the outside team. Patches considered the pieces one by one.

First off, he'd need to lay out a blueprint of Sing Sing in his mind. During walks in the 5 Building yard, Patches could have easily scanned the prison grounds dropping west downhill to the old section at the river. And while seated in the bleachers at games in Lawes Field by the water's edge, he could see the whole eastern section of the new prison spread uphill above him. According to McGale, the steam tunnel began in the basement of the prison hospital, diagonally uphill from the Administration Building, in the northern end of the compound. The tunnel exited at

a service trestle that spanned the New York Central railroad tracks, practically under the nose of 12 Post, the guard tower just below the Administration Building—smack between the new and old sections in the
prison's north end. If the men made it out of the tunnel without alerting
the tower guard and his Tommy gun, and then dropped by rope to the
tracks, where would they go? Where was the nearest place to plant a getaway car? Squinting north from the ball field bleachers, an inmate could
make out the Ossining railroad station, its red-clay tiled roof visible
above the tracks on a small transverse bridge, about a half mile upriver.
That would be the solution, then: they'd come out of the tunnel, slide
down to the track bed, and run like hell north. The train station would be
the perfect place to park the car.

Next came a more delicate question: whom could he trust to do that?
He had a lineup of acquaintances to consider, friends from the waterfront, and—of course—the Shopping Bag Gang. When the lights were
out and the breaks—hip-high levers that controlled the cell locks on each
side of the tier—were closed and padlocked, a man could put his mind to
work. The cells were just wide enough for a bed and a small desk and
chair, long enough for a toilet and sink. A window took up most of the
exterior wall, the tiny living space flat against a view of the Hudson at its
most expansive. Perfect for wide-open thinking. Cells were still single-
occupancy in the Big House—a man planning a breakout didn't have the
distraction of a cellmate in the bunk above him, somebody it took energy
to like or to hate. But overnight, the whole tier burred with the suspira-
tions of nearly three hundred men—coughs and wheezes, snores and
cries. The air quickly grew stale. For many inmates, if sleep didn't come at
once, it didn't come at all, and the mind got on its treadmill. His arms
behind his head, the metal bed frame cold on his wrists, Patches could fix
his blue eyes at the barred window—illuminated until dawn by the
prison's exterior halogens—and hone down his list of names like a movie
picture casting director. Who would set the car at the Ossining railroad
station? How might they be convinced to go along?

When Patches thought of cars, William Wade would have automatically come to mind. Wade was the Shopping Bag Gang's driver. He not
only drove the getaway car for the Con Ed Audubon job—he stole it first

and fitted it with lifted, out-of-state plates. That attention to detail would be needed for the current job as well. But even more important, Wade owed Patches a big favor. He was out walking the city streets that very evening because Patches, and Whitey, had both kept their mouths shut about Wade's involvement with the robberies. Billy Wade was waterfront Irish—he would honor, as a *Journal and American* reporter put it, "the strange tie of underworld gratitude."

But how could Patches plan a breakout with *any* former gang member? He couldn't very well write a letter to Wade—hey, planning a crash out, need your help. Inmate mail was read, both incoming and outgoing. That left the visiting room, not an ideal choice given the experienced convict's aversion to prying ears. Besides, criminal associates would never be allowed to visit one another in Sing Sing.

Anybody requesting to visit an inmate was fingerprinted first, and then Albany ran a check to see if those prints matched any convicted felon's; if they did, permission denied. Patches undoubtedly knew from previous stints at Sing Sing that the only visitors *not* fingerprinted were immediate family members—but Wade didn't look like kin. There was Robert Brown, Patches's pinball machine business partner. But he didn't resemble Patches, either. And anyway Brownie, though hauled in on various charges over the years, had never been an eager crook. He'd steered clear of any involvement in the Shopping Bag spree, after all. Brownie did have organizational ability, though, and that might be useful for other arrangements.

But what about Eddie Kiernan? Patches's old partner in crime—cellmate from Elmira and the Big House, alleged former gun mate from the Ardsley bank job—had been released from Auburn the previous month. With his small mouth and shapeless nose, Kiernan could easily pass for Patches's brother. Plus, Kiernan and Billy Wade went back twenty years, all the way to St. John's parochial school—they were bosom pals who trusted each other. Would Kiernan be game enough to jump right back into the mix? Patches thought so—as Eddie Kiernan's long police record demonstrated, the man lived and breathed for the angles.

Maybe Patches could make the visiting room work to their advantage—use the crowds, like on the Con Ed jobs, and hide in plain sight.

Carefully finessed, Kiernan could be his brains on the outside, using the well-worn thread of family visits to knit together a breakout plot that nobody would soon forget. Patches would talk to his girlfriend Gertrude Carlson the next time she came up to visit. Records show that she'd been his most regular visitor ever since he'd arrived upriver, posing as his wife almost every week. She'd help him get Kiernan up and running—what were wives for?

There was movement on the tier—the night keeper making his rounds, his footsteps squeaking softly, the jangling key ring clipped to his belt now cupped in his fist. Night staffers were so practiced in stealth that inmates would often throw pilfered salt on the tiers to hear the crunch of their approach. But Patches could relax for the night; the parts of his plan were cast. The next time Gertrude came to visit, they'd really have something to talk about.

———————

Thin and quiet, Gertrude Carlson was hardly a gun moll. Molls were maternal battle-axes like Ma Barker, so protective of her four outlaw sons—with whom she planned bank robberies—that she'd perjure herself rather than see them in prison. Or molls were highly sexed gunslingers like Bonnie Parker, who with her infamous boyfriend Clyde Barrow filled automobiles with weapons and pulled stickups in half a dozen midwestern states. Gertrude Carlson wasn't remotely in their league. She was more along the lines of Willie Sutton's loyal wife Louise, not at all violent but faithful in a pinch.

Gertrude was a plain West Side girl when she first met Patches, the two living edgewise like everyone else in Hell's Kitchen. Patches might not have been much to look at, but he had money and made the best of what he had—tailored sharkskin suits, a white shirt unbuttoned at the neck, the collar splayed across his lapels. But even so—the sharp clothes, chest hair at the V-neck—the man was thin, like a solid meal was always out of reach. A girl wanted to feed and take care of him.

Not that she would have had the cash. An economic situation like hers would have lent itself to the movies on Ninth Avenue in the West Thirties—the Nickel Dump it was called because of all the cheap first-, second-, and third-rate pictures showing there. But that's where Patches came in. Like lots of big spenders, he'd make up for the cut-rate entertainment with a steak at places like the Anchor Café on Twelfth—pretty nice for the waterfront crowd—or Jack Dempsey's on Broadway, the ex-prizefighter's classy joint, when he and Gertrude wanted to dance. John Waters showed Gert a time she might not have seen otherwise.

Stoic and soft-spoken, she almost certainly avoided the question of his money—who wanted to know? She'd keep her worries to herself. From the experiences in the neighborhood, though, she could imagine, and that was enough. But John offered to help change her situation, the monthly flipping through the bills, deciding which ones could wait. He had an apartment on West Eightieth Street, down the block from the Hayden Planetarium and the Museum of Natural History. He was one Hell's Kitchen kid who got away—but he couldn't stay away. In fact, Patches spent so much time at Gertrude's place on the corner of Forty-fifth Street and Ninth Avenue that most months he covered the rent there. Forget about what such an arrangement would imply about Gertrude's virtue—on the West Side in the late 1930s, nobody cared. This was the modern age running to ground; you did what you had to do. The past was done and they'd survived. The future—who knew what was coming? The time was now. Plain and simple, for a woman like Gert, John was a way out. And if she loved him, that was no one's business. When he ended up in Sing Sing, the least she could do was make every effort to visit him.

Sing Sing's visiting room was on the first floor of the Administration Building's south end. Decades later, the wide square room would become the lineup room, where officers arriving for their shifts would receive assignments and instructions. Sixty-five years ago, though, it buzzed with outsiders.

Inmates and visitors—wives and girlfriends, fathers and mothers and children—sat opposite one another on hardwood stools, separated from one another by only a brass rail. Under what was known as the Humane System, couples were allowed to hold hands and touch each other's faces.

Mothers wept, infants sat on the prison-gray laps of their fathers and wailed. Watchful officers were posted on raised platforms at either end of the room, and the barred windows gave long river views. The rear windows faced the scrubby hill behind the building, studded with rock from which the original prison was cut. A visitor and inmate were sealed off in this room—not at all in the outside world yet not completely in the prison, either.

According to Sing Sing Chief Clerk Don L. Parson's files, and later court testimony, Gertrude's first visit didn't go so well. She approached the visiting desk, soon after Patches had been admitted in February 1940, and told the officer she was Mrs. John Waters. The desk officer, Paul Wilson, a prison guard for fourteen years, many of them assigned to the visiting desk, asked Gertrude for her marriage certificate.

Gert admitted that she and John weren't officially married but insisted that they were common-law.

But that information wasn't listed in Patches's probation report, and Gert had no documentation to verify her relationship. She wasn't even sure about the particulars of the Waters family—John didn't talk much about anyone except an older sister, Catherine.

Gertrude's first visit hit a bureaucratic nerve. "For years and years," complained Chief Clerk Parsons in a contemporaneous memo to Warden Lawes, the prison had had a problem with common-law wives. Parsons had worked out a simple solution. He resolved that women presenting themselves to the visiting desk as inmates' wives would have to furnish proof of relationship. If they didn't have a marriage license, then some other evidence of cohabitation would have to be provided, such as automobile licenses, utility bills, or rent receipts. Lawes approved and the matter was put to rest to Parsons' satisfaction.

It must have been discouraging for Gertrude—an hour up on the train, only to be turned away for lack of documentation, the noise receding as she exited through the barred gates. But Gert was determined.

And when she did return within the week, she showed Officer Wilson a rent receipt for the apartment on Ninth Avenue and signed her name onto Patches's visiting card. She got her pass in return, sat on a stool against the wall, and waited. When she finally saw John at the beginning of March 1940—for the first time since the court appearances on the Con Ed robbery charges months before—she must have been jolted. The prison grays swam on him.

Subsequent visits went better. Gertrude got to see Patches thirty-two times over the next twelve months, about every eleven days. And Patches got what he needed, too. It's unclear exactly what he said in order to set his plan in motion. Most likely, as little as possible. For the thing to work, each link had to be secure, and that was best achieved by letting each participant know only his or her own part in the chain. Certainly he needed to tell Gert that he wanted to see Eddie Kiernan. But he didn't have to tell her why. He'd have to explain that Kiernan was an ex-con, though, because ex-cons weren't allowed to visit inmates, and they'd need to find a way around that. And they'd have to talk about the Waters family, because those details were essential to Kiernan's visiting. Patches was lucky. Gertrude was a West Side girl—he could depend on her not to ask too many questions and to keep her nerve. By the summer, she was con versant enough in visiting room procedure and Waters family particulars to instruct Eddie Kiernan on the best way for an ex-con—a guy who had been to Sing Sing himself twice before—to get into the prison visiting room.

Though Gertrude had never met Kiernan before the early months of 1940, he sat beside her twice that summer on the northbound train out of Grand Central, headed for Ossining. These hour-long rides gave Gert the perfect opportunity to fill Kiernan in on all he had to know. Eddie Kiernan had taken a last look at Sing Sing prison in 1936, as he climbed into the paddy wagon for his transfer upstate to Auburn prison. Now four years later, in June 1940, Kiernan was back, approaching Sing Sing's Administration Building as a civilian. His prison grays would have been replaced with a favorite suit—Eddie Kiernan was always stylish in police photos—the double-breasted blue wool, say, set off by a pearl tie and a charcoal fedora. The suit looked snug after years of starchy prison food, but that added an air of prosperity. His respectable appearance, though, masked a jumpy outlaw thrill, a gut-flutter sensation like in the seconds before pulling a job with a gun.

Since his release from Auburn in early March, Kiernan had been toeing the straight and narrow. He was living in Chelsea with his older sister, Margaret, who had practically raised him after their immigrant mother died when he was a baby and their grief-stricken father had turned more and more to drink. Every morning, Kiernan took the subway out to Greenpoint, Brooklyn, and his job with Jarka & Co., a stevedoring company. But aside from playing a few rackets, mostly low-stakes dice, he was working the docks and keeping his nose clean. Besides his parole officer, to whom Kiernan reported weekly, Margaret made going straight a condition before offering her little brother the lumpy sofa in her small apartment on West Twenty-first Street.

With all those demands on his honesty, though, Kiernan sometimes escaped into whiskey and beer. He wasn't really allowed alcohol while on parole, but he carried a burden going straight—and when he drank, anything seemed possible, even keeping on this side of the law. But now Patches had something in the works. Try as Eddie might, he couldn't help but be a part of it.

State police and prison records indicate that ever since he was a kid at St. John's parochial school on West Thirty-first Street, Kiernan and his partner Billy Wade were in almost constant trouble. Typical kid stuff, though, like boosting change from the collection boxes in the church or merchandise from the stores lining Seventh Avenue. But he wouldn't have thought of himself as a bad guy, compared to some of the hardboiled cases you met at Auburn and Sing Sing. He had never killed anyone, for instance, or even hurt anyone much in the course of his criminal career. Anyway, he made amends by going to Mass every Sunday with his sister Margaret. And besides, everybody was a finagler; any newspaper could tell you that. Eddie Kiernan simply found his kicks in thieving, be it armed robbery or burglary.

After Eddie was sentenced in 1936 for parole violation after the Ardsley bank job wouldn't stick, the system in its wisdom made sure to keep him and Patches separated. Patches went to Sing Sing; Kiernan went upstate. But the system was the system, lousy no matter where you went. Anything Patches had in mind couldn't be too good for this place, and Eddie Kiernan was there to help. He'd become Terrence Waters, arriving at Sing Sing to see his imprisoned brother John.

Kiernan and Gertrude followed the other visitors toward the visiting room, the prison's most public space. The gates banged and locked behind them, and they lined up before the visiting room guard's desk. The whole atmosphere—the echo of the voices, the scent of disinfectant—was oppressive. But Kiernan was a professional. He'd master his nerves as he would before any job. He'd be all business, calm and fully submerged in his role. Attitude made all the difference. Act as if you're supposed to be where you are and most people will accept it. Don't act shifty, but don't stare at anyone, either. Officers saw lots of convicts come and go, so Kiernan wouldn't be too worried about them. Inmates might remember him; certainly guys he knew would recognize him. So he'd keep an eye out. You couldn't trust many people inside. And when he removed his hat, stepped up to Officer Wilson, and correctly answered his questions, the precedent was established. Eddie Kiernan was Terrence Waters.

For the next year, he and Patches Waters schemed right under the prison's eyes and ears.

———————

Patches had spotted a flaw in the system, and he coolly shaped his plans to take full advantage. According to *Rules and Regulations Governing Inmates of the New York State Penal Institutions, December 1, 1940,* visits were limited to one per week, and male friends were permitted only once a month. Multiply that by a prison population of about twenty-five hundred, and Sing Sing's visiting room must have been one of the facility's busiest corners, with security dependent on two tireless guards. Despite Patches's claims to Gertrude that his family relations were strained, the entire Waters clan—his mother Delia; his sisters, Catherine, still at home, and the married Mary Schlicher—everyone it seems except the real brother Terrence—had all made visits to see Patches during his time in Sing Sing. In addition to Gertrude's more than thirty trips, Eddie

Kiernan's strategy sessions and near-monthly updates were made over the course of nine visits. Robert Brown, Patches's partner in the pinball business, also visited nine times. Tally up all of these visits, and it appears that John Waters enjoyed the very maximum number allowed by the state's rulebook. To the authorities, Patches Waters was just another popular inmate. But for Patches, this steady retinue of visitors, quietly parading among the room's buzzing throngs, provided him a solid scaffold from which to build his increasingly complex escape plot. Brainy and quiet, with a wide network of friends and associates, Waters simply sized up the overburdened system and used it to gain the upper hand.

The plan was working. In just a few months, the guards and even old Lawes himself would be left shaking their heads.

━━━━━

CHAPTER TEN

THE STEAM VAULT

As THE FRAGRANT SPRING OF 1940 TURNED into a stifling summer, Patches Waters and Charlie McGale crafted the two parts of their plan. While Patches finessed his visiting privileges, Charlie McGale continued leveraging the extraordinary design weakness he'd found in the prison hospital: the locked but almost unguarded 330-foot-long tunnel to the outside railroad cut. Each man seemed born to his distinct role—gregarious Patches with his steady relay of crony information through busy visiting room communications; and McGale, the picky little locksmith, armed with purloined tools for his lonely sneaks down to the hospital basement. A role reversal was unthinkable; it would have been remarkable indeed if, all of a sudden, Charlie was frequently called away from his repair assignments for a visit. He was known as a loner. Since his incarceration in mid-January 1936, Charlie McGale hadn't had a single visitor in more than four years.

In fact, he probably couldn't remember the last time he'd seen or heard from his family. It certainly must have been sometime before he'd pulled a gun and held up a card game for $40 in a parking lot on Eighth Avenue one warm summer night in 1935. The McGales had pretty much given up on their Charlie by then. Every time he was sentenced back to Sing Sing, McGale gave the chief clerk the name of a different "nearest living relative" to write down in the massive admittance book. Sometimes McGale said his closest relative was his father Bernard, living alone up in the

Bronx; other times, his brother Joseph. Sometimes McGale said that he was the youngest of four; other times, that he was one of seven, or nine. Nobody from the prison ever rifled through the records to compare earlier admittances, much less gumshoed out to check the facts—false answers to rote family questions were about the only control an arriving inmate had at that point. And anyway, as Charlie could see, nobody really cared.

Small and slight, McGale had spent much of his life passing unnoticed beneath the eyes of legitimate society. School had always been a struggle; and when he failed eighth grade, he dropped out at fifteen rather than face the shame of repeating the year again. He had a hopeful moment late in the Great War. Inspired by America's entry into the fight against imperial Germany, and vaguely hoping for glory, Charlie joined the U.S. Army. A skilled steamfitter by trade, Charlie was nevertheless bypassed by the 132nd Infantry's mechanical units and assigned to the medical corps. He had little time to brood over the slight. Within a year the carnage ended—too soon for Charlie to have been very effective, anyway—and he was honorably discharged. Back in New York City, scuffling around for work, Charlie McGale apparently felt that he had to make his own luck. Consequently, he began racking up convictions for burglary, assault, and robbery; and sentences to Welfare Island, the Tombs, and Sing Sing.

By 1940, on his fourth sentence up the river, McGale had come to feel almost at home in the Big House. During the mid-'30s, he'd been renting a bed at the Penn Post Hotel on West Thirty-first Street and Eighth Avenue, sharing the gamy, neon-splashed room with a civilization of cockroaches. His mechanic's skills overlooked yet again, McGale worked at busy Pennsylvania Station as a "baggage agent," according to one report, which meant lugging suitcases for traveling swells and their snooty wives. Pulling that gun on the Eighth Avenue card game seems to have been a stroke of desperate genius. It got him sent back to Sing Sing for the last time, where he again had an outlet for his mechanical know-how. As it turned out, he could even realize some potential.

Still though, it seems that whenever his life suddenly swept in on him, when thoughts about his situation flooded his mind—the loss of freedom that compounded the humiliation he'd lived all his life; the twisting corridors and tunnels between the prison buildings leading mazelike back around on themselves; the vaulting cellblocks echoing thousands of human voices; the thirty-foot walls that enclosed more than two thousand men on forty-five acres; all of this every day of his life and not a single word from anyone he knew on the outside—then Charlie McGale's heart would start to palpitate and sweat would bubble out of every pore. Then only leaning in a brick corner by himself would do, until the "bugs" passed him by. But those panicky moments, awful as they were, must have inspired him, too; they were the added incentive he needed to make good on his part of the escape plot.

As McGale told Patches in the yard, he had discovered the tunnel on an earlier stay at Sing Sing, back in 1934. Charlie was incarcerated on a parole violation and assigned to work at the powerhouse. Sing Sing was—and still is—a self-contained world, and nearly everyone worked. Factories turned out everything from shoes and socks to brushes and mattresses. The inmate sent up the river to bang out license plates is a tired cliché; more likely, he'd go deaf in the sheet metal shop hammering street cleaner pushcarts into shape. Besides operating the many workshops, the prison also generated its own light and heat, cooked and served its own food, made its own ice, wove and patched inmate clothing, ran a fleet of trucks, repaired its own buildings, and maintained heating, plumbing, telephone, and electric lines that stitched the whole grid together. Like the passages and corridors connecting the cellblocks, the power lines ran through a complex network of tunnels, and Charlie McGale knew the labyrinth well. Up until the 1940s, all the prison's mechanics—all the plumbers, all the steamfitters, all the machinists, even the locksmith—were inmate workers. To accommodate these many craftsmen, small repair shops and workbenches were scattered throughout the prison, in the basements and cellars of the facility's buildings. Like the large powerhouse and refrigeration plant, these widespread, tiny workshops were equipped with tools and repair materials, saving the workers trips back and forth, up and down the hill.

All those crowbars and screwdrivers in prisoners' hands—yet they were rarely even challenged to show their passes. The arrangement is unthinkable in modern times. The day would swiftly come when inmate mechanics, while still making prison repairs, would be scanned by metal detectors and frisked by officers before returning to their cells. The inmate work crews assigned to fix leaks and plaster walls eventually would be overseen not only by guards but by civilian contractors.

But in Charlie McGale's time, a clever convict had at his disposal a tool supply worthy of the finest hardware store.

————

McGale's job in the powerhouse gave him a measure of responsibility for maintaining power conduits and central heating lines throughout the prison. All of these lines branched off the main service tunnel from the powerhouse. The position was a dream come true for Charlie—bent over his tools, tinkering, lost to the world. After being passed over all his life, he must have felt an expert's pride arriving at a repair site, setting his toolbox on the floor, and carefully selecting the proper wrench for the job. When he was in a good mood, Charlie, fully immersed in the work, could expound his knowledge or ignore a kibitzing guard's commentary without getting into trouble.

McGale had seen nearly every corner of the prison and eventually was ordered to the hospital to repair a length of pipe in the sub-basement. No inmate was allowed down there unescorted. An officer unlocked the iron gate and wooden door to the sub-basement entrance, climbed down the iron rungs into the concrete pit, hit the lights, and motioned McGale through the entry into a large concrete vault for steam and power lines. Most officers were taller than Charlie's five-foot, six-inch height and would have had to stoop with a flashlight while Charlie sweated with the wrench, the cement ceiling inches above his head. Low-watt bulbs were threaded along the ceiling, sloping away to a point in the distance. The air in the vault was warm, furred with dust and the steam heat hissing through asbestos-wrapped pipes. The vault was really a tunnel, the pipes running west toward the river, if his sense of direction was right. You couldn't see to the end, but Charlie McGale had a good feel for Sing Sing's underground layout. He realized that he was in the main service tunnel from the powerhouse, across the railroad tracks in the lower prison. That meant there had to be an outside access. The thought was a revelation.

But before he could explore the utility tunnel any further, McGale's sentence was up and he was released. Charlie must have realized, however, that if he ever returned, as he reckoned he might if his past was any guide, there just might be a way out. And when he did return for the card game robbery a couple of years later, in 1936, the steam vault immediately came to mind. A tunnel straight out of the mighty Sing Sing—the thought would make any inmate giddy.

McGale's reconnaissance picked up where he'd left off. He knew where the tunnel began, but was it really a way out? McGale was assigned to work the refrigeration plant this time around, running a ten-ton compressor. He had a workbench in the "ice house," as the plant was known, where he could customize repairs. Then one afternoon, his experience as a steamfitter got him assigned to a two-man crew replacing a radiator in 12 Post. The tower post rose on the railroad cut just west of the Administration Building, directly above the front gate stockade and the railroad tracks right below to the west. While sliding the iron radiator into the tower's cramped, glassed-in observation deck, McGale could glance due south a few yards and see a large steam and power conduit elbowing from the top of the retaining wall in the railroad cut, thirty feet below. The conduit ran west across the rail bed on a small trestle bridge and into the prison's powerhouse in the old section. Looking back up the hill, he saw that the hospital was almost due east. That confirmed it. Charlie McGale had spotted his steam tunnel's other end—and it was outside. Although he was hefting a radiator up to the tower's deck, his heart surely skipped up a notch.

But could he get out that way? With the guard watching from the doorway to give the inmates room to work, Charlie and his companion knelt on the floor, grunting the new radiator into place and wrenching it tight. McGale's mind could hardly have been on the work, though, as he peeked at the railroad wall whenever he could. The conduit opening appeared much smaller than the entrance in the hospital basement, but that surely was the tunnel exit right above the tracks. An iron plate sealed off the opening not occupied by the exiting pipe. But from his vantage, McGale determined that the plate wasn't tight—a black sliver of space appeared to edge the sides. And best of all, there seemed to be rust stains around the plate, as if water had seeped through. If the plate's top and bottom were spot-welded—a light solder to hold the seal in place—then the solder was flaking and corroded with rust. In that case, a few jabs with a pinch bar, followed by a swift kick, and a man might be able to slip right through.

For the next four years, until Patches Waters arrived in 1940, Charlie McGale had thought and dreamed about the tunnel. Using his work assignments from the refrigeration plant, and his mechanic's skills, he cased the approaches to the steam vault and outlined a plan. Considering opportunities for a breakout took time—the mind had to evaluate the long-standing institutional weaknesses, so commonplace they were invisible to the administration, combined with any momentary lapses in security. You had to recognize a chance when one appeared and then immediately grab it.

To begin with, Charlie needed repeated entry to the hospital basement for careful inspections. From his one repair trip to the vault back in '34, he remembered the procedure. The guard used three keys to enter: one for an iron gate, one for a padlock, and one for a wooden door. A single fact was immediately clear: McGale's access to the hospital sub-basement would depend on meticulous locksmithing. But since inmates, even trusties, weren't allowed down into the steam vault without an escort, McGale would have to find another way in to begin his picking. He found the solution in the laundry building next door.

From his work on repairs in the laundry basement, McGale knew that a branch of the main steam vault under the hospital ran feed lines to the laundry building. But the laundry approach to the vault, also sealed behind a locked iron gate and padlock, was less guarded than the hospital route—the hospital, after all, housed inmates. What with all the pipes and lines snaking to the laundry's industrial-size machines, maybe McGale could pretend he was working. As a trusty mechanic, he'd just have to gamble that his frequent presence in the building wouldn't raise suspicion.

But he would need to cut blank keys to fit all the locks. Over time, he acquired a number of blanks—from where is unclear. Possibly he picked them up from among the many that were discarded or just "laying around," as he claimed. An extraordinary breach of security in any lockup, that was a tough story to swallow. But maybe a fellow inmate who worked in the powerhouse and was about to be released traded them for a pack of cigarettes. At the time, like the facility's other mechanics, Sing Sing's locksmith was an inmate who cut all the prison's keys at a guarded workshop. (Even more than sixty years later, according to one retired corrections officer, an inmate trusty was known to carry a ring of keys, although presumably they didn't fit security locks.) But whether this most trusted inmate would turn betrayer in the final days of his sentence, and in exchange for nothing more than cigarettes, is anyone's guess. Charlie McGale would never rat out such a valuable asset. In any event, once McGale had the blanks, he crafted a key at his workbench to fit the laundry cellar door.

Around the same time, Charlie scored another lucky break. He acquired enough rope to cover the nearly thirty-foot drop from the steam vault exit to the railroad tracks. Newspapers afterward were quick to print that the rope was lifted from the ice house, where Charlie worked. But McGale told another tale. He claimed that the rope came from a work crew cutting lengths for window sashes—he snatched up a coil of rope and stuck it in his shirt while the men were busy measuring the windows. He later hid the cord behind a stretch of pipe running along the steam vault ceiling. With these two components—the laundry key that got him closer to the hospital basement and the rope that would spin him away outside—McGale had the beginning and end of his master plan.

And then he languished.

Six years had passed since he'd first seen the steam vault, and all he had to show for it were one key and some rope. Even taking into consideration the patience and time needed to devise an out, Charlie McGale was lagging. That had always been his trouble, perhaps—difficulty plotting the big steps in life. The idea itself, it seems, had occupied him more than its execution. *A tunnel out of Sing Sing* had taken on a life of its own. But once he was out, then what? All he knew about was being inside prison. Even when he was outside, he always found a way back in. Despite the bugs that chased him from corner to corner, Charlie McGale lacked the foresight to fully imagine his great escape. He needed a spark to illuminate what came after. He needed Patches Waters.

After Patches was in on the plot McGale revved back into action. Each separate piece of the plan fit together like a perfect piece of plumbing, all the way to the end.

———

Later court records show that over the spring and summer of 1940 McGale worked out a careful schedule for his forays into the main steam vault. Dinnertime was best, he found, to use the approach from the laundry. When the inmate working stock and inventory in the laundry building basement went to eat, Charlie stuffed his pockets with tools from his ice house workbench. He used his homemade key to sneak down to the laundry basement, the air scented with detergent and dust; then he knelt in front of the gated entrance to the steam vault branch. The inmate would return from dinner in an hour; Charlie had nearly forty-five minutes to pick and file the locks. He just had to pray that the guards were focused on keeping order during mess hall.

The branch's iron gate was latched by key and doubly fastened with a fat Yale padlock and chain. From his pockets Charlie removed a small ice hook, similar to a buttonhook with a 45-degree angle; a small vise; some blank brass keys; and iron files. He picked up the ice hook and used it to pry off the gate's lock plate. He took a blank key and measured it against the lock's five brass levers, cutting notches in the blank with a file. Then he sat on the floor, the key fast in the vise, and started to file cuts, holding the blank up to the levers now and then for accuracy. When he was satisfied that the key was a fit, he tried it in the mechanism and saw the latch slip free. Another lock down. Only the padlock to go.

He looked at his watch—an hour had nearly passed. He would have liked to spring the padlock, enter the branch, and follow it to the hospital end. But there was no time. The laundry worker would be coming back from dinner any minute, and Charlie wouldn't want to stammer out any explanations. He refastened the gate's lock plate, pocketed his tools and the new key, and swept the filings away with his shoe. He'd have to come back another day to jimmy the padlock. When he did, a week or so later, using the dinner hour to fashion another blank key, Charlie McGale had his own private access through the branch to the main steam vault.

But the riskiest part of the job still lay ahead: access to the hospital basement to cut keys for *that* entrance to the steam vault. The plan was for both Patches and McGale to be admitted as patients, slip from their beds, go downstairs and disappear through the locked vault. The steam vault exited nearly at the foot of 12 Post, the tower above the railroad tracks, so the escape had to be made at night. But preparing the way—cutting the necessary keys that would unlock the hospital entrance to the vault—was dangerous. The hospital housed inmates round the clock, so the building had more guards than the laundry. McGale would have to work his locksmith magic fast, and silently, in the hospital basement to avoid being caught.

A few days later, McGale slipped away from his workbench. He climbed the hill to the laundry like he was on another job. Standing in front of the laundry branch entrance, he took a deep breath and stepped inside. The vault was tighter in the branch than he'd experienced on the hospital end, and warmer, the air sour with mildew. Rats squeaked in the dark, and water bugs prowled the damp walls. Charlie had to duck low as he walked. His two homemade keys had worked beautifully on the laundry cellar gate; he even locked the gate behind him. A light switch just inside illuminated a string of cloudy bulbs along the ceiling. This was his first trip into the vault alone to see what awaited him at the other end.

Again, McGale had less than an hour before the laundry worker returned from dinner.

Charlie came to a T in the vault. He'd have been walking south toward the hospital; a left turn led to the basement, a right down toward the tracks. The ambient light from the laundry branch faded as McGale turned left. He stretched one arm before him and felt along the cement wall with his other hand. It was now completely dark, and he could only guess how far it was to the hospital entrance. This would be about the worst time to panic, surrounded by concrete, rats, and fat insects, and buried under more than four stories of brick building. He rubbed the sweat from his face, his breath coming faster now. There was another light switch, a button box—the guard had pushed it when Charlie was down here years ago. But where was it? Somewhere along the wall, here, here, *there* it was. He hit the switch, and bulbs popped on all up and down the vault. He was at the hospital end of the steam vault.

McGale climbed the iron rungs onto the vault platform and stood within the vault's locked approach in the hospital basement. The small platform room was nearly black. If he remembered rightly, a wooden door was directly in front of him, with a gate on the other side. Thankfully, no light showed around the frame, which meant that no one was on the other side. He searched for the light switch beside the door and pressed the button on.

He stood in a small brick room. Pipes ran along the ceiling; wires from a square electrical box twisted up the wall. Planks of board lay on the floor. The air was close and dank. Charlie knelt in front of the wooden door and spread his tools beside him.

The lock looked easy, just a standard Sargent door lock above the worn brass knob. He used a screwdriver to loosen the setscrews in the jamb, then unscrewed the lock's barrel and pulled it free. With the barrel out, McGale lined up a blank key with the barrel's lock pins, made the notches, and filed them down. But when he tried the new key in the lock, he'd found he'd filed too far—the fit was loose and might not catch the pins when the time came. He looked at his wristwatch. There wasn't time to cut another key—the laundry worker would be coming back from dinner any minute, and Charlie had to get back if he wanted to avoid the man. He'd have to take the key back to his workbench and adjust it there. A disappointment but nothing too major—he was at the hospital locks, and that was good news.

McGale replaced the lock barrel and tightened the setscrews. He pocketed his tools and blew away the filings. Punching out the platform lights, he retraced his steps back down into the vault. He turned out the vault lights, and the tunnel went black. But that was no worry; Charlie just walked toward the glow fanning out from the laundry branch.

Step by step, McGale was breathing easier every day.

———————

Charlie McGale had a pretty good setup in the ice house. He ran a huge compressor, one of a number of ten-ton machines, manufacturing ice and pumping Sing Sing's refrigeration throughout the facility. Charlie was a diligent workman, and the compressor usually huffed along without much effort—he and a small crew of inmates were on hand just in case any problems arose. And if a seal did leak, or a pipe burst, McGale was usually able to make the repair on-site or at his workbench, under the smeared, pebble-glass windows along the wall.

On a given summer day in 1940, however, Charlie was bent over his worksite, peering into an entirely different matter. With small sections of pipe scattered across the nicked wooden surface, and a handy wrench for cover, McGale tinkered with the ill-fitting key from the wooden door on the steam vault platform. He'd filed the key too deeply but needed only a drop of solder to build up the cut. On his next trip down, he'd smooth away the excess and perfect the fit. With his ear cocked at his station for the guard who patrolled through the plant every twenty to thirty minutes or so, McGale used a soldering iron to melt a drop in the cut. He then leaned the key to dry behind a section of pipe on the table.

When the solder hardened, McGale put that key with the other keys hidden in the pants cuff of a pair of overalls hanging on a hook in his locker. Every inmate craftsman had a locker—though technically, because it didn't lock, it was more like a closet. The men needed a place to hang their greasy work clothes and to store other belongings. Charlie's keys would be safe there.

Eager to try the soldered key in the lock, McGale slipped back into the vault a few days later. Seated cross-legged before the wooden door on the steam vault platform in the hospital basement, the lock barrel in pieces in his lap, he filed the key down, tried the fit, and filed some more. At last, the match was good—still a little loose, but he and Patches could depend on it. Charlie replaced the lock barrel in the door and tightened the setscrews.

He jiggled the key and opened the door. The iron gate was right on the other side, fastened tight. A darkened storeroom was just beyond—a stack of old mattresses piled in the corner to the right of the doorway, the worn ticking sprouting like hair. McGale could hear voices and the clanging of pots and pans. The hospital kitchen was across the basement hallway outside, and a soupy steam drifted through the hall door. This close to inmates and officers, all Charlie could do was hope that a busy dinnertime would cover the sound of his work.

He pulled the Sargent padlock around through the bars of the gate, careful not to clank the heavy chain. He fixed the padlock steady against the lock plate with his vise. With a little compress hand drill, he bored a small hole in the padlock's side; the drill bit pressured the lock's tongue and sprang the latch. He took the padlock off and put it in his pocket. From his back pocket he pulled another Sargent padlock, perhaps acquired from his locksmith source, slipped the dummy through the chain, and locked it. Charlie hoped no one would need to come into the steam vault before he could fit a key for the official padlock at his workbench; he'd have to work fast to avoid that.

By dinnertime the next day, McGale had cut a key to fit the original padlock. With his signature attention to detail, he used a tiny piece of copper to plug the drill hole in the padlock's side. A guard would have to inspect the lock carefully, get right in there with a flashlight, to detect any tampering. Charlie was assuming that no officer would do that until he and Patches were long gone. McGale replaced the padlock on the gate and pocketed the dummy.

He checked his wristwatch. Dinnertime wasn't even half over. Using the small ice hook, McGale pried off the iron gate's lock plate, as he'd done in the laundry cellar, and cut a blank to fit. The work went faster on the hospital gate. By the time the kitchen noises were dying down,

McGale was done. He had six keys—three for the laundry approach, three for the hospital end of the vault.

He and Patches were practically home free.

By the middle of summer, McGale's part of the breakout plan was nearly complete. He had hidden all six keys in his locker in the refrigeration plant. To his surprise, the hallway door near the hospital kitchen was never locked—the prison guards apparently relied on the triple locks at the vault entrance for security. Charlie must have smiled at that. The final detail was at the other end of the steam vault, thirty feet above the tracks—the iron plate closing off the exit to the outside world.

From his first glimpse years ago while replacing the radiator in 12 Post, he knew that a corroding spot-weld held the plate in place. If it hadn't been reinforced in the meantime, Charlie reckoned that a few jabs with a pinch bar would open it right up. Although this job might have required the least skill, in some respects it was the most difficult.

As McGale had discovered walking the length of the tunnel, the vault's height and width varied in different sections. Near the hospital opening, the vault was over six feet tall and just as wide. But in the laundry branch, and deeper in the main vault, the height dropped to maybe five feet, and the air temperature rose. And nearest the exit above the railroad tracks, the passage funneled down to only eighteen inches—flush against the sweltering steam conduit, Charlie found there was barely room to work.

He heaved himself onto the narrow crawl-space ledge and inched forward nearly six feet toward the plate. Late afternoon light haloed through the loose sides; rills of fresh air evaporated in the tunnel's heat. He pulled the pinch bar from his waistband, careful not to burn his arms and hands on the steam-hot conduit, and began to chip. The work was slow, with little room for maneuvering and none for leverage. After just a few passes, Charlie was soaked in sweat. The summer sun on the plate's outside, and the hissing steam pipe inside, elevated the temperature in the crawl space to nearly 100 degrees.

McGale could hardly breathe. He kept straining forward, pushing his face toward the plate's edges for air. Afraid of suffocating, his heart starting to ram against his chest, he felt the panic rise. This was no time for an attack of the bugs. He wiggled backward out of the crawl space and doubled over on the floor of the main vault, coughing. He hurried back up to and through the laundry branch, locked the gate behind him, and took deep breaths of the laundry basement's cool, moldy air. The plate would take longer than he'd expected. The bottom weld wasn't even half done, and there was still the top; he'd have to go back. But he must have been relieved being out of there for now. So he'd underestimated the plate—that was nothing to worry about. Now that he knew what awaited him, he could prepare himself and take his sweet time to chip away at it. There was no rush.

Some weeks later, after a few more trips, McGale laid the pinch bar on the floor and reached his fingers around the plate. It jiggled freely in his hands—a good pull and it would come out cleanly. He pushed it carefully, firmly back into place. Charlie couldn't know for sure, but he trusted that from the outside there was no visible damage. From atop 12 Post, the plate looked as secure as it ever did—at least, the guards didn't indicate otherwise.

At last, everything was ready. The rope was waiting behind a twelve-inch electrical pipe, in easy reach above the conduit, and all the keys were made and hidden in his locker. Quiet and affable Charlie McGale had done it. Combining his mechanical expertise, his position as a trusted inmate worker, and the covert skills acquired from a life of street crime, he'd passed unnoticed beneath the trained eyes of the administration and opened the way for a crash out.

And from all that Charlie could tell, nobody suspected a thing.

————————

In August 1940, an unrelated development helped the plot along. Renovations began on cellblock B. Barely twenty years old and built above a natural spring, B-block had started to fall apart. According to the *New York Times,* fifty-one inmates were shackled in handcuffs and leg irons, moved out of the crumbling cellblock in a driving rain, and transported to Attica prison. Those remaining were bunked on the open tiers of other cellblocks until room opened up for them at Sing Sing or elsewhere. The renovation job was too big, and security clearly too great a concern, to leave repairs on a major cellblock to Sing Sing's army of inmate laborers. This meant that at the 12 Post gate—the prison's main vehicle entrance—the trucks and cars of contract carpenters, plumbers, and electricians arriving for the job would be queuing up.

Opening and closing the stockade gates, and searching each vehicle one by one, would keep the single guard there harried for the next eight months.

CHAPTER ELEVEN

―――――

MACHINE GUNS AND MILK TRUCKS

Patches wanted a Tommy gun.

As McGale crept through tunnels and filed away at his keys that summer, Patches worked up his end of the plan with Eddie Kiernan. Acquiring guns was part of that, and Patches wanted some serious firepower. It would've been hard to say so out loud in the visiting room. Maybe he had a code word or made a cutting motion with his hand. In any case, Kiernan got the message. A chopper. Kiernan's mind began to buzz. He knew a person or two, guys from the Brooklyn waterfront, who might have an idea where somebody could put his hands on a Tommy gun for a reasonable price.

The guns were de rigueur for bootleggers and Depression-era gangsters. Throughout the 1920s Thompson submachine guns were sold on the open market, even by mail, with the proviso that gun dealers would sell responsibly. They didn't. By 1934, federal regulations were in place, and only government agencies like law enforcement, the military, and, oddly, the post office, had legitimate access. Civilians and criminals were out of luck. But there was an underground market. Some outlaw circles even rented out weapons, which were returned like a Hertz automobile after a trip. Patches was working on a long-range plan, though, and a rental didn't fit the bill.

Kiernan was accommodating; he'd see what he could do. Billy Wade might know. But Kiernan hadn't seen Wade since Wade had gotten out of the Tombs, escaping conviction on the Con Ed job with his usual Irish luck. Kiernan probably appreciated being the top guy in a maneuver for a change. Wade had always been the one with the glib tongue when the heat descended from one of their school-day capers. Why bring him in until it was absolutely necessary? Another fellow came to Kiernan's mind, Alfred Catelan, aka "Steve Collins," who would sell Kiernan a machine gun that summer for $100. Right off the bat, the heavy stuff was set.

By January 1941, ice floes the size of cars, the size of parking lots, crusted the Hudson. From a cell in 5 Building, an inmate could imagine a chilly walk across the ice to the gray Palisades. On Friday the seventeenth, a snowstorm turned to freezing rain, snapping power lines and tree limbs, even killing people up and down the East Coast. The next day, howling gusts pelted the cell window. With weather like that, Patches was almost sorry to leave his job in the steaming mess hall.

But he had managed another leap forward. He had positioned himself closer to the tunnel. The previous autumn, seeing the need for an even closer eye, he'd put in a request to the Assignment Board for an orderly job in the hospital, hoping his experience banging around in the prison mess hall would be an advantage—who better to roll food carts up and down the sick wards? Apparently, the Board agreed. When a position opened up, Patches was reassigned to the hospital in January 1941.

He brought meals up from the basement kitchen, and fresh linens and towels from the laundry. He quickly memorized the hospital's layout and routines. And the next time Kiernan visited, Patches gave him his most important assignment: he put him on the trail of the milk truck.

By then, the phony Waters brothers must have become quite comfortable in their masquerade. Experienced thieves, they knew the value of keeping secrets and maintaining roles. They kept glad expressions on their faces while they fabricated normal conversation about mom and sisters, home and work. Kiernan knew so much about the Waters family by January that he almost felt part of it. But when the guard passed by and returned to his platform perch at the end of the room, or when the adjoining cubicle had cleared of occupants, the men's discussion dropped to tight-lipped mutterings, sparsely worded code.

Kiernan had bought the machine gun and hidden it safely in his basement. But Patches needed handguns inside. He wasn't sure how many yet, two at least. Patches had kept Whitey in mind but hadn't said a thing to him about the progress of the plan over the preceeding months. He intended to approach him again later, closer to the break; he was still sure he needed an experienced strong-arm on a job like this. He'd worry about how many guns later; right now, he had to figure out a way to get them inside.

Every morning, a milk truck stopped at the hospital. Crowley's Dairy. Patches asked Kiernan to take a look, see if it was even possible.

From repeated observation, Patches and McGale determined that the milk truck made daily, daybreak deliveries. It entered the prison at the 12 Post gate, under the tower right outside the Administration Building, and stopped to be searched inside the stockade. A lone officer was assigned to check every vehicle that came inside, even Warden Lawes's automobile. Years ago, the warden suspected that four revolvers were smuggled in tied to the chassis of his car; he was determined that would not happen again. But there was no pit from which the guard could check vehicle undercarriages, and there were no mirrors to slide under the truck in order to fully examine the chassis. The uniformed officer had to wriggle under the vehicle on his back.

Up until now, Eddie Kiernan had been laying the groundwork alone. But now he needed help—it was time to give Billy Wade a call. Kiernan didn't want to follow a milk truck by himself, get lost up in Newburgh, for instance, or break down beside the apple orchards in Marlboro. That would be all he'd need. Billy Wade knew vehicles—he was a trucker's helper on the West Side docks, when he wasn't a getaway driver for armed robberies. Kiernan evidently accepted that he'd have to give up some of the control he'd been enjoying while working alone. So be it.

According to the New York State Police report, Kiernan and Wade began meeting to discuss the escape plot sometime in February 1941. They usually met at a saloon in the mid West Thirties, off Eighth Avenue. The report doesn't specify the address. It wasn't the Yankee Tavern or the

Hudson Hofbrau, the Shopping Bag Gang's usual haunts, but the West Side was dotted with ancient tap rooms. Open a tavern door on any street, and you'd find scuffed wooden bars, their brass rails bolted to the checkerboard linoleum, beneath tin ceilings grimed by decades of unfiltered cigarette smoke. Narrow places serving shots and beer, where men could talk in private.

Kiernan was in his element. "They have some keys for some doors up there," he said, telling Wade the whole idea. "Can you get a car?"

Wade was thirty-two years old, skinny, his reddish pompadour in need of a comb after the February wind. Pictures show him with a square chin and an impish expression, like he had the smart answer before you asked a stupid question. Besides working the docks, he was known in the rackets for taking numbers on the horses. He had five arrests dating back twelve years but no convictions. The latest pickup, for the Con Ed robbery, put him in the Tombs for ten months. Now he was free, and he surely appreciated why. If Patches Waters needed a car, Billy Wade could not say no.

But Kiernan wasn't finished. Patches also needed guns, and he thought he'd figured a way to get them inside. Wade was a driver. Could he help Kiernan case a milk route? Wade could.

Kiernan must have been relieved. He'd known Wade for years. He wouldn't have figured on any problems. But guys could get funny sometimes, even old pals—especially when they owed.

The following Friday night, around midnight, Kiernan and Wade crossed the Henry Hudson Bridge into Riverdale. They followed the Albany Post Road north and, after about an hour, passed through Ossining. Driving just about the only car on the road at that time of night, they'd have kept well within the speed limit. Eventually they crossed the Bear Mountain Bridge, wound up and down Storm King Mountain, passed West Point, and reached Newburgh just before one o'clock. They turned off the headlights and parked down the street from the truck entrance to the Crowley Dairy, on the opposite side of the street.

And then they waited. The plant stood behind a bending chain-link fence. Exterior lights above the loading dock showed a long, flat-roofed, two-story brick building. Nearest to the car, a fleet of trucks sat warming up in a gravel lot adjacent to a loading platform, their exhaust spiraling into the freezing dark. A couple of men in heavy coats loaded wire crates and large metal canisters of product into the back of a truck. The trucks were mostly small, residential deliverers, but there were also a few large vehicles for the dairy's industrial accounts.

How could they tell which truck went to Sing Sing? The Crowley Dairy served the entire Hudson Valley, making deliveries to the prison seven days a week. Patches was interested only in the truck that came on Saturdays—because he worked Saturdays unloading the truck at the hospital, or because McGale would have the best access on that day. There were maybe half a dozen trucks in the industrial fleet. Either Patches had been quite specific about which milk truck made the Saturday delivery, providing Kiernan and Wade with an identifying vehicle or license plate number. Or the men may have had to follow the trucks one by one until they found the truck that delivered to Sing Sing. In either case, this surveillance took about eight weeks—time enough to allow for false starts, identify the correct truck, and confirm its routine. The exact scheme was never revealed, but when the right truck slowed for Sing Sing's front entrance, the boys knew enough to steer past it and proceed up the hill that curved around the great limestone wall.

On the tenth of March, Kiernan signed into the visiting room and told Patches they had the milk truck cold. What next? Patches needed to talk to Whitey Riordan one more time to answer that question.

Patches had been right. A year in Sing Sing had changed Whitey again. The young kid who eleven months ago had accepted years in Sing Sing before him, who had wanted nothing to do with Patches's plan, had had a change of heart. They met in mid-March 1941 to discuss it. The ice floes had melted but the river was still leaden. The bare Palisades looked rounded with the cold. Whitey had passed his first anniversary in Sing Sing without fanfare. It must have felt far longer than that. Only eight more years to go before parole.

Patches almost certainly noticed the change in his young pal. The brawny stevedore had softened: prison food thickened his middle, and the long year had creased his forehead, turned his face jowly before its time. Warden Lawes could preach all he wanted to about respecting an inmate's humanity, but time in Sing Sing took its toll.

"How would you like to go home?" Patches said.

Home. Whitey didn't hesitate this time. "Sure, if it's not too big a risk."

"There's no risk."

"What have you got?"

The whole design, building up piece by piece over the months, tumbled out in a rush. "Through the hospital. In the cellar, I have a tunnel. You check into the hospital, and when the keeper comes around on the count you watch him. He calls up every half-hour, and then he goes into a room and sits there. At two-thirty in the morning, after the rounds, you can sneak out and go downstairs. You go through the tunnel and you can make it. There is a hole there and I have the keys to all the doors, so we can go out through there." For the moment, Patches kept it simple—he didn't mention McGale's name. And as if to clinch the deal he added, "Nobody will get hurt or nothing."

Whitey must have heard that before. Nobody ever gets hurt; there's never any risk; no one ever finds out. His life was a broken record stuck on that refrain. Still, what did he have here? Work on a general laboring crew, and nights alone behind bars in his cement cell. Lining up for breakfast, lunch, and dinner, officers barking at you when you didn't move fast enough; a quick boot in your pants not unusual. Eating at long tables surrounded by the same faces; the cons and guards as sick of each other as you were of all of them. The bright spots? On the weekends, there were ball games to watch, movies in the chapel, radio shows through headphones at night. Things that people on the outside did with their family and friends.

But what was normal on the outside was bizarre inside the walls—a reminder of what was gone, like the dreams of lost loved ones that depress you when you wake up. Those treats showed you how things weren't anymore, and wouldn't be anytime soon. Whitey wouldn't be eligible for parole until 1949. Impulsive all his life, he probably couldn't even see that far ahead. Time in Sing Sing was dead air for him. No beginning, no middle, no end. Just this constant, awful always. A year ago, he might have thought he could do his sentence standing on his head. How wrong could he be? He'd never make it through the next eight years until parole.

"Do you want to go?" Patches said.

"You can sneak out?"

"Yes."

"All right."

It sounded so easy.

But then, it always did.

Over midnight, into the early morning of Saturday, March 22, Kiernan and Wade drove back up to Newburgh for the last time. A red cardboard-bound package was stuffed under the passenger seat. A smoker, Wade kept the driver's-side window inched open and a cigarette held up to the edge. Kiernan was dressed for dirty work in a dark jacket and work pants. Concentrating on the job in front of them, the men let the car radio speak for them, crackling in and out as they steered through the Hudson hills: *Selective Service Talk*; an advertisement for Dr. West's Water-Proofed Toothbrush; *The Lombardo Orchestra*.

In Newburgh, they circled around the block, drove past the dairy, and parked down the street on the same side. Kiernan, twisted around in his seat, reconnoitered with a pair of binoculars; Wade kept watch through the rearview mirror. Around 1 A.M., the delivery trucks growled to life and began backing up to the loading platform.

Kiernan reached under the seat and retrieved the red cardboard package and zipped it into his leather jacket. He opened the door and climbed into the dark.

The chain-link fence around the dairy was old and bent. From a previous observation, Kiernan had found a wide rip in the mesh. He squeezed through. A scrub-grass lot bordered the loading area. Hunched low, Kiernan kept in the building's shadow and approached the loading platform from the side. He paused against the dairy's brick wall. He could hear the men working, mutters and laughs, clanking bottles and cans.

Kiernan crouched and scuttled to the end of the platform. No one saw him, covered in shadow, crawl under the loading dock.

The ground was damp, soaking through the knees of his black work pants. The stench of sour milk filled his nose. He could see the truck tires backed against the platform, men's boots walking across the gravel lot. Bad luck for Kiernan if a driver dropped his keys.

Behind the truck, he unzipped his jacket and took out the package. He lay on his back and used his elbows to shift from side to side, wriggling under the truck. The truck bed rocked and boomed as the workmen loaded wire crates and five-gallon milk canisters. The ambient light from the spots on the roof above the platform showed Eddie as much of the chassis as he needed to see. A spare tire was set almost flush against the rear axle. He took off his black gloves, wedged the package into a niche, and buckled it tight with leather thongs like the straps a kid would use to hold schoolbooks together. He was satisfied that the package was there to stay until someone removed it.

Kiernan inched back under the loading platform and crawled back to the end. He watched for approaching boots, then emerged from underneath and hurried back across the scrub lot to the hole in the fence. Wade started the car when he saw him.

They didn't follow the milk truck that night. Kiernan and Wade took their time driving back to New York City; this part was done and they were relieved. They kept the radio off and made jokes all the way home. The sky was bluing into a nice spring dawn when they crossed into Manhattan.

Around eight o'clock that morning, Sing Sing officer Harry Effenberger waved the Crowley Dairy truck into the high-walled stockade. The 12 Post gate closed, and the driver, Harold Smart, shut off the engine. He got out of the cab, said hi to Harry, lit a cigarette, and opened the engine hood. Officer Effenberger looked into the engine well and nodded. Smart shut the hood.

The officer followed the driver to the side of the truck, then to the rear, and waited while Smart unlatched the side and rear cargo doors and swung them open. Officer Effenberger craned his neck and peered inside, shined a flashlight around the large metal canisters. But he didn't climb up inside. The officer walked around the truck, crouched low, and looked underneath, shined his light over the chassis and along the muffler system. He did not lie on his back and shimmy under the truck. The gate was already backing up with contractors arriving for B-block repairs and with the normal traffic. Officer Harry Effenberger was forty-five years old and had been on the job fourteen years. His only company at the gate was the officer in the 12 Post tower above. Effenberger was not about to bounce up and down all day long, crawling under almost thirty arriving and departing trucks, without coveralls, in a uniform for which he was responsible.

When the inspection was done, Officer Effenberger opened the interior gate into the prison, waved the truck through, closed the gate, and climbed into the passenger seat beside Smart. The officer in the tower would watch over the trucks gathering at the gate, while Effenberger rode with Smart. The milk truck drove down to the Death House first, isolated in the prison's southwest corner, hard by the river. Officer Effenberger stood by the front of the truck and watched Smart unload a tall can of milk from the truck's side doors. An inmate worker received the can and wheeled it inside.

The men got back in the cab and drove up the hill. Outside 5 Building, they passed under the arched "horse block gate," named for the old horse path that now lay paved under the road, and they continued on to the hospital. After the main storehouse, the hospital was the biggest delivery. They pulled to a stop alongside the building's south end. The side entrance led into the basement storeroom, past the entrance to the steam vault, and into the hallway, where the hospital kitchen steamed. Officer Effenberger stood between the truck and the building and watched Smart unload four milk cans from the truck's side cargo door. A couple of kitchen workers rolled the canisters inside. The work would have taken from three to five minutes.

In that short time, somebody managed a rendezvous. Either Charlie McGale approached the truck from the road, keeping the vehicle between him and the men on its other side; or hospital orderly Patches Waters, assigned to help unload the truck, evaded Officer Effenberger and the rest of the workers. Someone slipped under the rear of the truck, spotted the red cardboard package fastened to the axle, unbuckled the straps, and stowed the package under his shirt. Whoever retrieved the package kept it hidden for three weeks—McGale in the steam vault or Patches somewhere in the hospital—until the night of the break.

After the hospital delivery, Officer Effenberger got back aboard the milk truck as it made its final prison rounds for the day. When he arrived back at the 12 Post gate, a line of trucks stood idling for admission. Effenberger quickly went through the motions of reinspecting the milk truck and waved so long to Harold Smart. As the truck left, another vehicle ground into gear and moved into the stockade.

Officer Effenberger had no idea that the heavy traffic would soon be the least of everyone's troubles.

CHAPTER TWELVE

TO THE HOSPITAL

Patches Waters and Charlie McGale were all ready. They had the keys, they had the guns, and they had the ruse. A whole year ago they'd first discussed the possibility of a crash out—then months of planning without a hitch. As if to accentuate their good fortune, a holiday was approaching. What better time to break the stone walls of Sing Sing than on a sleepy Easter Sunday night?

As Whitey would later tell it, around Wednesday, April 9, Patches and he had their last conversation about the break. It was Holy Week 1941. Moods were up in the mess hall; the visiting room was busy. Even the Hudson didn't look so gray from the 5 Building yard.

"Well, everything is set," Patches said. "We can go this weekend."

So they were really doing it. "All right. Anybody else going?"

"Yes. Charles McGale."

Whitey pictured a little dark-haired guy with big knobby hands, sitting next to him at a basketball game the previous fall. His fingernails were like a mechanic's. "How is he?"

Patches's plan was soldered to McGale's, and he wanted Whitey in on it. "All right."

"Okay."

"I have guns," Patches said, "I'll hand you a package in the hospital. But we won't have to use them. You just check into the hospital on Saturday, and I'll get in on Sunday." Patches would have to check in as a patient, too. He wouldn't be scheduled to work overnight; there'd only be a trusty on duty. "The keeper makes his rounds, he passes your bed, and he goes out in the hall. At 2:30 in the morning, after he takes the count, he'll go in a room on the side. We'll go out in the hall, go downstairs, and sneak out."

"Okay."

And that was it—they had to break up. A guard taking notice, a con sidling up; conversation over.

Lots of times questions occurred after a job was discussed. The business about the guns, for instance. That was the first time Patches had said anything about guns. Not that Whitey was squeamish; he'd handled weapons before. But that wasn't the point. Maybe he'd liked to have known about the guns before he'd said yes. That's what was good about the Shopping Bag jobs—you could pick up a phone when something came to mind, or meet a guy at the bar if you forgot a point. Inside, even talking wasn't easy. He'd have to meet up with Patches at the hospital. This Saturday. In three days.

———————

Patches worked the hospital the rest of that week with the secret held inside of him. At times, he must have felt it would bust right out. Compared to his old position in the sweating mess hall, an orderly job in the hospital was a breeze. True, there were four tall stories of brick and steel to cover. And sometimes the doctors and nurses, frantic and bloody with the scores of monthly surgeries pumping away on the fourth floor, would hold up the elevator for emergencies. Then orderlies had to run ragged up and down the wire-caged staircase that rose flight after flight through the center of the building. Aside from the moans and the medicinal stink, it wasn't bad. But in his remaining days, even that small complaint must have faded into deep background.

Patches just did his usual: he kept his head down, did his job, and continued adding to his mental checklist. There were about fifteen inmate nurses on staff, but only a skeleton crew overnight, and an orderly did whatever they asked. One of the nurses was even good for a laugh— David Kaplan, a Jewish immigrant with a thick accent, doing forever on an arson count. The patients were mostly regular cons, yeggs and grifters like everybody else, and because they were sick, you tried to be nice.

A bronze inscription nailed up in the hospital foyer declared *Nihil Humani Probis Alienum*—"Nothing Human Is Foreign." But probably not always to Patches Waters. There was McGowan Miller, for instance, a Negro with a heart condition, doing time for rape. African American inmates were still a minority in Sing Sing in 1940; and Patches, like most convicts, likely held sex crimes to be the lowest of the low. McGowan Miller, with two strikes against him, would have certainly kept as low a profile as possible among the Irish, Italian, and Jewish crooks and gangsters. As far as Patches was concerned, Miller could make his own goddamn bed. Another distasteful part of hospital work, at least to contemporaries locked in Sing Sing's macho environment, was the homosexuals. One old-time officer recalled that he hated to work the hospital and have to rouse male lovers out of each other's beds. A Catholic inmate raised in Hell's Kitchen would have kept his eyes open when he was around them, unless he went that way himself. Patches didn't, and surely made that clear. For the rest of the week, he'd have to hide his growing excitement by acting his usual sullen self.

He kept note of the guards making their half-hourly counts and then taking a load off in their office. He'd have tried to spend the bulk of his shift on the bustling third floor, the medical and convalescent wards, watching the routine. That was the main floor as far as he was concerned—he, McGale, and Whitey would slip out from there come Sunday night.

Saturday, April 12. A holiday weekend. Whitey and the rest of the population not assigned to work had yard-out privileges all afternoon. The weather was sunny in the 5 Building yard, but Whitey would have turned up his collar against the cool wind off the river. Working on and living near the Hudson all of his life, he must have found it strange to see that water from a Sing Sing hilltop. A completely different river from what flowed past the West Side, different for a lot of reasons, and not only the wooded Palisades in place of New Jersey warehouses. Somehow, watching the river up here was like seeing some version of your childhood, now grown into a better man. But the Hudson was what Whitey knew; and working on the water was what he figured he'd do again when he got out tomorrow night. He'd get a job on a steamer. He couldn't work the merchant marine, not with German U-boats targeting cargo ships in the North Atlantic. No, he'd go somewhere safer than Nazi Europe. Someplace warm. South America. A whole continent to get lost in. The way it looked in *National Geographic,* a guy could live like a king down there on hardly any money at all.

If he got out, that was. All his life, everybody—including him—had nothing but grand dreams. And they never, ever, came to a thing. But where he came from, a person never gave up. Anybody could tell you that's when Sing Sing won. But assuming they did get out, there was no going home. He'd have to get far away. Who knew when he'd see his family again?

His mother had been to visit a couple of weeks before. Every time she came up, Whitey must have been struck by how old she looked. The past year might have been hard on him, but his mother seemed nearly done in. She would turn sixty-five on April 30. Well, none of their lives had been any picnic. But he had helped her pile up troubles, he surely recognized that, he and his brothers. She'd never admit it, though. Kept the family news coming instead, mostly how cute his nephew was, his sister Margaret's boy, how smart for a four-year-old. Her hope for the future, perhaps. With Whitey, she'd keep a vacant poker face on, as though her boy hadn't dealt her a bad hand. And Whitey almost certainly did his best to make the past year in Sing Sing sound easy. But nobody would have been fooled.

Whitey checked his watch—a little after two. Patches had said to check into the hospital today; that way, they all wouldn't come in at once. Well, if he was going, now was the time. He looked at his watch again. Don't think about what was at stake. Just go.

He walked across the yard to the presiding officer. Playing up the dodge, Whitey pressed a hand to his lower gut as he drew closer. The guard watched him approach. Whitey told the officer that he didn't feel well. The officer gave him another once-over and then wrote him a pass for the admittance nurse at the hospital. Whitey walked over to the building next door.

A civilian nurse at the desk, William Taylor, would remember admitting him.

"What's the matter with you?"

"I feel sick."

Well, of course. "What is the *matter*?"

"My stomach. I throw up. When I eat I throw up."

"How do you feel now?"

"I don't feel so good." Whitey rubbed the right side of his abdomen.

The nurse wrote something on a piece of paper, made a telephone call, and told Whitey to wait on a bench along the wall. Pretty soon, an orderly wearing a white jacket over his prison grays rolled up with a wheelchair. He told Whitey to get in and wheeled him to the elevator up to the third-floor Medical 1 ward. They stopped beside an empty bed halfway down the row, the number 5 stenciled on the white metal frame. There was a nice view of the river out the windows across the room.

Down the row, on the other side, Charlie McGale lay in a bed. He'd checked in that morning at 11:45 after reporting that his back hurt. At the hospital, McGale had been alternating between a soft bed and a hot sitz bath. If he was any kind of crook, he didn't even glance at Whitey Riordan when he was wheeled in.

The orderly handed Whitey a cotton gown, told him to put it on. Whitey could put his jacket and grays here, and the orderly opened a door on a small bedside cabinet. He gave Whitey a thermometer, wrote down that Whitey's temperature was 100 degrees. Thanks to his nerves, perhaps, Whitey had his alibi. The orderly told Whitey that the doctor would be around shortly, then left.

Whitey settled into bed, the gown smoothed below his knees. Ready to go, he left his socks on. The mattress was twice as thick as the one on his cell bunk, and the crisp linens smelled of chlorine bleach. Lying in that nice bed, he must have dozed. Then the doctor was bedside, flipping a paper on a clipboard. He lifted Whitey's wrist, took his pulse, listened to his heart and lungs with a stethoscope. The examination was quick.

Whitey repeated the lie he'd told the nurse.

The doctor decided to hold Whitey for observation. His symptoms might be appendicitis. If they got worse, Whitey should call for the nurse. Then the doctor walked down the row.

Well, he was in it now. Whitey would have to keep up this pretense until tomorrow night. If the plan didn't come off, he could tell the doctor that he was feeling much better and return to the cellblock on Monday. Nobody would know the difference. But if they did manage to pull it off . . .

There were fourteen beds in two rows down the length of the room, more beds on his side—the opposite row was divided by a nurse's station. Almost all the beds were taken—guys curled on their sides sleeping, or lounging on plumped-up pillows reading papers and magazines. The ward was bright, three sets of three windows in the east and west walls. If it weren't for the bars on the windows, and the uniformed guard walking through on the half hour counting everyone, you'd think it was a regular hospital. Quiet and peaceful. A real good setup for a breakout.

One night and one more day would tell.

The next morning was Easter Sunday. After his holiday Mass in the chapel, Sing Sing's Catholic chaplain Father Bernard Martin came through the ward with Communion. His faith was remarkable, considering his parish. Thin and balding, Father Martin was a dedicated prison priest, giving hopeless men the benefit of the doubt. Above and beyond the call of his priestly duties, he was in the middle of a private investigation that spring, tracking down clues of innocence in a condemned man's murder conviction. At his own expense, the priest followed leads to other prisons and interviewed detectives. He was overstepping his bounds, prosecuting attorneys told him; but Father Martin was becoming convinced the doomed man was not guilty. And he ultimately earned his own headline in the *New York Times* when he cleared the man's name. Surely every convict in Sing Sing knew about Father Martin's activities. He must have been their hero. Just receiving the Host from such a priest would have calmed your guilty nerves.

Father Martin went down the row of beds and up the other side. He stopped beside McGale's bed. He finished up, stopping to chat with one man and another. Then he left.

Back home in Inwood, Whitey's mother would have gone to early Mass at Good Shepherd Church. Could Whitey even picture the last time he'd gone to church with her? When he was a kid, probably. Once he was sent to Sing Sing, though, he went to Mass often enough, every week at first. But lately, it had been more occasional—Christmas, maybe a Holy Day. Certainly not every Sunday, like some guys. A lot of inmates found religion in prison—Warden Lawes encouraged it. But Whitey hadn't, despite Father Martin's sanctity. Whitey had looked at first, perhaps thought for a moment, *maybe;* but like everything else, religion eluded him. He went to Mass out of habit more than anything else; the Catholic Church was part of his physical makeup, like his blond hair, nothing more. It wasn't that he didn't believe; he did, sort of. He even wore a saint's medallion on a silver chain around his neck. But there was an awful lot in his life that didn't square with what Father Martin, for one, was always talking about. Love and kindness, for instance. The Christian Brothers at the Catholic Protectory were full of something, but it hadn't seemed like love and kindness. Contrary to Father Martin's example, if you showed love and kindness in Hell's Kitchen or on the docks, at Welfare Island or at Elmira, or anywhere else Whitey had spent time, you wouldn't last very long.

Still, he took Communion. Why not? If God forgave sinners, he was one, and in need of forgiveness. If God didn't, then nothing mattered anyway. If they busted out tonight, or even if he lay there goldbricking the rest of the weekend, Whitey felt better going through the motions of a religion he didn't embrace but couldn't abandon. He felt he'd made the effort, at least, regardless of the result.

———

By the second afternoon, Whitey must have grown accustomed to ward life. The comfortable bed and soothing, attendant routine—he'd never been in a hospital before, and the new experience anesthetized him. He drowsed away the hours, perhaps forgetting sometimes why he was there. After the lunch trays were cleared, Nurse Kaplan, the trusty, came through with newspapers and magazines. Whitey would look at the Sunday *News* for the sports pages. The Yanks had clipped the Dodgers, 3–2, in a ninth-inning squeaker at Ebbets Field the day before. DiMaggio killed a Dodger rally with a 400-foot double, driving Tommy Heinrich home. There were nearly nineteen thousand fans at that game. How great it would be to get out to the ball field again. But not anytime soon. Certainly not from South America.

Late in the afternoon, the sunlight gray behind lowering clouds, Whitey woke up from a nap and got out of bed. He went to the bathroom in the hallway. After he was finished and was washing his hands at the sink, Patches appeared beside him, dressed in a white gown. He must have been admitted while Whitey was asleep.

Patches pushed a small brown paper bag into Whitey's stomach.

Whitey took it, held it against his thigh. The bag was heavy and tied with string. All he could think of to say was "Okay." He returned to the ward, put the package in the bedside cabinet under his folded clothes, and got back into bed. The paper bag's density, its metallic heft. There were no more *ifs*.

Patches came back into the ward, got into the bed next to McGale's, on the other side of the nurse's station. Nobody looked at anybody else. What goes through a convict's mind before a crash out? McGale lay with his arms crossed, undoubtedly turning over his locks and keys in his mind for the millionth time. Patches, too, was probably mentally rehearsing as he pretended to read a magazine. Whitey might have tried to doze, but he was done sleeping.

The rest of the evening, they waited. Experienced at high-pressure preludes, they surely knew not to thrash around. But there would be no stopping a steady thrumming in a man's chest, an adrenaline tingle in his arms and legs. Now each routine event—dinner, nurse and orderly visits, but especially the guard's clockwork rounds—instead of lulling Whitey, would have wound him tighter, as each action marked another step closer toward 2:30 A.M. After lights-out, at 10 P.M., one dim red bulb burned above the ward entrance. In the gloom, as the breathing from the beds around him deepened, Whitey could follow the hulking shape of the guard through half-closed eyes, each time he passed through the ward.

The keeper's rounds were soft-soled half hours that Whitey and the others counted down.

The Shopping Bag Gang. Seated, left to right, William Wade, William Athalis, aka "Willie the Greek," Little Joe Salvatore; standing, left to right, Whitey Riordan, Patches Waters. *Courtesy of Ossining Historical Society*

Joseph Riordan, aka "Whitey"
*Courtesy of Ossining
Historical Society*

John Waters, aka "Patches"
*Courtesy of Ossining
Historical Society*

Members and Associates of the Shopping Bag Gang

Thomas Gentles,
aka "Lulu"

Eugene Mello,
aka "Rusty"

Jacob Maislish,
aka "Jake the Butch"

John Hanley, aka "Mac"

Emilio Spagniolo, aka
"Little Joe Salvatore"

All photographs courtesy of New York City Municipal Archives

Aerial view of Sing Sing

Courtesy of Ossining Historical Society

1. Steam tunnel exit at power line trestle

2. 12 Post and delivery entrance stockade

3. Administration Building

4. Laundry Building

5. Hospital

6. 5 Building

7. Chapel

8. A-Block

9. Mess Hall

10. B-Block

11. Warden's Residence

12. Old Cellblock

13. Death House (the Dance House is the angular structure in the center of the building)

14. Lawes Field

Stockade entrance and 12 Post tower. The milk truck entered here.
Courtesy of Ossining Historical Society

Warden Lewis E. Lawes in a publicity photo for his memoir *Twenty-thousand Years in Sing Sing.*
Courtesy of Ossining Historical Society

A typical cell in 5 Building, the cell block where Whitey, Patches, and McGale were housed.
Courtesy of Ossining Historical Society

Sing Sing's old visiting room, where the escape was planned.
Courtesy of Ossining Historical Society

Charles McGale, the locksmith.
Courtesy of Ossining Historical Society

The Sing Sing hospital ward,
with unidentified inmates.
The break started here.
Courtesy of Ossining Historical Society

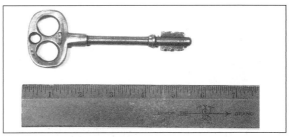

One of Charlie's homemade keys
to the hospital steam vault.
Courtesy of Ossining Historical Society

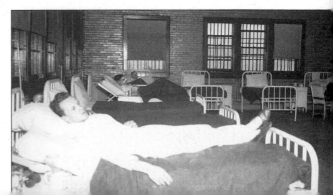

X

Trial exhibit photo: the railroad tracks through the prison. The "X" marks where the steam tunnel exited. *Courtesy of Ossining Historical Society*

James Fagan
*Courtesy of New York
Public Library*

John Hartye
*Courtesy of New York
Public Library*

Edward Kiernan, left, and William Wade
Courtesy of New York Public Library

The escape route: (1) Indicates Administration Building. (A) Shows prison hospital with dotted white line to (B) indicating steam vault route to exit above the tracks. White line along tracks leads past (C) where the getaway car was parked at the railroad station, and continues on to (D), where the fugitives engaged police in a gunfight. Whitey and McGale fled west toward the river and encountered fisherman Rohr at his shack (E) and forced him to row them across the Hudson. *Courtesy of Ossining Historical Society*

Whitey and McGale in the hands of police.
Courtesy of New York Public Library

Fisherman Charles Rohr
Courtesy of New York Public Library

Execution Chamber Viewing Area. *Courtesy of Ossining Historical Society*

Sing Sing's electric chair. *Courtesy of Ossining Historical Society*

PART THREE

CRASH OUT

MARIE: *Mister. What's it mean when a man crashes out?*
REPORTER: *Crashes out?*
That's a funny question for you to ask now, sister.
Means he's free.

—JOHN HUSTON AND W. R. BURNETT
High Sierra

CHAPTER THIRTEEN

―――

MURDER AND REPRIEVE

THE TOWN OF OSSINING rises above a wide section of the Hudson River that early Dutch settlers called Tappanese Zee, or Tappan's Bay. The river has always been the life force of the town. Back in the nineteenth century, fishermen rowed out in skiffs from docks knitted up and down the shoreline, returning home with bursting nets of sturgeon, striped bass, and shad. Early villagers depended on the Hudson River for their daily supplies, as well as for their news, and the green water constantly churned with the comings and goings of steamboats and sloops. A trading hub developed along the waterfront as area farmers and local manufacturers, like Brandreth's Medicine Factory, shipped their goods down to New York Harbor and out to the wider world, or bartered with other riverside towns up north, like Poughkeepsie, Kingston, and Albany.

Sing Sing penitentiary was the limestone anchor in the village's southwest corner through most of the 1800s. By midcentury the small prison town had grown. Individual fishermen still caught a livelihood from the river, but Isaac Smith & Son Shipyard employed far more folks. Grocers, apothecaries, and haberdasheries—busy merchants catering to a nineteenth-century boomtown—had also taken root and spread up Main Street's hill, their customers dodging the horse carts rattling through the dirt streets, or stepping gingerly, kerchiefs pressed to noses, when the spring thaw made avenues impassable. Over one hundred saloons swelled along Ossining's tree-shaded lanes, serving a growing population of thirsty prison guards, shipbuilders, and factory workers.

By the end of the nineteenth century, the town was important enough for the Hudson River Railroad, as the carrier was then known, to extend the tracks north from Yonkers to a new terminus at Ossining, just north of the prison. When the red ribbon was cut, local entrepreneurs seized the opportunity brought by the increased commuter traffic, and opened two new restaurants, even crowning the broad new Depot Plaza with a hotel. In 1914, to accommodate the additional business, the town built a red-brick train station that spanned the tracks a full story above the ground, designed in the Classical style, with a "hipped roof" of clay tiles.

The station has not changed much in more than ninety years. Today, businesspeople, tourists, and families making visits to loved ones serving time in the prison climb the steps from the train platform up to the station and cross the concrete bridge that straddles the tracks. From the center of the bridge, these travelers can look south, the Hudson on their right blue beneath a clear sky, the gleaming tracks curving around a bend. From up there you can see Sing Sing prison's old powerhouse and smokestack, but you can't see any walls.

The town has worked hard to file down its rough edges. Rechristened Ossining-on-the-Hudson in 2004 to capture some river-village flair, it erected faux-rustic, gilt-edged boundary signs to welcome New York City commuters to their spacious condo homes. And while the railroad station's worldly importance has been scaled back—Amtrak ignores the station altogether, its daily express roaring past, heading for capital cities like Albany and Toronto—Metro-North trains make commuter stops, serving a white-collar population whose bulging salaries account for the cabin cruisers that steam out of the local yacht club.

New residents may find it easy to turn a blind eye to the fact that some of the country's toughest criminals are caged no more than a few miles away. After all, Sing Sing sits in a pocket corner of the dolled-up town, deep by the river. All they have to do is ignore the squat shape and umbrella roof of the gun towers pushing up from the water's edge. But sooner or later, Sing Sing commands attention. Whenever the prison whistles' wail signifies an escape, jarring sleeping citizens awake in the middle of the night, the fact comes thudding home—whether in the nineteenth century fishing hamlet or in the popular modern-day suburb—that Ossining is and has always been a prison town. The threat of escape was and remains something you live with, like Californians with earth-quakes, or heavy smokers with heart attacks. You can forget about it until that first jolt under your feet, or until the pain strikes.

When Warden Lawes first arrived in 1920, relations between Sing Sing and the town were thorny. Residents along State Street, bordering the prison's eastern wall, for instance, griped to the newspaper that the Sing Sing property was "unsightly and unsanitary." Lawes fired back that the complainants themselves were the ones dumping trash and debris on penitentiary land. Nevertheless, the warden dispatched crews wearing inmate gray to pick up the refuse under armed guard.

However, within a few years, the relationship between the prison and the town became more cordial, even complimentary, like the affinity between any major industry and its village base. Cinders from the coal that was burned in Sing Sing's powerhouse were spread over Ossining's icy streets each winter. Twice a week, a guard would drive up to the Victoria Theatre on Church Street and pick up a print of the motion picture playing there. The film, whether *Strike Up the Band* with Judy Garland and Mickey Rooney or *We Who Are Young* with Lana Turner, would be taken down to the prison and projected on a screen in the chapel for the inmate audience.

In the years before and after the Second World War, most Sing Sing guards kissed their families goodbye and left their neighborhood homes for the short drive down the hill to work. Back then, the state required that guards live within the confines of Ossining. Close enough, anyway, to hear the prison whistle when it blew every afternoon at 5 P.M., notify-ing the officers—and everyone else within earshot—that the last count of the day was secure.

Prison guards' lives were threaded into the uniform of the town, as were the lives of the workers at the Ossining Hospital, the Hudson Wire Mill, or Rand McNally, the town's other large employers. Like other local workers, Sing Sing officers played baseball in a town league. The Prison Keepers often made it to the league championship playoffs under their soft-spoken coach Ed Siebern. Guards also competed with area law enforcement, such as the Ossining Police Department—their great rivals—in Westchester County–wide pistol marksmanship con-tests. After Pearl Harbor, Ossining's young men—Sing Sing guards and others—marched in monthly parades down Main Street for Selective Service mobilization, accompanied by the VFW drum corps. Prison guards were always the rougher cords in the town's fabric, though, the braid that stood out.

By the early years of the twenty-first century, officers hardly fit into town life at all. A Sing Sing corrections officer starting out on $28,444 a year would be hard-pressed to pay modern-day Ossining's average monthly rent of $900 for a studio apartment—or far more for a place that could accommodate a family—and often would be forced to commute from less-gentrified neighborhoods such as Beacon, New York, or the Bronx. Some officers would consider themselves lucky to live alone in one of the shabby small trailers backed against the prison's long east wall—a grim colony that officers nicknamed "Jellystone Park," after a TV cartoon.

Like the strained relations between a university and its provincial host, a blue-collar, gold-badge version of town-versus-gown rankles in the modern era, the frosty tones of the early twentieth century resurfacing. You can see it clearest, perhaps, in the overlapping jurisdictions of the town's resident lawmen—cops and guards. A retired Sing Sing officer tells the story of working with the Ossining police in a search party for a prison escapee in the 1980s. The corrections officer was alone with two policemen who believed the fugitive was hiding in an abandoned house. The Ossining cops had him cornered, but it became the corrections officer's responsibility to capture him. The cops would stay outside and provide cover with drawn guns. Not about to lose face, the officer drew his .38 and kicked in the door. Luckily for everyone, the unarmed inmate hiding in the basement gave up without a fight.

But the cops could hardly be blamed. They'd likely heard the stories. You didn't know what an escaped con would do. Besides, if Sing Sing was inept enough to let 'em get out, Sing Sing could round 'em up.

On the run, convicts might try to kill anyone brave enough to stop them.

———

Eddie Kiernan and Billy Wade would never admit it themselves—the official police version says it for them—but in the final hours of Easter

Sunday, April 13, 1941, they stole a beige 1939 Plymouth two-door sedan. Local thieves with some semblance of loyalty, the two wouldn't have wanted to hot-wire a car from their own threadbare Chelsea neighborhood. Instead, around nine thirty, they took the IRT up to West Seventy-ninth Street and walked over to quiet, residential West End Avenue, where the quality of goods was better. People on the Upper West Side could afford to lose a car. The cool spring afternoon clouded over by nightfall, and the air became muggy. A photo taken later shows Kiernan still wearing his Easter suit and pearl tie. Standing lookout on the sidewalk in front of 411 West End Avenue, he must have been sweating in his overcoat and fedora. Wade, dressed for the job in dark work pants and a nylon windbreaker, jimmied the Plymouth's passenger-side door, leaned across the front seat, and stripped and twisted the ignition wires to start the engine.

Patches Waters had instructed them to park the car under the Ossining railroad station ramp, ready to go with the loaded machine gun, by 1:30 A.M. The break was scheduled for 2:30, and the extra hour would allow time to straighten out any snafus that might arise. Would Kiernan and Wade have been gutsy or foolish enough to attempt a car theft with a Tommy gun in their possession? That might explain Kiernan's long coat in the mild weather. Or perhaps they drove back downtown to Chelsea and retrieved the gun from Kiernan's basement. In either case, by eleven o'clock, the men were headed north on the Albany Post Road to Ossining, the Plymouth fitted with a pair of license plates Wade had commissioned a Hell's Kitchen kid to steal for him back in February. Wade kept to the speed limit, while Kiernan snapped together the Tommy gun in the backseat.

The Plymouth's rearview mirror flashed with the reflected headlights of an Oldsmobile swinging around the curves behind them. In the Olds' front seat, thirty-nine-year-old Brooklyn longshoreman Charles Bergstrom rode beside the driver, moon-faced Robert Brown, Patches's pinball machine business partner. Charles Bergstrom was a game but low-stakes crony of the gang, friendly with both Wade and Kiernan. Bergstrom had a long police record, but his role in this plot was minor at best. He may have assisted in the purchase of the machine gun, or just come along for the ride.

Robert Brown, for his part, must have learned over the years to limit his involvement in Patches's wilder schemes. Careful, dark-haired Brownie had a police record of eight arrests but no convictions—pinball machines were one thing, but apparently he'd never gone in for armed robbery. In visits to Patches during the break's planning stages, Brownie walked the dime-thin line between loyalty to a partner and self-preservation. In the end, he agreed to handle the vital though peripheral arrangements for Wade and Kiernan's return trip to the city. Visiting Patches one last time on Good Friday, Brownie also finalized the agreement to secure a hide-out for the fugitives. On Saturday he went up to Harlem to shell out $14 for a studio apartment, far west on 124th Street. The block between Amsterdam and Broadway was perfect—just north of quiet Columbia University, in a building soon slated for the wrecking ball. They'd all meet there in the dead predawn, when Sing Sing was ripping itself apart looking for them.

The cars motored up the lower Hudson Valley. But somewhere between the traffic lights in the sleeping villages, the two cars became separated. Wade and Kiernan continued north, steering the Plymouth left onto Ossining's deserted Main Street and cruising down past darkened storefronts toward the river. Brownie and Bergstrom's car was gone. Wade braked the Plymouth down steep Secor Road, which descended to the train station plaza. Directly in front of them, Depot Plaza's ramp ascended to the train station and the bridge over the railroad tracks. Wade turned right, drove around and under the ramp, and pulled the car to a stop at the curb. He untangled the ignition wires and the engine died.

Beside the car, iron fence pickets divided the plaza from the New York Central Railroad's northbound and southbound tracks, which were separated by long, concrete passenger platforms. Wondering about their ride back home and concerned about being on time, the men checked their watches—about 1:20 A.M. They were right on schedule.

There were always nerves before a job. They wouldn't panic, though. Wade had his cigarettes. Kiernan would check one more time to see that the machine gun was hidden under the backseat. River air came through the rolled-down window. Then, a moment of relief. Behind them, at the plaza's north end, headlights entered the parking lot. They beamed through a gathering mist and came closer. That had to be Brownie and Bergstrom.

But the Packard snapped on a roof light, circled around, and went back up Secor Road. A taxicab, looking for midnight fares—a train must have blown through minutes before. They waited another few minutes, but no more cars came.

There was a small tavern on Depot Plaza's northern boundary. The men had told Bergstrom and Brownie to meet them there for the return trip downtown, in case they got separated. Wade and Kiernan left the car unlocked. They walked across the parking lot toward the neon lights. After all the work so far that night, all the tension, a cold beer would taste pretty good right about then, maybe chased down by a warm shot. Anyway, they had plenty of time.

———————

On the third floor of the prison hospital, Whitey Riordan lay on his iron bed. His wristwatch was on the bedside cabinet. The only light in the ward was a small red bulb burning above the entrance. Whitey later recalled that after Waters passed him the package in the bathroom in the afternoon—nearly ten hours earlier—he "lay in bed waiting for 2:30," the package right there, unopened in his bedside cabinet. He didn't snap the string that bound it or rip apart the paper. He didn't even feel the outline of the contents. The heft could have come from a hammer, for all he knew. Patches, however, had told him he'd deliver guns, and Patches was a man of his word.

Not only was the package unopened. Whitey wasn't even dressed. He hadn't pulled on his clothes under the blankets, as McGale and Waters had done. His pants and lumber jacket were still balled up in the bedside cabinet, on top of the unopened package. Whitey might have been suspicious of being observed by snitches. The hospital, even more than the general population, was known for its stool pigeons. Four or five of the men around him, in Whitey's estimation, "had hollered on somebody." They were kept in the ward as protection cases. But the worry of being ratted out certainly diminished as the hour got later. Whitey Riordan had been part of a holdup gang known for its precision timing. Why wasn't he ready to go?

Maybe he'd decided to sit this one out. The anxiety must have been tremendous, after all, compared to what he'd felt before pulling a robbery. The guard was a nearly constant presence on his rounds, passing through the ward counting everyone over and over—twenty times in ten hours. Usually, holdup men aren't under constant watch on the outside. If they are, their instinct is to lay low. Plus, a stickup has an element of surprise—most civilians never expect guns in their faces. But inside Sing Sing, with guards trained to be on the lookout, eyeballing you for the slightest indication of what was really on your mind—certainly aware, at least, of what kind of people surrounded them—well, that was different.

A breakout from prison was like a holdup from inside a vault.

———

Officer John Hartye finished the one–thirty count in Medical Ward 1—at the south end of the hallway, where Whitey, Patches, and McGale lay waiting—and walked to the north end of the hallway to count through Ward 2. He called both counts in to the desk operator on the hall telephone and went back into his office. The Sunday *Daily News* sport pages were spread across the desktop, full of items on the weekend's games—the New York Giants playing Indiana, the Washington Senators whaling the Baltimore Orioles. But the real story for a Brooklyn Dodgers fan was the victory the Yankees had stolen from them once again. That damn DiMaggio, of course, flattening the Dodgers rally in the ninth inning. Jolting Joe had increased his hitting streak to eighteen games with the win. In the paper's "Roundup" column, Dodgers manager Larry MacPhail insisted his team was still the "best-conditioned club in either league." No Dodgers fan would disagree. Officer Hartye puffed his pipe back to life and finished the grim details.

Most officers dreaded working overnight shifts, especially men with wives and young children at home, and the rookies to whom the graveyard watch was usually assigned. Not remarkably, many found it hard to stay awake. The sergeant on duty certainly knew that and would make unannounced visits to different posts. Nobody wanted to get written up, so the guards devised an unofficial warning system. When the sergeant left for a surprise round, the operator sounded the alert by ringing up various posts. In a prison, you wanted somebody watching your back, no matter where the threat came from.

But John Hartye, a veteran Sing Sing officer approaching twenty years' service, preferred overnight shifts. He could stay awake and apparently wasn't bored by the quiet. He even seemed to enjoy it. Each work night he drove up without complaint from the Bronx, where he shared a large apartment with his sister and her husband in tree-lined Mott Haven. At fifty-five, he was still unmarried, and the nighttime peace and quiet fit his genial personality. Day shifts were often too hectic, not to mention too supervised, to catch up on sports and world affairs, or to enjoy a meditative pipe over a black river view.

Hartye was a big man, easily carrying his 225 pounds on a six-foot, two-inch frame. The rookies under him appreciated his willingness to work midnights, weekends, or holidays. He was always amenable to shift swaps when a wife was expecting or a child was sick (*Sure, boyo, of course,* in his reassuring brogue). He'd taught many of them the ropes when they'd first come on the job—the most comfortable, quietest boots to wear, still bruising enough to an unruly convict if you had to kick him; or the best way to count a cellblock swarming with inmates. The young rookies nicknamed him "Old John." Even an institutional staff photograph couldn't hide Hartye's kindly disposition: the picture shows a full-faced man with graying temples, a high forehead rising above no-nonsense eyes that are tempered by laugh lines, and a broad mouth shaped by smiles.

Officer Hartye linked the new officers to Sing Sing's storied past, almost back to the era when guards and keepers were distinct positions. Hartye would have worked with veteran officers who remembered the difference. According to an old prison handbook, up until 1902 keepers "had custodial charge of contractors' shops and maintenance groups, and performed cell hall and gate duty. Guards were stationed about the grounds and did strictly guard duty, having no control over inmates." The titles were still in use in 1941, but they were synonymous terms by then, residual language that tied Sing Sing to the turn of the century. Whether called a keeper or a guard, every officer dealt with convicts these days.

Through the office window, the spotlighted prison grounds rolled downhill, dipping in and out of shadow all the way to the river. Blue and green lights shimmered on the water, fishing skiffs working the midnight catch. Hartye's two o'clock count was coming up, nothing complicated about it—tally up the inmates in Medical 1 and 2, make sure they matched the numbers from the previous count, and call it in. Certainly the numbers would add up; they usually did. If they didn't, it most likely meant that you missed one, and you'd check again. But Old John was an old pro; he wouldn't make a mistake like that. Afterward, he'd open his Thermos bottle and pour a cup of hot coffee, relight his pipe, and enjoy the view for a while. Officer Hartye turned out the desk lamp and stood up. On a tranquil night like this, he probably couldn't understand why more officers didn't prefer the graveyard shift.

Whitey was lying on his back when Officer Hartye made his round. He passed down the row in silhouette and up the other side. As he passed Whitey's bed, the guard's thick index finger could be seen beating in time to the count. He counted through Ward 1 in about a minute and left. Whitey reached over for his wristwatch on the bedside cabinet, held it close in the dim light. 2 A.M. Almost time.

He must have felt that last half hour crank up right then, a final countdown pumping through his veins. The ward was still. At least he never mentioned hearing anything. No movement or rustling fabric, like people throwing back the covers and rushing for the door. Just dead quiet for a minute or two.

Then two gunshots boomed across the third floor. Whitey froze.

He had carried a loaded revolver on at least half a dozen armed robberies. He had pointed the gun at regular people working their jobs and made them wide-eyed with fear. He had even once held a struggling man so his old partner Bandit Gregory could slice open the guy's nose with a knife. But Whitey Riordan had never shot anyone.

For half a minute or more, he lay in bed with his thoughts racing, "everything . . . running through my mind." Patches and McGale had shot somebody, the officer, the nurse; someone was bleeding. Whitey had no idea what to do. But then it occurred to him. Those shots would bring guards running. They would search the ward and find the package, still unopened in the bedside cabinet. That gun made him an accessory before the fact, unwrapped or not. He jumped up, pulled on his pants, stepped into shoes, and grabbed his lumber jacket. He headed for the hallway. The rest of the ward was staying put; no one else was crazy enough to run into gunfire.

The hallway was empty. Just the mineral burn of gunpowder and a blue pall of smoke up at the other end of the hall. No sign of Patches or McGale. There should have been another guard upstairs on the top floor. But a minute or two after the shooting, there was still no sign of him either, investigating the gunfire one floor below. Whitey figured he was probably calling in the alarm. Soon, the building would be overrun with officers.

"What the hell?" Whitey said out loud. "Are they going to leave me here?"

A cement stairway dropped through the center of the building. Whitey took the steps two at a time, grabbing the mesh surrounding the stairwell for balance. In the basement, a sixty-foot-long hallway ran north and south, identical to the floor plan upstairs. Whitey wasn't sure where to turn in the gray light, but there were whispers to his left. He pushed open a door into a storeroom at the south end of the hall. Patches and McGale stood at a wooden door in the left-hand wall, beside a stack of old mattresses. McGale was fumbling through his pockets. Patches was pointing a .38 revolver at Nurse David Kaplan, who was backed up flat against the wall opposite the entry.

A valued trusty serving a long sentence for arson, Kaplan had been assigned overnight duty at the hospital; the civilian nursing staff of fifteen were home in bed. He'd been asleep like the rest of Ward 1 when he was awakened by the gunshot. Rushing into the hallway, he came face-to-face with Patches, wielding his revolver. Patches stuck the gun in Kaplan's gut and steered him toward the stairwell. Glancing into Medical Ward 2, the startled Kaplan surely blanched at what he described as "Officer Hartye . . . leaning over the side of a bed," bleeding.

Now Kaplan was alone in the basement with two armed cons trying to make a break. The sight of arriving officers would have been welcome. But Whitey's sudden appearance couldn't have been much relief.

"It is supposed to happen at 2:30," Whitey said. "What is the matter?"

No one had an answer.

McGale searched his pants pockets and came up empty-handed.

"I dropped the keys," he said, "I left the keys upstairs."

They'd never get farther than this if those keys were lost.

Whitey blurted that he didn't have his gun. "I didn't think it was going to happen," he explained.

They couldn't afford to lose any more time. Whitey and McGale ran back to the stairs, leaving Patches alone, pointing his gun at the nurse.

"Jesus, we made a mistake," McGale said, listening for approaching footsteps and scanning the stairs for the missing keys as he climbed. "He started off too soon."

According to McGale, this was all Patches's fault. For whatever reason, the mastermind hadn't waited. He'd crept out of bed right after the two o'clock count, having already dressed under the bed sheets. He went out to the hallway bathroom. McGale followed him, trying to talk him back to bed, reminding him that it was too early. But then Patches handed him a gun. McGale said they didn't need guns, that this was a clean sneak. But he took the revolver. Patches told him to come on and rushed out. Now a keeper was dead, they had a hostage in the basement, and McGale had lost the precious keys in the scuffle.

At the third-floor landing, they caught a break. McGale spotted the missing keys and scooped them up. Despite hearing voices in the hallway, the two came out of the stairway onto the ward. A group of inmates stood squabbling around the hall telephone, barelegged in their gowns. They shut up when they saw Whitey and McGale, who waved his gun and moved toward them. Whitey turned away, sprinted into Ward 1, and retrieved the package from the cabinet. He ripped the paper open, unfolded a white cloth inside, and found a snub-nosed .38 and a pair of handcuffs. He tucked the gun and cuffs into his pants pockets. Now they really had to get out of there. The prison whistle could howl at any second.

Back out in the hallway, Whitey found McGale with his gun trained on the inmates. Officer Matteo DeSimone, the fourth-floor guard, stood among them with his hands raised. He had come downstairs at last, only to find Officer Hartye on his back in Medical Ward 2, blood pooling around him. When DeSimone hurried back out to call in an emergency, he walked right into McGale's gun.

Despite the constant risk, DeSimone had to know that dying violently on the job at Sing Sing actually was a rare occurrence. The guard would have had to think a moment, counting back twenty-five years to June 1916—the last time a keeper had been killed at Sing Sing. That night thirty-five-year-old Daniel McCarthy was shot dead by a condemned man breaking out from the Death House. The inmate's sister had smuggled in a gun—as in 1941, there were no female officers to frisk visiting women. And before McCarthy, DeSimone would have had to go back to the nineteenth century. A few years after the Civil War, in 1869, five convicts escaped from the mess hall by strangling Keeper Edwin A. Craft to death. Just two murders in seventy-two years.

Yet when a bolt *did* strike from the blue, it was gruesome. There DeSimone was, surrounded by inmates, one of whom held a gun on him. Hartye was dead or dying; and now the officer watched another inmate barrel down the hall, a husky kid with blond hair wild in his face, looking DeSimone right in the eye and pulling a revolver from his pocket. DeSimone wasn't a big man, and he possessed a nervous disposition. He was, however, a crack shot with a handgun. He scored fourth overall in the countywide pistol competitions, against the Ossining police among others, an especially sweet victory. But that was little solace now. Prison officers carry only a hardwood club while on duty behind the walls— there's too much risk that an inmate could get possession of a firearm. Still, DeSimone knew his weapons. The gun in the inmate's hand appeared to be a Colt .38 Detective Special, short-barreled for easy concealment under plainclothes and quite deadly at such close range. The blond kid pushed it into DeSimone's stomach.

"This is a break," the blond kid said, taking away the officer's club. "Don't worry, nothing will happen to you. Just go downstairs and everything will be all right."

DeSimone had to hope so. It looked as though they'd just killed an unarmed guard. They might try to use DeSimone to barter their way out and then shoot him. Or other officers, sighting down their barrels at the fugitives in the dark, might not see him before they opened fire. The blond kid's gun moved him toward the stairs.

In the basement Whitey and McGale pushed DeSimone into the storeroom. Patches still held his gun on Nurse Kaplan. Patches's gun hand was shaking, and Kaplan was drenched in sweat. The waiting had been long for both of them.

Whitey must have worried that McGale, with his reputation as a bug, would be the one to watch. But there was Patches, his reliable partner, the dollars-and-cents entrepreneur—as cool as could be when sticking up a crowded cash business—standing in a wrinkled hospital gown and trousers, trembling like the palsied. The gun was all over the place. Whitey couldn't find the words.

But then Patches settled on Officer DeSimone. Maybe he didn't like his features, the dark wavy hair and olive complexion, the wide, full lips— too much like Little Joe Salvatore, perhaps, and all he represented. Patches went up to the officer and punched him in the jaw, then turned and slapped Kaplan. "Let's kill the screw," he said, using the inmate slang for *guard* and pointing his gun at DeSimone.

Whitey told them to wait.

McGale was still having trouble with the keys, and Patches grabbed them. He wasn't much steadier, Whitey noticed, but Patches had to be in charge. He managed to unlock the wooden door, get the padlock off the gate, and then he turned a key in the lock plate. He and McGale pushed their captives into the entry room to the steam vault, shut and locked the door and gate behind them, and pressed on the light switch. Then, Patches turned on the hostages.

"Let's give it to them," he said.

McGale chimed in. Without more witnesses, they might have a chance.

Kaplan backed away, and DeSimone put up his hands as if to ward off another blow. "For what?" the officer said. "If you do that and get caught you'll burn. You've already shot one man. You're on your way out now."

The guard was right. Time was wasting. Officers might be storming the hospital right now. Whitey knew that they had to get going, and fast. "We got no time," he insisted.

But Patches stood there, skinnier than he ever looked in his pricey suits, the gun shuddering in his hand, his pitted face enflamed. Patches was the brainy moneyman, everything carefully thought through, his every maneuver pointing to the results on the bottom line. When did he turn cold killer?

He had been assembling an intricate, covert plan under intense obser-vation for a year. Could waiting the last half hour in the hospital bed have been too much for him? Patches would never say. All Whitey knew was that things were slipping. A guard upstairs was dead. Two more lives hung by threads in front of him. Any more killing and they were finished.

"If we do that," Whitey said, "we might as well put the guns to our own heads. Less noise, less killing. Let's go."

Patches seemed to tally up Whitey's reasons one by one. In a moment, the sum was clear. He put his gun away and took out his handcuffs. Then he and McGale pushed DeSimone and Kaplan against a railing that encircled the pit above the steam vault and handcuffed them there. The fugitives clambered down the iron rungs, Patches first, then McGale. Whitey glanced at the handcuffed captives staring back at him. There wasn't anything more to say. He turned away and climbed into the con-crete vault after his partners. McGale pushed on the light switch.

The vault's opening was large, over six feet, but the steam conduit and power lines running the length of the ceiling took up room. Whitey ducked his head and followed the others. The cool air of the sub-basement was gone, replaced by a powdery heat. When the tunnel tight-ened, they bent their backs and knees, and their breathing and scuffling echoed. Patches stripped off his hospital gown, made the rest of the way bare-chested. Three hundred thirty feet later, McGale squeezed around Patches and heaved himself onto the crawl-space ledge at the tunnel's end. He inched toward the iron plate he'd loosened months before. It came free in his hands, and the tunnel cooled with the smell of rain.

The rope, he said, up behind the steam pipe.

Patches felt around and pulled the length of rope down, handed it to McGale. He leaned out and felt the drizzle on his face. In the thick river fog, 12 Post loomed behind him forty feet to the north, its spotlight beaming across the compound toward the hospital. Guards focused tower spots on trouble. Did that mean they'd found Hartye? The fugitives would have to hurry, creeping out past another wall tower—3 Post—diagonally across the tracks due south. McGale reached out for a stan-chion on the trestle that carried the power lines over the railroad. He tied the rope tight, let it dangle down to the dark rail bed. He listened for the siren, or the dogs.

There was only silence.

McGale climbed out onto the trestle's mouth and slithered down the rope. Patches went next, then Whitey. The rope was gray cloth cord, and thin—good for window sashes but murder on the palms. McGale had been able to steal only about twenty-feet of it, so they had to jump the last three yards or so, landing hard on the rail bed's cinders. But there were no twisted ankles or broken bones. Their frayed luck was holding, barely.

McGale and Patches hit the ground running, and Whitey hurried to catch up. They scrambled north up the tracks, in the gloom against the wall, past another tower, 2 Post. The prison walls on either side tapered to iron fencing and then nothing. Soon they were running full-out, and Sing Sing fell behind them. Up ahead about a third of a mile, the lights of the Ossining railroad station burned in the fog. The long-planned-for escape had begun—half an hour early, and mayhem in their wake. But no one was shooting at them, and the loud prison whistle was mute.

They were out.

CHAPTER FOURTEEN

A CRACK SHOT

THE INMATES LEFT BEHIND on the hospital's third floor were in a jam. Minutes after Whitey and McGale had left with DeSimone, smoke still hung in the air, and a keeper lay bleeding to death on the ward floor. Kaplan the nurse had been abducted also, and he and DeSimone might be dead soon, too. Complicating things further was thirty-five-year-old McGowan Miller, the black convict finishing a sentence for rape. He'd been admitted to Medical Ward 2 with a heart condition; in fact, his parole had been delayed until he got a medical release. But now Miller's hands were limp on his chest, and he wasn't moving. As far as anyone could tell, he was dead. Miller apparently had sat up in bed at the sound of a scuffle and seen Officer Hartye gunned down. In a fright, the inmate collapsed back on his bed in cardiac arrest. This might have been just desserts for a sex pervert, in prison opinion. But what about the nurse and the two guards?

The inmates around the hallway telephone were in the thick of it. Simply picking up the phone and calling for help was not a clear-cut option: there were prison reputations to consider. Yet, if the inmates didn't make the call, they'd surely be implicated. But nobody wanted to telephone and get fingered as a rat. Back and forth they went, until one bright individual came up with the perfect solution: take the receiver off the hook and let it dangle. Let the prison switchboard operator on the other end, hearing no caller at that time of night, sound the alarm. Five minutes after the abduction and escape, that's exactly what they did.

After receiving the dead call and helloing over and over into the receiver, the switchboard operator tried to return the call to Officer Hartye. According to the *Journal and American* account, the phone just kept ringing. Then the operator dialed DeSimone's fourth-floor line. No answer there, either. Such silence at the hospital meant calling the officer in charge of the night guard, Sergeant Maynard Darrow. But before the prison operator could place the call, an officer in one of the tower posts— evidence points to 12 Post hard by the steam vault exit—called the sergeant first. The officer thought he had heard something. In the stillness it sounded like gunshots, near the hospital. Sergeant Darrow told the officer to shine his spotlight on the hospital and keep it there, goddamn it. The tower guard did so, removing the light from the wall.

Moments later, Patches, McGale, and Whitey slipped away in the dark.

When Sergeant Darrow hung up his phone, it rang again immediately. The switchboard operator told him that something funny was going on at the hospital. Darrow had heard enough. Shots, nobody answering either guard's telephone—he rushed over to the hospital building. When he entered, he heard commotion upstairs and headed for the quickest way to the third floor—the elevator. If he had used the stairs, he might have heard the heated debate about killing the hostages going on one floor below, in the basement.

Upstairs, the inmates pointed the sergeant to Ward 2. Ashen-faced, Officer Hartye lay on a bed near the door, where worried convicts had placed him. He was dead—shot twice, one bullet fired close enough to leave powder burns. The sergeant hurried to the phone, told the switchboard to patch him through to the warden's residence, fast.

Up at the mansion, Lawes had just dropped off to sleep after hosting a small Easter party. The bedside telephone trilled, and Lawes fumbled for the receiver. The sergeant's tense voice on the other end of the line instantly brought Lawes wide-awake. Darrow had the worst news a warden could hear: an officer was dead, and prisoners were missing. Lawes was dressed and down at the scene in moments.

Bit by bit, the warden and Darrow drew the story from the inmates. In the basement, the warden and sergeant soon found DeSimone and Kaplan—terrified but alive—handcuffed together in the steam vault entry room. The lights in the vault were still on. The warden was encouraged. If this was the escape route, the attempt was a dead end. Lawes was confident that the steam tunnel was sealed at the outside end.

"They can't get out," Warden Lawes said. "We have them."

Lawes of all people knew how infrequent actual breaks were. Only three men had made it out and disappeared in his whole twenty-year career. Most likely, he thought, these inmates had been able to get only so far and were now holed up, hiding someplace behind the walls, like that wretch whose skeleton they found years ago. So there was no need at that point, the warden reasoned, to sound Big Ben, as the prison's alarm siren atop A-block was known. Its wail was powerful and could be heard up and down the Hudson River Valley. If Sing Sing blew Big Ben every time there was a miscount or a man went missing, the neighboring towns would be in an uproar, and the villagers would get so used to false alarms that they'd ignore the siren when it really mattered. Warden Lawes was certain of this judgment call. Unless the prison knew *for sure* that inmates had gotten out, Big Ben would remain silent. And right then, Lawes would have staked his life on his belief that the men were still behind the walls, trapped like rats in the steam vault.

So the warden focused his attention inward. He summoned every officer into service and began a complete search of the facility and grounds. About two hundred seventy men joined in. They began with a thorough hunt through the hospital basement, steam vault, and laundry. The sleeping prison was already locked down for the night, but all exterior lights were switched on, and the tower spots—usually reserved for trouble in the dark—crisscrossed the murky hillside. Cellblocks were recounted, and every inch of every building was combed—basements and rooftops, crawl spaces and stairwells.

The extra officers augmented the night staff already on duty—about fifty men—who were ordered to remain at their posts until further notice. But despite the thoroughness, the procedure was agitated. Officer Fred Starler, stationed in 7 Building throughout the night—two hundred feet north of the hospital—told of complete confusion. He hadn't heard the shots, but the telephone rang incessantly with calls from other officers wondering if there was any news. Searching guards kept coming through, but they, too, didn't seem to have a clear idea of what was going on. Not until the following day did Starler and other officers hear that a guard had been shot. Even then, they weren't told Hartye's name.

The tower guards must have been especially concerned. Even today, one of their biggest worries is falling asleep on the overnight shift. They remain at their stations for the entire eight-hour shift, forbidden to leave even for a restroom break (flush toilets were installed in the towers in 1967; before then, tower guards used a slop bucket). There are no lights in the tower, no radio playing; the guard is expected to remain vigilant in the quiet dark. The officer in charge of the night guard would routinely blink a flashlight at a tower—at random—and expect an answering flash. For anyone found to be dozing when the break occurred, there would be hell to pay. And if someone had slipped out right under the guards' noses, it would be even worse.

Worry increased when Warden Lawes's fine-tooth probe came up empty.

In the time it took to get the search up and running, Waters, McGale, and Riordan were far up the tracks, nearing the Ossining train station. At about the same time, a village police car on routine patrol was cruising lower Main Street, slowing downhill toward Depot Plaza's northwest corner. A report of loiterers had been received at headquarters—Brownie and Bergstrom had arrived at last and were parked at the curb near the bar waiting for Kiernan and Wade to appear. Officers William Nelson and James W. Fagan were dispatched. The two patrolmen braked their car to the curb at the corner of Main and Water Streets, two blocks from the train station and just east of a small tavern.

Unbeknownst to the officers, three armed fugitives were bearing right down on them.

———————

As Officer Nelson settled his wire-rims on the bridge of his nose and heaved himself from the car to investigate what the dispatcher referred to only as "characters," his partner, thirty-five-year-old Jim Fagan, checked his wristwatch and noted the time and complaint in his report book. More than likely, the call was nothing—some drunks stopping to slur each other good night. But you never knew, even in sleepy Ossining. Police work often took unexpected turns. Maybe that's why Officer Fagan was still in the game.

Jim Fagan hadn't always wanted to be a cop. But he'd always felt a strong pulse of civic pride and responsibility. Born and raised in town, a handsome, blue-eyed high school football star and former Ossining tennis champion, Fagan volunteered with the Holla Hose firehouse right out of high school. In his spare time, he played the cornet and sometimes performed with local bands. Young Jim Fagan did it all—but there was little money in any of it. He tried running a greengrocery with his brother. He'd even taken a law course offered by the Blackstone Institute in Chicago. But for Jim Fagan, clerking and even lawyering lacked the necessary zest. He needed something smart and dazzling, something to complement his dark Irish looks, a career that would blend the glamour of sports and show business with the true service of volunteering. Jim Fagan found both in police work.

His idealism, however, collided almost immediately with raw experience, and he told friends he thought the job was gruesome. Only two days after Fagan officially joined the force in March 1934, an old man died in his arms. Not long after that, the young officer was rushing three injured kids to Ossining Hospital when one child expired en route in the backseat. But Jim Fagan's darkest impression of police work came on a bright summer day, July 23, 1934, only four months after proudly pinning badge number 13 to his midnight blue tunic.

On a mild Sunday afternoon—the same day FBI agents shot John Dillinger dead outside a Chicago movie house—a tour bus carrying members and supporters of Brooklyn's Young Men's Democratic League wound its way up to Ossining to play Sing Sing's celebrated inmate baseball team. The bus never made it to the prison. During the entire trip from the city, the high-spirited passengers grew increasingly worried. The bus driver kept stopping to adjust the brakes—at one point, actually screwing the pedal back on. Once the bus reached Ossining and started down steep Secor Road toward the train station, the brakes failed completely, and the bus picked up speed. Stuck in high gear, it skidded wildly downhill, bouncing off a retaining wall, and careened up Depot Plaza's train station ramp. The bus screamed past the elevated railroad station, crashed through the cement guardrail, and hurtled through the air, landing upside down in a fiery explosion in the middle of a lumberyard on the other side of the tracks.

People with their clothes and hair on fire staggered from the wreckage, ran for the river, and jumped in as the lumberyard burst into flames. The yard's locked gates hampered rescuers—fishermen at first, horrified out of a quiet afternoon. Twelve passengers were killed outright, and ten others died over the next few days. Officer James Fagan, among the first on the scene, helped pull bodies from the inferno, many burned beyond recognition. Two days later, still on round-the-clock duty since the crash, and reeking from the catastrophe, Fagan was on hand at dawn to pull the final body from the Hudson River.

The incident brought the young policeman the renown he seemed to crave—his picture on the front page of the local newspaper. But the ghastly bus crash had scorched the glamorous sheen off police work. Fellow officers had ribbed Fagan about his unlucky badge number, and he'd always laughed it off. But now this horror. He was twenty-eight years old at the time, and the appalling and senseless deaths would have challenged any young man's faith. But Officer Fagan didn't falter or resign from the force. If anything, he seemed to feel an even deeper commitment to service. Still, the images lingered. Would anyone who had witnessed that awful day ever sit by the curb near the train station, say, without seeing in his mind's eye the charred bodies and the twisted wreckage?

Patches Waters continued up the tracks, with Charlie McGale at his heels. Whitey had fallen behind. As they had been from the start of this escapade, Patches and McGale were way ahead of him, passing into the blackness beneath the station. The fog was dense, blurring light and shadow. Maybe that's why they missed the car.

The Plymouth was parked to their right, at the curb on the street side of the iron fence, beneath the station ramp. Or perhaps that precise detail hadn't been communicated to Patches by Kiernan during all the visiting room planning. Whitey surely was wondering where the hell the car that

Patches had mentioned was supposed to be. But he couldn't know. This was Patches's plan. Perhaps Patches had devised the same fallback that Kiernan and Wade had, to meet Brownie and Bergstrom at the bar. That might have been the case, because just north of the station, Whitey saw Patches and McGale climb the iron fence out of the rail bed and start east across the plaza. He followed.

They were hurrying north up a side street, in and out of the yellow cones of light cast by wooden lampposts, past houses shuttered for the night. To Whitey, Patches seemed lost—the station was behind them. At an intersection at the top of the street, near a tavern, an automobile was parked at the curb. Patches and McGale stopped. Whitey kept running to catch up. Somebody had to tell them that they were headed in the wrong direction, that the car at the curb couldn't have been left for them. That the car, in fact, looked like a cop's.

———————

Officer Fagan must have smiled. Two men had appeared in the intersection from out of the gloom, opposite the direction from where Officer Nelson had gone inspecting. They both looked as if they'd been shot out of a cannon—one small and wild-haired, the other shirtless, his bare chest white and scrawny. Obviously a couple of drunks keeping the neighbors awake, just as Fagan had thought. He rolled down the car window to yell at them and noticed both men were wearing similar trousers. Uniform gray and shapeless. State issue. Fagan's smile disappeared.

"Hey, you," Fagan called, his fingers closing around the door handle. "What are you guys . . ."

Without a word, the two men raised guns and opened fire.

A bullet flattened a gold button on Fagan's uniform and slammed into his heart. Another pierced the car door and shattered a kidney. Officer James Fagan, like the cool-headed hero he'd trained all his life to be, the crack-shot marksman and trophy winner at county meets, pulled his sidearm as he tumbled from the car. He emptied his revolver as he collapsed to the pavement mortally wounded. Hearing the gunfire, Officer Nelson abandoned questioning Brownie and Bergstrom. He drew his .38 and sprinted back down the block. From two hundred feet away, the bespectacled policeman squinted down his gun sight and sent a bullet through Patches Waters's temple, dropping him dead. McGale turned and ran.

Whitey saw the policeman roll from the car, saw Patches fall, and he fled. He pointed his gun behind him and fired blindly three times. Luckily for McGale, who was running right at him, the shots went wild. Whitey legged it back across the plaza. He raced over a footbridge that crossed the tracks north of the station, heading toward lights haloed beside the black stretch of river.

Maybe he could find a dock, with a boat—anything to get them to the other side. That was their only chance now.

———————

Officer Nelson lifted his bleeding partner into the backseat of the patrol car, switched on the bubble light and siren, and raced to Ossining Hospital, five minutes away. Steering with one hand, he called frantically over the radio and alerted headquarters. But, like the injured kid he'd tried to save years before, and the many more he couldn't help in the fiery bus crash, Officer James Fagan died in the backseat of the squad car on the way to the hospital.

The alarm went out—at least two suspects, desperate and heavily armed. Every policeman in the town of Ossining responded. The Teletype also chattered out warnings to the State Police, as well as to every police station in the surrounding towns and villages. But no Sing Sing officers joined the hundreds of lawmen converging on Depot Plaza in the largest manhunt ever seen locally. On Lawes's orders, the penitentiary was still searching for the men the warden believed were inside the walls.

And Big Ben remained silent.

———————

Billy Wade and Eddie Kiernan perched at the bar on the north edge of the plaza, working their way through glasses of beer and shots, undoubtedly wondering where the hell Brownie and Bergstrom were. Kiernan and Wade had no idea that their accomplices were at that moment parked up the street, being questioned by Officer Nelson. All they knew was that their ride home was an hour late. The neon clock above the shelved liquor bottles showed about 2:15. In less than fifteen minutes, Waters, Whitey, and the other fellow were scheduled to make their break. Wade and Kiernan needed to leave *now*. They couldn't risk being on the scene when the inmates arrived. Experienced at passing unnoticed (as much as that was possible: they were probably the only ones in the bar at that hour of a Monday morning), they'd have kept their hats on, hunched over their drinks. But the light was low, and the bartender likely ignored them in the hopes that they'd leave so he could lock up.

As the two worried, they heard loud pops outside, lots of them, close by.

The bartender went to the window at the end of the bar, pulled aside the dusty curtain, and stared through the beer lights. That sounded like gunshots.

Wade and Kiernan looked at each other, then back down at their drinks. They put a couple of dollars on the bar, slid off their stools, and hurried out.

The bar was west of the intersection of Main and Water Streets, but Wade and Kiernan didn't even look to the left, up the street. They skirted the north end of Depot Plaza, then scooted around the block. A taxicab had passed them when they were parking the getaway car under the ramp. The cab had turned and gone up the hill—there must be a taxi stand up there. They'd have to work their way uphill and around the pandemonium breaking right behind them. They pulled their hats low and hurried into the fog as police sirens began to wail.

———————

Taxi driver Cliff Ellsworthy heard the shots, too. He was behind the desk in the company office on Spring Street, off Main, probably flipping through the Sunday *Citizen Register* for the hundredth time. On the odd chance that a fare stood stranded at the train station, he'd driven the Packard through Depot Plaza about forty-five minutes earlier. But the plaza was empty—except for a beige Plymouth parked under the ramp. Cliff's headlights had swept across the car, and he thought he'd seen two figures silhouetted in the front seat. Unless they were waving him down, though, that was none of his business. He'd driven back to the newspaper in the taxi office—a slow night, and there was nothing to do about it.

But now those shots. Not too close, but not faraway, either—down the hill, near the plaza, it sounded like. The clock on the desk read about 2:15. Cliff got up and stood in the doorway. Spring Street was dark and gloomy, not a soul around. Then there was a police siren, wailing and fading away; a few minutes later, other sirens joined in. That many sirens meant it must be big. He'd have loved to jump in the car and go see, but he couldn't do that. He was the only driver on duty, and he had to stay by the phone.

But soon these two guys walked in, breathing heavy like they'd been pushing it. One of them was skinny, with a long face like a leprechaun. The other one was pudgier, fixed up neat in a suit and overcoat. The shots, the sirens, and then these two. Cliff was spooked.

"How much to take us to White Plains right away?" the leprechaun asked.

"Three dollars."

The pudgy one pulled out a roll, peeled off three singles. "Come on."

Cliff said okay. The last thing he was going to do was drive these two to White Plains at nearly three in the morning. A twelve-mile trip over pitch dark roads with two strangers who showed up right after gunshots and sirens? Cliff had better think fast. "Say, one of you guys have a cigarette?"

The leprechaun took a pack from his windbreaker, shook one out. "Okay, let's go."

Cliff lit the cigarette, stood up, and ambled from behind the desk. He walked over to the wall where his coat was pegged. "Go out and get in the Packard. I'll be along right away."

The two hustled out, and Cliff heard the car doors slam. He didn't know what to do; it felt all wrong. He called his boss, who had no idea what was going on and was of no help. Cliff couldn't see another choice. He went out, hoping another idea would come to him before he started the engine. He couldn't imagine these two didn't suspect something fishy, the way Cliff was moseying. They might kill him just for lagging, as soon as they got to White Plains. He opened the driver's-side door, stretched one last time, and saw Ossining patrolman Vincent Kelly hurrying his way. Cliff almost swooned with relief but waved him over instead.

Officer Kelly was flushed and breathless, too. He'd been walking his beat on Main Street, a block north of the taxi stand, when the shots echoed across the darkness. On the force less than a year, Kelly was a beefy foot patrolman reputed by the local paper to "know his potatoes" when it came to unsnarling traffic at the intersection of Spring and Main. But the confusion and violent excitement of the evening had rattled him. Trying to keep up with the rapidly unfolding events, Kelly used the street callbox to speak to headquarters; he flagged down passing cars to speed him to the scene. On his way downhill, Kelly spotted two figures hurrying through the fog. Turning right around, he waved down another car headed back uphill—driven by Wade and Kiernan's bartender, of all people, who likely described his recent customers. Officer Kelly was about to make the most important collar of his young career.

He put a thick hand on his holstered revolver and pulled open the back door of Cliff Ellsworthy's taxicab. "Okay you, get out," he ordered. "I want to talk to you."

The men climbed out. "What's wrong?" the skinny one asked. They were cool but kept their faces wrinkled in concern like anyone would.

"There's some trouble in town and we're checking everything. What's your name?"

"Wade. This is Kiernan." Confident with alcohol that they could bluff their way out, perhaps, or confused by the night's turn of events, they didn't give false names.

"You have identification?"

"What's this about, officer?" Wade said, rifling through his wallet and handing over a bill of sale and car registration made out to somebody named William Arkin.

Kelly stared at it and frowned. "Is this your name?"

"No, my name is Wade."

"What are you doing in Ossining?"

Wade put on the impish expression he used to charm people. He calmly started telling the policeman how he and Kiernan had come to town with a couple of pickups named Betty and Peggy. Kiernan and Wade ended up fighting with them, and the girls got mad. They hopped in Wade's car and left them flat. The stranded Romeos were hoping to catch a cab home.

Kiernan, accustomed to letting Wade do the talking, smiled and nodded. He had nothing to add.

Officer Kelly had had enough of their routine. The men had no true identification, and tonight that was more than enough reason to run them in. He frisked them both and found them unarmed. Officer Kelly had Cliff drive them all to headquarters. For Cliff Ellsworthy, it turned out to be not such a slow night after all.

In fact, for everyone within earshot of the screaming sirens, the small-town stillness was shattered beyond repair.

CHAPTER FIFTEEN

HOOK MOUNTAIN

Fᴉꜱʜᴇʀᴍᴀɴ Cʜᴀʀʟᴇꜱ Rᴏʜʀ Jʀ., crating a fresh catch of shad in his riverside shack north of Sing Sing, paused for a moment. A small fusillade was echoing across the night. Then silence again. Just the river lapping against the pilings of Holden's Dock. Rohr shrugged and went back to work—probably a couple of drunks setting off a pack of firecrackers. Rohr should have such fun. He'd need to step on it if he wanted to get these fish downtown in good time. The Fulton Fish Market opened in a couple of hours in southern Manhattan, and this was the money season.

A miles-long school of the biggest herring—the local papers called it the "shad brigade"—was swarming up the Hudson River in what looked to be the best run in a quarter of a century. After nearing extinction only five years ago, the seven-pound, lavender-scaled bucks and roes could bring a total of nearly $250,000 for the local fishing business by June. Even the U.S. War Department had designated and licensed crews to spread nets from Fifty-seventh Street in Manhattan all the way north to Poughkeepsie. The shad run would last only six weeks, and most fishermen worked around the clock. Charles Rohr was no different—he definitely wanted a piece of that much action.

He clamped his cigar between his teeth and puffed as he fastened the wire clasps on the lid of a crate. Not that a professional fisherman minded the essence of cold shad. But if his news photo is any indication—a cigar butt angled between his fingers like a sixth digit—Rohr clearly preferred his stogie to the smell of wet fish. He stacked the box by the door and retrieved another empty box. Rohr shaved some ice off a melting block and layered it along the bottom of the crate. He'd finish this last box by the time his partner got back with the truck; then they'd load up and drive downtown. With any luck, Rohr would be back home, with a chilled beer, and in bed by 8 A.M.

But then a siren was wailing, like a police car's fading away into the hills. Rohr took the cigar out of his mouth and listened. Maybe that was more than firecrackers. There was something else then. Another sound, this one closer. It sounded like crunching, right outside—in fact, like someone walking around. He crossed the shack and pushed open the door. The outside light barely illuminated the gravel shore a few feet below the dock, his sixteen-foot skiff pulled up from the water. Somebody was down there, messing with his boat. Hey, he called, jumping down.

Two men rushed him, a little dark-haired fellow and a bigger blond. They were breathing hard, and they stuck something in Rohr's stomach. Guns.

"Is that your rowboat?" the little guy asked.

"Yes," Rohr said. "You can have it."

"We just shot a cop," the blond said, "we need to get to the other side."

"Take it."

"Nothing doing. You're going to row us over," the little one said and drew Rohr toward the boat with his gun.

"We're escaped convicts," the blond explained, in case the fisherman was wondering.

The fisherman's weathered face tried to register the shock. Rohr's high cheekbones and boxy forehead were lined by the long, seasonal hours, and a lifetime of deaths and disappointments pushed out a full lower lip. But for a hardscrabble fisherman, guns in the stomach were off the scale. He could think of nothing to do but throw the wooden block anchor under the seat in the bow and push the rowboat off the gravel and into the dark water. One gunman climbed into the bow, Rohr hurried to settle between the oars, and the blond hunkered down in the stern. They kept their guns trained on him as he pushed and pulled, the oarlocks click-clacking in a steadying rhythm as the boat moved away from shore. More and more sirens called across the dark. But the fog was thick, and the sirens died quickly. The depot lights vanished, too, the fog hushing everything but the men's dry breathing and the uniform splash of the oars.

—————

Ossining police lieutenant Frank D. Carlson was furious. Taking initial command of the investigation into Officer Fagan's death, he stood above the John Doe sprawled in the intersection of Main and Water Streets. It didn't matter that the stiff was shirtless—if you were a lawman in Ossining, home of the Big House, you recognized the trousers. Gray and baggy: that was convict wear. The standing order was, whenever an inmate got loose, prison officials telephoned police headquarters and sounded Big Ben. That had been the procedure for twenty-one years, ever since Warden Lawes arrived. But Lieutenant Carlson had heard no prison siren, and headquarters had received no call. Sing Sing was silent. A policeman was dead. And there the guy lay, those pants as good as a tattoo.

Carlson about-faced as they loaded the body into a police wagon for the trip to Ossining Hospital. Medical examiner Dr. Amos O. Squire was waiting. With cold-eyed precision, Carlson coordinated the growing police presence spreading into the plaza. Hundreds of patrolmen from neighboring Pleasantville and Briarcliff, as well as state troopers from the Hawthorne Barracks, sped to the scene and joined the fifty-man Ossining force. Croton-on-Hudson's chief of police, bedridden with a nagging fever, dragged himself into clothes and overcoat and hurried four miles down the Post Road to the station. The chief's men commandeered a locomotive from the Harmon Yards and clung to the engine, pistols drawn and electric torches flashing, as it chugged for miles up and down the tracks. A hundred newsmen and picture snappers, maybe more, who were dialed in to the police radio frequencies were alerted by the crackling reports. Smelling headlines, the press men converged on Ossining, too, coming from as far away as New York City; they clogged the streets

threading downhill and boiled with rumors of a mass escape at Sing Sing
and the murder of many guards.

––––––––––––

Warden Lawes, still orchestrating Sing Sing's internal search from
behind his office desk, hung up the telephone. The State Police commander at Hawthorne Barracks had called, needing confirmation about a
gunfight near the Ossining train station and the killing of a local policeman. This was the first Lawes had heard of either. But what struck the
warden dumb was the commander's suspicion that the other dead man—
in baggy gray trousers and clutching a .38—was a convict. Lawes con-
ceded that there had been some trouble that evening at Sing Sing but said
he knew of no inmate getting out. He assured the commander that he'd
get back to him as soon as he got to the bottom of it. The warden must
have known by then, however, that some of his boys *had* gotten out. And
they were armed.

This was big trouble. Lawes didn't need to be as finely tuned to the
newswires as he was to know that soon anyone who could read or listen
would learn of this blunder. A famous warden for twenty years; a man of
national reputation. There'd be the initial hollowness in the pit of the
stomach, maybe; then an adrenaline flooding. And the question: was the
end of his career at hand?

Why had Lawes misread the clues? All the witnesses in the hospital
had pointed the way downstairs, right to the tunnel. DeSimone and
Kaplan had told how the fugitives had disappeared into the vault. The
escapees had apparently locked the gate behind them—they had not only
guns but keys, too. Yet Lawes had refused to accept the possibility that
these resourceful men would get out. Experience had told him it was
highly unlikely—90 percent of the men who tried failed. This was *his*
prison, after all, and these were his men. He knew every inch of the place
because he'd rebuilt it from the ground up. Every one of his books and
every broadcast testified to his understanding of human nature in general
and of the men behind bars in particular. These inmates were not extraordinary. And that meant they were still inside.

So Lawes had stuck with established policy. And like the hidden flaws in prison security, unseen to all but the enterprising convict with escape on his mind, the well-worn policy was revealed as flimsy only when men crashed through it.

The thing to do now was to correct the situation. Then, with luck, he'd get out of this with a reprimand and a simple retirement. He certainly couldn't allow these events to blow up into a disgraceful dismissal. A state investigation was on the way, and Lawes badly need some information to save his reputation.

The warden placed a call to Ossining police headquarters and confirmed what he now knew was true. He'd heard sirens wailing through town for a while now, but for all he knew they were fire trucks. Wrong again. Lawes continued the prison search just to be safe, but he scaled it back, sending a contingent of guards to the depot to join the manhunt. With one inmate down, that meant two armed men were still on the loose. What remained of his career depended on his bringing those two men, *his* men, back before any more lives were lost.

A little before three o'clock—nearly an hour after the break—Big Ben growled to life.

————

The rowboat was halfway across the river's four-mile span, but Whitey and McGale couldn't see that. Landmarks were vague at best. The chalky smudge in the fog behind them must have been the lights of Ossining. But ahead, all was murk. They couldn't have been in the rowboat for more than thirty, maybe forty-five minutes. But it seemed like hours, bobbing up and down, the oars cutting through water black as pitch, the fisherman panting. And to top it off, it had begun to rain, a muggy drizzle in the 50-degree predawn.

"Is this the fastest you can go?" Whitey said.

"Shake it up, buddy, shake it up!" McGale joined in, up in the bow behind the fisherman, nudging the man's back with his gun.

Rohr blamed their slow progress on the tide, and he wasn't lying. The Algonkins knew the Hudson as the "river-that-flows-two-ways." The hijacked rowboat couldn't help but rock in the northbound tidal flow from the Atlantic, which sometimes pushed salt water as far up as

Poughkeepsie, sixty-five miles away, and the river's southward current, streaming hundreds of miles from deep in the Adirondacks.

But McGale was out of patience. Running for his life from flying bullets was not what the locksmith mastermind had bargained for. And it was all Patches's fault. No car, no machine gun, just cops with blazing pistols. McGale couldn't take his anger out on Patches, though. He was dead. This stinking fisherman would have to do. It made good sense, too. They could never let him live after this.

Off starboard, Whitey spied faint blue and green pinpoints, maybe police boats in hot pursuit. "What are the lights?"

Rohr glanced north, to his left. "They're some fishing boats." Their nets full of shad, to be sure, full of cold, wriggling treasure. But that wasn't so key right then. A cold beer from the cooler they no doubt kept in the cuddy, though, that was another matter. The heavy work of rowing had parched Rohr. The rain on his face, the water all around them, made the thirst unbearable. But focusing on how thirsty he was, and on the ache that developed in his back and burned his arms, was better than staring at one gun muzzle while another pressed into his spine.

Whitey watched the lights of the fishing boats brighten and dim through the drifting fog. He probably would have traded places with those unknown fishermen in a second if he could have. He'd worked the river, and he knew his way around a boat. But then there was the river's mackerel scent. So distinct from the sewage and chemical-laced waters he'd swum in, worked on, back in his waterfront days. This river was unknown to a man like Whitey Riordan. And there would be no trading spots with anyone now.

Their best hope lay on the other side, whatever was over there. From a Sing Sing cell, the Hudson's western shore was a wooded ridgeline with outcroppings of steep rock emerging from the water—a blank, in other words, to urban convicts. No buildings or roads were visible in daylight, nor were there lights at night. From Nyack, eight miles southwest of the prison, up to Haverstraw, about five miles northwest, Palisades Interstate Park was a dominating wilderness. The darkness, the fog, even the rain, though, would surely all work in their favor to hide them. If anything could pull them out of this, they must have realized, it was reaching the far shore as soon as possible and running like hell.

But then a howl rose above the splash of the oars. It carried high above their breathing and echoed up and down the Hudson River Valley, drumming the fogbank around them so hard that they might have felt themselves deep in the throat of it.

Big Ben.

———————

Lieutenant Carlson had to put his face next to people's ears to be heard above the prison siren just down the road. He ordered officers to commandeer any boats not in use and patrol the shoreline. The police didn't realize that the fugitives were fleeing across the river, but they figured that the men could easily be hiding among the boulders and flotsam that littered the riverside. Luckily, a local boat club had its dock just north of the train station. Club members would know what that siren meant, like everyone else in town; but they'd be surprised to find their boats gone in the morning.

As the search widened, the State Police contacted New York City detectives and arranged for a city police airplane to take off in two hours, at dawn. The plane would fly north and cover the river from the air in back and forth sweeps. But the state's most immediate contribution, besides 150 officers, was its prize bloodhounds. State Police Trooper W. W. Horton, the trainer and handler of the Hawthorne Barracks's renowned bloodhound pack, leashed up his two best dogs, Sappho and Monk, and piled into the station wagon. The dogs may have panted in anticipation of a long trip, as they were often loaned out to aid searches in the tri-state area, even as far away as Maine and Pennsylvania. But perhaps too soon for them, they hit Ossining, and the bloodhounds bounded from the car. The siren was piercing to a dog's sensitive ears; but Sappho and Monk were disciplined veterans of more than fifty cases a year.

They were eager to get to work. Bloodhounds, with the keenest noses of all the canines, have been used as trackers since the fourteenth century. But in 1941, the unit harnessed to find fugitives and lost children alike was relatively new to the New York State Police. The six-dog pack was initiated in 1935 by the forward-looking superintendent, Major John Warner, the son-in-law of former governor Al Smith and a concert pianist who had once played Carnegie Hall. Among fugitives on the run, the ninety-pound dogs had a fearsome reputation as maulers, which couldn't have been further from the truth. Bloodhounds were more likely to pounce on their prey with tails wagging and tongues slopping hello. But men running for their lives, hearing the throaty baying at their heels, found that hard to believe.

Warden Lawes and his guards arrived and waved the sheets from Whitey's and McGale's hospital beds under the animals' jowls. The dogs took off. When a trail is fresh—eight hours old or newer—bloodhounds show great excitement. Sappho and Monk pulled lanky Trooper Horton across the train station plaza toward the shoreline, yapping in their glee. Bloodhounds have been known to concentrate so strongly on the scent that they ram headfirst into walls and parked cars if the track leads that way. Perhaps luckily for Horton, the trail went cold at the water's edge twenty-five yards away. Horton tugged back on the six-foot leashes, as Sappho and Monk loped from side to side, sniffing for the scent.

"A wild goose chase," a local cop wisecracked, panting to keep up. "Those two cons are probably miles away by this time."

"They'll find them," Trooper Horton pronounced. He knew his dogs.

Big Ben echoed off the mountain rising in front of the rowboat. A sandy little beach appeared out of the gloom, and the smell of wet woods emanated from the bank. The boat glided, then bumped something about ten feet from shore. The fisherman maneuvered the boat around the obstruction. He rowed closer and jumped out, grabbed the rope and block, and pulled the craft in. His shoulders were burning, the convicts sitting like lumps, the rain falling harder now.

"I think there's a highway here," Rohr said, dropping the anchor and craning his neck up the incline. When he turned back the convicts were on the sand a few feet away, their guns pointed at his waist.

"Let's bump him off," the little dark-haired one said.

So that was that. There was the rowboat, the shack, a partner with a truck. There were shad and sturgeon in the spring, striped bass in the early summer, and herring in the fall. If you were lucky, there was enough left after the overhead to celebrate. God forbid you got sick, or something.

But now everything had come down to this: gut shot to die alone in the rain, a body swept downriver, swollen by the tide or pulled to pieces by animals here on this driftwood-strewn beach.

"That won't do you no good," Rohr blurted. "Everybody in Ossining knows my boat. If they find it here, they'll know where you landed. Better for you to let me go, you won't have another life on your conscience. I'll keep my mouth shut, it'll take me an hour to get back." It must have sounded like babbling. The fisherman stopped, afraid that if he said any more they'd shoot just to shut him up.

The men turned away and huddled, the big blond with an arm around the little guy's shoulder, talking into his ear. The little guy kept turning to face Rohr; then he dropped his eyes. They broke apart and faced the fisherman again.

"You ain't going to hurt me, are you?"

"Don't worry," the blond said, "you're going right back."

Rohr's knees went wobbly, and he threw his arms around Whitey.

"We're not going to do anything," Whitey said, unwrapping himself from the guy. He must have known it was risky letting the fisherman go. But Whitey couldn't let McGale shoot the man. Maybe it was the shock of seeing his friend Patches fall with a bullet through his head, or a twinge of conscience that even Sing Sing couldn't erase. Whatever the motive, for the second time that night Whitey Riordan stepped in to stop murder. If they let the guy free, maybe their luck would hold long enough to get them out of this. Maybe not. But as Whitey saw it, their only chance wasn't more killing; it was a highway with cars headed north or south. "So there are roads around here?"

"Up on the hill."

"How do we get up from here?"

"Keep going north. You'll find a place with a path over the rocks, up the cliff." Rohr wished there was more to tell them, he was so grateful.

The little guy still looked mad. It's unknown what Whitey said to

him. But for McGale, eager to kill Rohr and right the wrong he felt this
night had done him, Whitey's words were strong enough to persuade him
otherwise. Still, McGale wanted something for his pains. He asked Rohr
if he had any cigarettes. Rohr had a tin of tobacco.

"Okay," McGale said, snatching and pocketing it, "get in your boat
and scram."

Rohr sprang to his boat, cast off, and jumped between the oars. The
prison siren was winding down as he settled the oars into a rhythm. A
minute later, when he glanced back to the beach, the men were gone.

———————

The rain had ended, and the fog was bronze with dawn when Rohr
reached Ossining sometime after five o'clock. The train plaza was ablaze
with searchlights, the red bubbles twirling on dozens of police cars—he
hadn't seen such action since the bus crash seven years ago. He put his
boat in at Holden's Dock and dragged himself ashore, his lips white he
was so dry. The first cop he saw, he grabbed. Palisades Interstate Park, he
told him, about two miles north of Rockland Lake. There's a little beach
at the foot of Hook Mountain, the bend below Haverstraw. The cop hustled Rohr over to Lieutenant Carlson standing by a radio car, where Rohr
told his story again. After all, he hadn't made those convicts any lasting
promise—they'd almost killed him.

Rohr's gasps touched off a manhunt that extended twenty-six air
miles from the New Jersey approach to the George Washington Bridge,
up Route 9W through Rockland County, and on up to the Bear Mountain Bridge, twelve miles north of Ossining. Roadblocks were manned by
shotgun-toting cops, their black rubber slickers and jackboots glistening.
Search parties wouldn't add helicopters to their fleets for another decade
or more, but New York City's Coast Guard station was radioed for its airplane (local and state authorities apparently figured the military craft
would be sufficient and canceled the New York police airplane). The
Coast Guard also sent two patrol boats and two launches north from its
headquarters on Staten Island. As a hazy sun began to rise, the Interstate
Park Police joined the more than one thousand officers from the state,
county, city, village, and town, riding out north, south, and west from the
train plaza. Two dozen grim-faced Sing Sing guards, armed with

Thompsons and .45s, took a private launch and joined the flotilla heading four miles west across the river. The guards hoped they spotted Riordan and McGale first—they'd shoot them dead and save the state some
money. And State Trooper Horton loaded Sappho and Monk onto a
Coast Guard cutter, the launch growling through the water, as the dogs
took deep draughts of the bed sheets held under their snouts and squinted
into the fragrant morning breeze.

Basalt cliffs towered above Whitey and McGale, rusty in the first light.
Boulders had tumbled down ages ago. The piles of rock were overgrown
with trees and saplings, vines and brambles, still sharp without spring
leaves. They'd gone north like the fisherman had told them, slapping
through the dark, but then they could go no farther. Up what path,
Whitey might have wondered. You couldn't walk it if you tried, the
shoreline curving away from the river, then reversing, so disorienting to
two city boys that even morning light didn't help. If there were a highway
up there, they'd need a Gimbals's escalator to reach it.

They could hear powerful engines rumbling across the Hudson and a
droning airplane circling overhead. Uniforms were coming, with guns to
kill them outright or with chains to drag them back behind bars and
straight to the electric chair. So they started to climb, hand over hand,
leather soles slipping on the still-wet ground. Soft from prison food, they
straddled crevices that dead-ended at sheer rock faces two hundred feet
tall, and they clung to the underbrush. Scraped and soaked to the skin,
Whitey and McGale inched into a crag and leaned panting against the
rock. Awake for nearly twenty-four hours, their bodies throbbed, any
adrenaline long since boiled away. That fisherman was out of his mind—
there was no climbing this rock. You'd need to be in better shape than you
got from shuffling around the 5 Building yard. A steady thrum echoed on
the river. A hundred yards below was a white boat, a ship really, shuttling
up and down the shoreline.

Somebody had called the Coast Guard.

Whitey took the revolver from his jacket pocket, clicked open the
cylinder, pulled out the three spent shells. Maybe he could tell them he
never fired the gun, that Patches gave it to him half loaded. Maybe they'd

even believe it. He threw the empty shells away down the hill and closed a fist around the saint's medallion hanging on a chain from his neck. A gift from his mother, most likely. A prayer couldn't hurt now.

———————

The Coast Guard cutter cruised back and forth along the wild riverside for half an hour, looking for the exact spot Rohr had described. The Ossining fisherman couldn't be coaxed aboard to help. He'd done his bit, and he was all cashed in. Finally, the authorities determined the precise beach and dropped anchor. They were up there in the rocks, and Lieutenant Carlson was determined to get them. Sappho and Monk, splashing ashore with long-armed Trooper Horton, immediately sniffed at the ground and at the shoe prints stamped into the sand.

Carlson stood with Horton, looking up the rock face, his mouth an unfriendly line, his pale eyes expressionless. The bloodhounds were necessary, but Carlson had also enlisted the help of the Interstate Park Police, headquartered at Bear Mountain. These woods were wild, and you needed an expert to find your way around. Carlson turned to his.

Forty-two-year-old patrolman Wallace Mullen, a genial, eleven-year veteran of the Park Police, knew the Palisades better than anyone on the force. When Rohr had sculled back to Ossining with the news, it was Mullen the professional tracker who was routed from bed to study the topographical maps. He stood with Carlson, their flashlights playing over the footprints, while Horton tied the eager bloodhounds to a tree.

Shoeprints—two pairs of them—led north along the beach and into the woods. That heads over to North Park Trail, Mullen told the others. But he didn't think they could have gotten far—this stretch of woods was a real tangle. The posse had better get moving, just the same, though. These crevices and crags, all these brambles—guys could hide out here for days. Trooper Horton untied Sappho and Monk and gave the dogs their lead. He clomped into the woods after them, Mullen at his shoulder, Carlson right behind.

Sappho and Monk led the men north. The scent gathered in the folds of their jowls, and they smelled the direction. In town and city searches they could determine whether their prey had jumped into a car or was hiding in a crowd. But in the woods, after a rain, the trail was diluted. Two miles up, where an ancient rockfall had cleared the trees, the woods opened out to jagged boulders in a sloping pile to the cliff. The bloodhounds sniffed along the rocks but weren't satisfied. They pulled Horton south again, and then they stopped. Their jowls flopped; their long ears swung around for the scent. But Horton wasn't worried. Then Sappho and Monk circled decisively and bayed at the southern foot of the cliff.

"You'll find McGale and Riordan up on those rocks somewhere," Horton told the officers.

Carlson and Mullen paused for breath. Then they started climbing up the rock pile.

Bloodhounds. Whitey and McGale heard their baying echoing off the rocks, sounding like a hundred of the dogs. The fugitives were huddled in a crevice, nowhere near the mountaintop. It didn't matter—cops were probably all over that road by now, anyway. The dogs were after them, too, and getting closer. What else could they do but keep running until the end?

Whitey crept out, McGale behind him. They grabbed branches and hunched low as they tried to climb higher. Whitey's wristwatch showed a little after nine. His tongue was thick like a rag in his mouth—neither man had had any water since early the night before. A blurry sun was already steaming against the hillside, the temperature suddenly like July's. But the sunlight just illuminated the haze, made the woods softer, harder to focus on. They couldn't see anyone after them, and that scared them more. Maybe the cops were right behind them, or about to pop up in front. Even worse, the dogs' baying rose and fell, an echo that threw their cries up and down the mountainside.

So they did what they'd done on the streets all their lives, what they'd done all night on cinders and concrete. They tried to sneak. It might have worked in the city or the town, but what did they know about the woods? The fallen leaves and branches around their feet, the noise they made? You could get away down an alley, flat against the shadows of a brick wall, hop the fence at the end, and then you were gone. But trees and bushes? Forget it. They might as well be blowing trumpets.

And sure enough, Whitey took a step and cracked a branch. It sounded like another gunshot. He and McGale ducked into the underbrush.

————————

Mullen dropped to his knees, held up the back of his hand to Carlson and Horton. The trooper shushed his dogs. Mullen peered uphill about one hundred yards. A blond head ducked between some bushes. Mullen looked back at his companions, pointed, and nodded. Then he took a deep breath and shouted, "Stop where you are!"

Whitey and McGale didn't move. Unlikely, but maybe the voice was yelling at something else.

"Come down here," Mullen called again. "You're surrounded. You haven't a chance!"

The same voice, deep, and meaning it like every other cop's. Who the hell else were they talking to? Probably had them in their gun sights right now. "Okay, okay," Whitey called. "We'll come down, don't shoot!"

They tried to keep their hands up as they slipped and slid down the way they'd climbed. The posse emerged from the underbrush on a landing below the cliff, shotguns and Thompsons leveled. Some cops were holding back a red-faced Sing Sing guard, nobody Whitey or McGale knew. The police officers had the guard's arms pinned to his sides, his Colt revolver contained. A trooper in a raincoat, his ten-gallon hat stained with sweat and rain, held the bloodhounds on a tight leash—two dogs, that was all, barking and wagging their tails, happy as hell to see them. Sappho and Monk seemed to know the good work they'd done and were looking forward to their usual reward—a chocolate bar with almonds.

Just above the landing, McGale lost his footing; his arms pinwheeling, he rolled practically into the cops' arms. Whitey watched his partner disappear into a scrum. When they dragged him to his feet, his left cheek was scraped, and he was already manacled. Whitey kept his balance, though, showing his palms all the way down to them.

He was still on his feet when the first fists began to fall.

CHAPTER SIXTEEN

THE THIRD DEGREE

THE WHITE COAST GUARD CUTTER scored the blinding water as Whitey and McGale sat cross-legged on the bright metal deck. Their hands were pulled behind them and shackled to a railing. A posse glared. Sailor-capped Guardsmen, .45 automatics in white leather holsters; detectives in trench coats and neckties or the first clothes they had grabbed in the dark; cops in patent leather and dark blue wool. Everybody bloodshot and drawn, and in no kind of mood. Every now and then, somebody would swing a fist, and with any luck there was time to duck, flinch away at least. But the worst was the haze, the brightest morning in the world, it had to be, eyes squeezed tight and light still getting in, orange like a lit match.

After maybe a seven-minute voyage, Whitey and McGale were dragged ashore and thrown into the back of a police car. Flashbulbs popped the whole time, dozens of them. The newspapermen, dropping their cigarettes, finally had something to show for their long night waiting. One lucky photographer assigned to the Interstate Park Police got a shot of the capture, the beached fugitives with a smug-looking cop framed behind them. The picture catches the temper of the moment: a ramrod stoic McGale, and Whitey looking hang-dog as he always did when caught, his blond hair spiked in his face. But the agency staff photo revealed nothing compared to what awaited them in Ossining. All McGale's stickups and even the Shopping Bag robberies never earned this kind of attention. Apparently, they had to kill people to get the wide limelight. But they sure had everybody's interest now, especially the cops—they were rolling up their sleeves to show how much they cared.

A crowd was rustling at the Ossining police station. Townspeople shocked awake all night and outraged at the murders of Officers Fagan and Hartye heard the police car screaming up the hill and were eager to see the culprits. Chained together, Whitey and McGale had trouble climbing from the car. But three officers moved in, one grabbing Whitey by the forelock to pull him straight as he stumbled. The cop had him by the roots, but Whitey showed nothing, his face a blank. After a lifetime, he knew what came next; maybe he had to go deep down to face it. McGale, though, a head shorter than the circling strong-arms, was wide-eyed. He'd scuttled between the bigger boots stomping around him all his life, sometimes getting out of the way, most times not. The way they had a bigger guy like Whitey, though, this looked to be about the worst. The townsfolk, seeing action at last, yelled for more. But the prisoners were fast-walked through the police station's main entrance, the morning-bright sandstone facade like a slap in the eye.

It was cool and dark inside, and their eyes saw green. They were shoved through the foyer and into a back room. Black metal file drawers, bulging manila folders stacked on top of them; a sharp-cornered desk with a Bakelite telephone; the whole room musty and smelling of paper and ink. Crowded, too. Six detectives, some from the boat; a Sing Sing keeper, still uniformed from the night; a rumpled *Daily Mirror* photographer, reaching into a suit coat pocket, screwing a bulb into his camera's flash attachment. Then the keeper threw a fist, and McGale's head snapped back. He started going down.

Whitey tried to hold him up by the handcuffs on their wrists, but McGale had fallen against him. A detective's fist landed against Whitey's cheek, and he went down, too. The camera flashed.

"Stand up, what's the matter with you?"

The two were flattened against the file drawers as the detectives and the keeper swung in. The photographer kept snapping, unscrewing the hot bulbs, screwing in new ones, and flashing away. Punches were landing on Whitey's still expressionless face, on his body. A jackboot landed in McGale's groin, and he doubled, his eyes rolling white.

"Stop, here comes Gallagher."

The detectives scraped back, breathing hard and rolling their shoulders to adjust their suits as a natty Irishman entered. Westchester County District Attorney Elbert T. Gallagher was fresh to the power. He'd made his name six years ago as chief assistant D.A., prosecuting child sex-killer and cannibal Albert Fish. Gallagher had triumphantly watched Fish burn in Sing Sing's chair. Maybe these two cop killers would be next.

Gallagher stood there looking down at them, his wide forehead smooth, his blue eyes calm. But he wore a funny smile, slight and thinking, as though the wheels behind that empty slate were already turning.

He wanted to know if everything was all right.

Whitey said he slipped and started to get up. McGale was struggling, still bent, his breath retching.

What's your name, Gallagher asked of Whitey first, then McGale, his expression never changing. He knew, of course. He'd have been provided with their police and prison records before entering the room. He was just taking measurements, perhaps his opening statement to the jury outlining in his mind, even his summation arising.

They told him their names.

Gallagher nodded. He mentioned how much trouble they were in and glanced at the detectives. The State Police were taking control of the investigation, so the questioning would continue at the Hawthorne Barracks. Then he left the room.

The detectives pulled Whitey and McGale to their feet, propped them against the file drawers, told them to smile for the camera. The photographer took one last shot; the hunting party stone-faced with their game. The two were hustled back out into the sun and the waiting car, the crowd cheering the marks on their faces, the back of the cop car a glass and steel oven.

———————

Despite the pounding fists, Whitey and McGale's beating at the Ossining police station doesn't qualify as the infamous third degree. The term traces back to the Freemasons, circa 1772, denoting the intense questioning a Mason undergoes to achieve the rank of Master Mason, or Third

Degree. Within a hundred years, the phrase "third degree" became synonymous with tough interrogations, and by the twentieth century it was
applied almost solely to bare-knuckle police questioning. The Ossining
cops and Sing Sing guards, however, didn't care about getting answers
from Whitey and McGale. They simply thought the two suspected cop-
killers deserved a thorough battering. Their treatment in the Ossining
police station suggests another etymology, though, one that connects
harsh police methods to disfiguring third-degree burns—a metaphorical
scorching nearly down to the bone. That's what awaited them at the
hands of the State Police at Hawthorne Barracks.

Whitey and McGale caught their breath on the five-mile ride to the
Troop K barracks off Saw Mill Road. They didn't speak in the car, and
nobody said anything to them. They closed their eyes and let their heads
roll with the bumps in the road.

Inside the brick station house, someone produced a key and unlocked
the handcuffs. A couple of uniforms pulled McGale down one hallway
off the main desk. A state trooper in civilian clothes shoved Whitey down
the other. They put him in the station's photographic darkroom.

A very small room, with a ceramic sink and faucets in a black marble
countertop running along a wall without windows. Clothesline hung
from wall to wall above the counter. A chemical stink that stayed on your
clothes and in your hair. Hot. In the old days—say, thirty years before—
the barracks darkroom would have needed a potbellied stove burning a
mixture of trash, rubber, coal, and bones to be called a traditional sweat-
box. In 1941, at least in Hawthorne, the age-old technique of sweating
suspects had been modernized; fuming jars of acetic acid and potassium
bromide replaced the smoking stove. The trooper with Whitey took his
jacket off and hung it on a hook behind the door.

The door opened, and a man entered, his dark blue suit a slight cut
above the others.

Inspector, the state trooper said.

The inspector unbuttoned his suit coat, shook out of it, and hung it
over the trooper's jacket behind the door. He loosened his necktie, unbuttoned his collar, rolled his sleeves above his wrists. He stepped up to
Whitey. The inspector was taller, as cops always seemed to be. He stood

too close and ran his eyes over Whitey's face, peering down a long nose, as though he was deciding something.

"I don't know," he said at last. "You're a wise guy." He hit Whitey in the ribs, doubled him up, and threw another punch at Whitey's jaw. The inspector kept swinging rights and lefts, over and over. Whitey put his hands up, trying to cover his face and gut. When the inspector paused, the trooper stepped in and punched Whitey in the ribs. They didn't seem to like Whitey's trying to ward off the blows.

"This guy is too wise," the inspector breathed. "Get a pair of handcuffs."

The trooper opened a pair of handcuffs and snapped them onto Whitey's wrists. He held onto them as the inspector went back to work from the side, slower, more deliberately this time. Finally he stopped, took his suit coat off the hook, threw it over an arm, and closed the door behind him. Whitey slumped against the counter, alone with the trooper.

For the next half hour or so, troopers would walk in and out, throwing punches. Some officers were in uniform, some in plainclothes. Everybody seemed to want a piece of the infamous outlaw. Whitey had no choice, and he took it. It didn't matter. If he said something, he'd get hit. If he kept his mouth shut, he got hit. The procedure was almost a tradition. Only a few decades earlier, police routinely whaled on suspects with lengths of rubber hose and thick phone books. Suspects were shot up with drugs and hung out of windows by their ankles. The questioning would go on for days, without food or water or sleep. Any confession forced out of you at the end of the ordeal could be used against you in court. Whitey was lucky. The State Police were using only their fists. Eventually, they decided he was ready for the official interrogation.

In another room across the hall, District Attorney Gallagher perched on the edge of a wooden desk, his bland face serene. A couple of troopers put Whitey on a straight-backed chair before the desk, then stood by the door. A court reporter sat behind his Stenotype machine, a pair of glasses on the end of his nose. This room had windows, open to a summer breeze in April. Gallagher's smile was barely skin deep. "So tell us about this prison break," he asked, as though he wanted to know about Whitey's big promotion at work.

Whitey held his cuffed hands in his lap, his legs aching with relief. "I don't know nothing about this," he said.

Gallagher squeezed his eyes shut and beamed. "Tell us what happened," he nodded.

"I was in bed at the time when this keeper was shot."

"What do you mean you were in bed?"

"I was laying in bed and the next thing I knew I heard two shots. I knew there was to be a break but when I heard—"

Gallagher held up a palm and shook his head. He looked at the troopers, who lifted Whitey from the chair and brought him back across the hall into the dark room. The inspector was waiting. After only a couple of punches, Whitey began gagging.

"What's the matter?"

"You knocked my teeth down my throat." Whitey's bridgework, an upper and bottom partial, were choking him.

"Take them out before I knock them down your belly."

Whitey spit his dental plates into a trooper's handkerchief. The trooper slipped them into his coat pocket. Whitey asked for some water.

The trooper glanced at the darkroom sink, back at Whitey, and shook his head. "That water is no good; you can't drink it." He turned on the tap. When the water was nice and cold, he leaned over the sink and slurped from a cupped hand. "Anyway, it is no good for *you*," he said, straightening and wiping his mouth.

They took Whitey back to Gallagher, leaning against the desk, a yellow legal pad beside him. The district attorney kept referring to his notes as he spoke. Who shot Hartye? How long have you known McGale? Where did the car come from? How did the guns get inside? Who are Edward Kiernan and William Wade? Did you make the keys? Whose idea was it, anyway? Attuned to any hint of deception—flushed face, hesitancy, fidgeting—the troopers swooped in every time Whitey paused, practically carrying him back to the darkroom and the inspector's fists. After some threats and punches, it was back across the hall to Gallagher, cool and smooth in his light blue suit, his back to a breeze of fresh air through the window. Half the time, the stenographer lifted his fingers from the Stenotype and picked up a paperback, flipping through to where he left off, as Whitey continued denying he knew anything. In the darkroom again, even the inspector seemed to wear down and took a less physical tack. "If you tell us the names of the other fellows in this with you, I'll see to it you get a nice steak and a couple of glasses of beer."

The promise was another strategy. But Whitey couldn't even shake his head by then. "I was in bed before the shooting happened." His speech was loose and whistling without his teeth. He let his head fall. "It ain't going to make any difference in my life; I'll probably get the chair anyway." He looked up, his eyes swimming. "Do you want me to say I was there?" But he couldn't. All the times in his life when he'd lied; now here he was telling the truth, and nobody believed him. "I . . . wasn't in there when that man got shot—I was laying in bed."

Back out with Gallagher, sometime in the afternoon. The court reporter put down his book and waited. The district attorney set aside his notes and calmly regarded the prisoner drooping before him. Gallagher had an open-and-shut case, of that he was sure. Besides the physical evidence, there was powerful emotional value: beloved Old John Hartye murdered in cold blood, shot in the back; the community's fear of escaped convicts; Officer Fagan's grief-stricken young widow. But the D.A. had been around long enough to see such ironclad indictments picked apart by nimble defense lawyers. If the county prosecutor's office wasn't to be Gallagher's last stop, he'd have to avoid any mistakes. Gallagher looked at the abrasions on Whitey's hands.

"How did that happen?" the D.A. asked, as the stenographer tapped his black metal keys.

Whitey glanced down. His hands, manacled on his lap, were burned raw. "Sliding down a rope."

Gallagher nodded, then took note of Whitey's cheeks and mouth. "Your face is pretty well bunged up, isn't it?"

"Yes."

"How'd that happen?"

"I fell down a mountain when I was on the other side."

"Nobody touched you, did they?"

"No sir."

"Anything you say here, you are making of your own free will and

accord?" Gallagher heard the Stenotype clicking the words into the official record.

"That is right," Whitey nodded. He hadn't much, but there was that—
the West Side code against squealing, running too deep for their fists
to reach.

Whitey couldn't even rat out a cop.

———————

The police beat all four of them, of course—suspects in the murders of
two lawmen, no one expected they'd receive anything less—despite the
illegality of the third degree. This was twenty-five years before *Miranda
v. Arizona*—the famous 1966 U.S. Supreme Court decision guaranteeing
a suspect's right to remain silent and to an attorney—and law enforcement was deep in the new wilderness of suspect rights. Only four years
before Whitey, McGale, Kiernan, and Wade were brought into custody,
the Supreme Court in 1937 had handed down its first decision on the
unconstitutionality of coerced confessions. The law said they violated the
Sixth Amendment against due process. Just the year before, in 1940, the
Court had extended that violation to include confessions based on sleep
deprivation. Clearly, District Attorney Gallagher was aware of all that.

But as long as the D.A. didn't *see* anyone getting hit or kicked, he
could plausibly deny being witness to any brutality. And as long as the
transcripts contained suspects' assurances that their statements were vol-
untary, the law was satisfied. Gallagher would still have to deal with the
bruises and lacerations on both Wade and Kiernan. Not to mention the
Daily Mirror photographer snapping flash pictures of Whitey and
McGale ducking punches at the Ossining station house. But the D.A.
would worry about all that later. In an important case like this, a beating—an official third degree—was sometimes the only way to get tough
guys to talk. Besides, if the townsfolk outside the police station were any
measure, public opinion was on his side.

The method, though, was inexact. As the fists fell through the day in
another part of the barracks, for instance, Billy Wade's story was sounding pretty convoluted. He and Kiernan had been kept at the Ossining
police station all night. They'd been surrounded by commotion as the

cops investigated Fagan's murder and sought Whitey and McGale. But when the getaway car was found, and the taxi driver was questioned again, Wade and Kiernan were brought to the State Police barracks. And their real troubles began.

First, Wade told the D.A. the story he had given Officer Kelly—the Ossining cop who arrested him and Kiernan—about the two pickups Betty and Peggy. How he and Kiernan had argued with the girls, and how they'd taken Wade's car and left him and Kiernan flat in Ossining. But then Gallagher asked about the car registration Wade had shown Kelly. Why was it made out to a fellow named Arkin—what was that all about? Wade tried to explain that he'd just bought the car the girls had stolen—that very night, as a matter of fact—from a fellow he'd met in a West Side bar. Gallagher held up a palm, shook his head, and the troopers dragged Wade back to the inspector before he could finish.

The inspector seemed to delight in Wade's twists and turns. He told the troopers guarding Wade not to damage his face. "That's going to be my pleasure," he smiled and then went to work, splitting Wade's lip, blacking his eye, boxing his ears.

Still, the slightly built Wade held his own. When he refused to deviate from the Betty and Peggy story, the inspector ordered Wade taken out back. The old State Police stables were behind the barracks house.

A record-breaking heat, 84-plus degrees, when they pushed Wade ahead of them across the concrete and into the animal dark. The lights hanging from the pitched roof showed abandoned stalls, ancient hay moldering on the floor. Somebody wove a yellow rope into a noose, slipped it around Wade's wrists, threw the loose end over a rafter, and leaned back. Wade was pulled to his tiptoes, and he began to scream.

"Gag that bum," the inspector said, "he's disturbing the D.A."

A trooper shoved a rag into Wade's mouth, and they started hitting him about the body. Eventually, they pulled the rag out and asked if he was ready to talk.

"I'll say anything you want," he pleaded. "I didn't come up on no break, but I'll tell you anything."

He'd admit to killing Lincoln, one trooper joked. But as long as it was on the record, that was good enough for the inspector and his men. Wade answered everything they asked him—but it took a noose to finally loosen his tongue.

———

By the early evening of April 14, New York City police had scoured the North River docks, Piers 83 and 84 at the end of West Forty-third and West Forty-fourth Streets. "We want to talk to anyone who ever had any connection of any kind with the old Shopping Bag gang," a detective told a *Journal and American* reporter. The police believed that the crash out had been "hatched" in Hell's Kitchen, possibly with mob support, but there weren't many members of the old gang left. David "The Beetle" Beadle, Whitey's old dock boss who'd taken his percentage of the robberies, was dead. So was Patches Waters. Whitey and Wade were in custody. Rusty Mello and Mac Hanley were in Clinton prison, up in Dannemora. Willie the Greek was also imprisoned upstate, and Lulu was in Rikers on an extortion charge. The gang was finished. The New York cops had to content themselves with rounding up Whitey's brothers, John and Andrew; his childhood pal, Johnny Clinton, the ex-boxer, longshoreman, and offspring of the Kitchen's notorious Clinton-Sheehan gang; and Tommy Waters, a loyal visitor to Whitey at Sing Sing.

Irish Johnny Clinton, a material witness in an unrelated murder case linked to the gang war started by Davie Beadle's killing, had nothing at all to add to the Sing Sing break. He was friendly with John Riordan, but he hadn't seen Whitey in a long time. Tommy Waters said, sure, he visited Whitey—he liked the guy, so what? But Tommy Waters was no relation to Patches, and that was easy enough to prove.

The inspector was undeterred. He threatened to throw Whitey's brothers in prison if Whitey didn't come clean. Both John and Andrew were on years-long parole for adolescent thieving and had been keeping out of trouble. They had steady jobs on the docks, were taking care of their mother, and were thinking of raising families. Prison would have ruined them.

Whitey was stuck with the truth. He didn't know who else was involved; he knew nothing of the plan; he'd only gone along in the last few weeks.

But he wanted it over.

Just before seven o'clock that evening, Whitey signed a written statement. He admitted to being involved in the break, which automatically meant complicity in Officer Hartye's murder. McGale signed his statement shortly after. Once the police had their statements, and it was clear that the four men they'd rounded up had nothing to do with the break and even less to do with the Shopping Bag Gang, the men were released.

Whitey and McGale were brought back to police court at the Ossining station house handcuffed to Fagan's partner, bespectacled Officer Nelson. Nelson was limping by then from a broken bone in his foot, injured while chasing the fugitives up Hook Mountain. But he was stoked on pain and rage. He'd see these sons-of-bitches arraigned before he took a seat. Police judge Vincent Fuller obliged.

Besides the many policemen and newspaper reporters, over twenty picture boys crowded around the bench, their flashbulbs strobe-like in the small courtroom. Above a *Daily News* photo caption on the next day's front page, "End of Desperate Break," a bedraggled McGale stares out from under his brows. Whitey, just behind him with a bruise on his cheek, has found an expression at last: bitter and defiant. Also caught in the hot glare, Warden Lewis Lawes stands to the judge's right and slightly behind the bench. He is somber in a dark suit, and his jowls look freshly shaved. He tilts back his head and casts his eyes sidelong at the complaint on the judge's desk.

So many questions the warden had yet to answer; perhaps he dreaded glimpsing his name there, too.

CHAPTER SEVENTEEN

"LOOK OUT WARDEN"

HE WAS A DRAMATIST; he knew a climax when he saw one. This was his—sound music, roll credits. Thank God he was still healthy, just shy of fifty-eight. There was plenty else he wanted to do. Offers came in almost daily, for books, for articles, for radio appearances; he had to turn down most of them, there were so many. But maybe the time had come to sweep back another velvet curtain. Hadn't he been complaining about so little time to write? His bio-picture, with Bogey in the lead? Well, it looked as if Lawes would get his wish after all. If this was his finale, though, Warden Lawes was hearing little applause.

Albany was eager to know how the hell such a colossal misjudgment could have occurred. Corrections Commissioner John A. Lyons ordered Lawes to conduct an immediate investigation, and he expected a report, complete with intended improvements and safeguards, on his desk "without unnecessary delay." The Ossining police commissioner also demanded an explanation as to why "Ossining Police were not notified by telephone of the escape." The statement's text was printed on page two of the *Citizen Register* for everyone in town to read. And then there was the warden's personal dismay. Officers Hartye and Fagan; inmates Waters and Miller: four dead. Guns smuggled in right under their noses. The warden was questioned and derided by the state and local lawmen— practically a laughingstock. Shocked that any of his "boys" would betray him like this. The situation needed more than simple damage control. If the warden was going to avoid retiring in complete disgrace, he'd have to summon all his public relations skills.

His secretary, Clement Ferling, quickly telephoned a local reporter at the *Citizen Register*. The warden had an official statement. Interested? Quite simply, Warden Lawes told the reporter, the police "were not notified immediately" because the "machinery at the prison failed to function." Vital time was lost while Sergeant Darrow, the night supervisor, tried to reach the officers in the hospital. DeSimone was "locked in the building and we had to get to him before we knew what had happened. As soon as we contacted him, he said the men had run into the basement." Furthermore, Lawes claimed, "as soon as we found that they had gotten out and that they had killed Guard Hartye, police were notified." The reporter, with his notes collected around him, must have scratched his head at the warden's inconsistencies.

First off, DeSimone was handcuffed in the basement, right beside the steam vault entrance. Didn't he tell the warden that the fugitives had gone through the tunnel? Moreover, Lawes knew the men were armed the moment Sergeant Darrow awakened him by telephone and told him that Hartye had been shot dead. Lawes saw the officer's bullet-riddled body. Shouldn't that have been enough to call the local police? But the reporter didn't ask. He just scribbled down the warden's version for the townsfolk to decipher. When all the reports were put together, it appeared that the warden had relied on his twenty years of experience that night, rather than on his own eyes or the statements of firsthand witnesses, one of them a uniformed guard. Lawes had presumed the men were still inside the walls—as nearly all missing men turned out to be. The warden was clear about one thing, though. For some time now he had "tried in vain to get a boat—but it was too late when we did get one." In fact, he'd been pestering the state for years that Sing Sing, a waterfront prison, needed a patrol boat. But he'd never gotten the appropriation.

Lawes's official statement did little to quell the growing controversy. Meanwhile, the warden issued a blizzard of internal memos over the next few days. He wrote to Principal Keeper Sheehy, to the officers on Posts 12 through 18, and to those assigned to the visiting room. He wrote also to the chief engineer, to the storekeeper, to Dr. Sweet at the hospital, and to others. Two dozen memos in all. They covered everything from the thorough search and cataloging of all delivery trucks and their drivers; to randomly challenging inmates in the yard to show their passes; to frisking all inmates upon their return from the yard; to issuing identification photographs for all trusties with jobs outside the enclosure; to the distribution and collection of every tool; to the weekly—no, make that *daily*—checking and rechecking of all utility tunnels in the institution. In fact, when the warden got right down on his hands and knees and took a really close look, he saw that an awful lot of play had come into the system over the years and had loosened it up. Well, all that would change. He might be on his way out, but, by God, the next fellow coming in wouldn't have grounds to complain about the way Warden Lewis Lawes had left the place.

The steam vault exit that Charlie McGale had so completely chipped free was immediately welded shut. An illuminated pit was constructed in the stockade, from which a guard could thoroughly inspect all vehicle undercarriage. A mechanically handy guard, who Lawes believed could be trained to become the facility's locksmith, was found at last, replacing the inmate trusty. Visitor fingerprinting was extended to the inmates' families, "with the possible exception of a mother," the warden allowed. And most important to Sing Sing's neighbors, a system was established for sounding the prison siren. Ossining police and the State Police would be notified whenever "a man or men are missing from the count." But Big Ben would sound *only* when anyone had actually escaped. It seemed a practical compromise to Lawes. There was no admission of wrongdoing, and the procedure differed little from the previous policy. This communication just articulated it better, put it in black and white.

Lawes completed his report to Commissioner Lyons by the last week of April. Citing institutional weaknesses while deflecting blame for them away from himself, Lawes cast Sing Sing as a "medium security prison, attempting to function as a maximum security prison." The structural faults included the "cheap, low fence" along the riverfront; the "weak and inefficient" entrances to the Administration and 5 Buildings; and the railroad tracks dividing the facility. His litany of personal grievances outlined a career-long dispute over appropriations with the state legislature, where, Lawes believed, "the responsibility should be placed." The state kept sending inmates to Lawes, he complained, even though Attica, Auburn, Clinton, and Green Haven "are all structurally secure," certainly more so than Sing Sing, which he said was "an insecure plant, badly designed and poorly located." In contrast to *Twenty-Thousand Years in Sing Sing,* which was stuffed with the bright details of his proud achievement in prison renovation, the April report on the '41 break condemns the facility that he himself had rebuilt and fortified over the decades.

It had been a sweaty couple of weeks. There was local criticism, as well as an anonymous letter to the warden's office. Even a tiny paragraph in the *Citizen Register* seemed unnecessarily snide. Headlined "LOOK OUT WARDEN," the piece warned that inmates denied sleep for two nights because of the breakout were threatening to picket the warden's office. Striking convicts? That sounded an awful lot like coddling. The warden's generosity had become a mean joke. But Lawes also had his backers. His wife Elise, of course. Also, a petition was circulating through the prison, gathering page after page of officers' signatures in support of their boss. His wife and family beside him and the firm backing of his men inspired Lawes. He'd weather this, he knew he would; and then he'd move on.

The very week of the break, as a matter of fact, as the warden authorized prisonwide investigations and hurried to and from funerals—Officer Fagan's at St. Augustine's in Ossining, the largest requiem for a policeman Westchester County had ever seen; then down to St. Ann's in the Bronx for Guard Hartye—Lawes also found time to negotiate his show-business future. On April 15, the day after the break, Frank Cooper of the General Amusement Corporation in Rockefeller Center wrote to Lawes wondering if the warden was "available to do a radio program . . . [something] similar to the one you did before." Lawes penned right back. He had "some excellent material for radio presentation." Despite the "considerable fireworks" of the past few days, the warden invited Mr. Cooper up to Sing Sing to take a look at the "tremendous amount of very fine material" that the warden had collected. Three days later a deal was inked—General Amusement Inc. was Lawes's new agent for radio work.

The warden might have paused to reflect on his timing. But he had his family's future to consider. He wasn't going to second-guess luck where business was concerned—he was looking forward to being back on the air. Thanks to his writing and speaking schedule, Warden Lawes would be able to make his own way out of Sing Sing, just in the nick of time. He would tender his resignation to Commissioner Lyons as soon as Whitey Riordan and Charles McGale were tried for murder.

———————

The Sing Sing break was a high-profile case, and New York City's crime-busting district attorney, Thomas E. Dewey, weighed in. By the spring of '41, he was a national star with a Republican presidential try under his belt—at the age of thirty-seven—and a popular radio show, *Mr. District Attorney,* inspired by his derring-do. Publicity-savvy Dewey couldn't resist commenting while the flashbulbs popped around Whitey and McGale. He was in the middle of an investigation into corruption on the New York waterfront—the first city D.A. to use hidden cameras in a criminal probe—and probably hoped to find a West Side link to the crash out. Dewey had prosecuted the Shopping Bag robberies, he told the scribbling newsmen, and he knew the character of these desperadoes. In comparison with the big names he'd gone after—crooks like Lucky Luciano, Dutch Schultz, and Harlem Tammany boss Jimmy Hines—Whitey and McGale were the "worst criminals" ever brought to justice by his busy office.

And from their reception at the county courthouse in White Plains, a week after the break, you'd have thought the bedraggled remnants of the Shopping Bag Gang were Dillinger's own men. They were escorted two at a time by transport van from the Westchester County Penitentiary in Eastview to their plea hearings, their hands shackled to thick leather belts buckled around their waists. A carload of six sheriff's deputies, armed with shotguns and machine guns, followed close behind. Reporters and photographers pressed around the courthouse entrance in the glaring sun, jotting and snapping away. First Whitey and Wade, then Kiernan and McGale, in rumpled prison grays—unshaved, uncombed, unwashed, without socks on their feet or laces in their shoes—shambled before county judge Frank Coyne. Whitey's and McGale's hands were still bandaged from the rope burns suffered a week earlier; Kiernan and Wade were still bruised and cut. They kept their heads bowed and spoke so low that Westchester County District Attorney Gallagher, looking sharp in his summer suit, had to lean in to hear their mumbled "not guilty." Only Wade said he had retained his own counsel.

Lucky Wade. Attorney Henry Lowenberg of New York City was a street-smart criminal lawyer who had successfully sprung Wade two years before from all charges related to the Shopping Bag spree. Lowenberg avoided the limelight; at least he managed to duck the photographers mobbing the courthouse entrance. But he can probably best be envisioned from the case notes he left behind—scratched with a sharp pencil in a spiky hand, the yellow legal pages smudged and redolent of stale cigarette smoke sixty-two years later—and in the vigorous, tenacious defense he mounted. Seeing the magic that Lowenberg had worked for Wade and might work again, Whitey wrote to the attorney pleading for representation. Lowenberg even drove up to Eastview to talk it over with Whitey, tell him what his fee would be.

Never before in such dire need of a good lawyer, Whitey immediately got in touch with his mother. But Elizabeth Riordan scuttled all hope. She was at her rope's end with her middle son—the many visits to Sing Sing to keep his spirits up, only to see him caught up in the worst disaster of his life. Not to mention that he almost dragged his brothers into his troubles, just when they were doing so well. And now he wanted a private attorney? She had sacrificed her life for her children after her husband died; she was a loving mother who had done all she could. Now she told Whitey plainly that "she didn't have no money."

Whitey didn't give up and asked the court to assign Lowenberg to him. But the lawyer, estimating the caseload, told the court he'd already been retained by Wade. The lawyer probably recognized Wade's as the stronger case. No documentation linked Wade to the breakout, for instance, but Whitey's faked illness was noted on the hospital admittance sheet. Besides, Whitey had confessed being in the hospital when Officer Hartye's murder occurred. Moreover, the recently fired revolver in Whitey's possession when he was captured had three empty chambers.

Lowenberg passed on the long shot and told the court he "wasn't interested" in representing Whitey. Instead, the judge assigned Gerald
FitzGerald of Tarrytown to Whitey. A former president of the Westchester County Bar Association, FitzGerald was now playing the role of
public defender.

Another New York lawyer, Herbert Rosenberg of lower Broadway,
showed up in White Plains seeking a writ of habeas corpus and demand-
ing that Eddie Kiernan be released immediately. Rosenberg told the
court that he'd been given the runaround when trying to interview Kiernan. First he went to Ossining, then he was sent to Hawthorne, and
finally he tracked the proceedings down to White Plains. D.A. Gallagher
smelled a shark—the kind of mouthpiece who hung around the night
court, looking for work when the waterfront racketeers were paraded
through. Gallagher believed the West Side was full of lawyers like that,
their wallets full of mob cash. The D.A. wouldn't stand for that kind of
interference in his bailiwick, and he demanded to know who had hired
Rosenberg. Defendant Kiernan had said he'd "never heard of him" and
didn't have any money anyway. The New York attorney refused to
respond, even when Gallagher threatened to bring him before the grand
jury "with the other defendants." When the D.A. and Rosenberg
appeared in the judge's chambers, and the judge also questioned Rosenberg about the mysterious retainer, Rosenberg withdrew his application
and drove back home to the city.

Having won that display of public muscle, Gallagher was ready to
proceed. He wanted a speedy trial, within a month. The public demanded
swift justice for such cold-blooded crimes. He'd like this matter wrapped
up by summer, if possible. Judge Coyne granted his wish. Within days a
grand jury was convened. First-degree murder indictments were handed
down in the killing of Officer Hartye, and jury selection got underway.
The second murder, Fagan's death, wasn't prosecuted; the men could be
executed only once.

Gallagher may have brushed off the questionable Rosenberg, but the
defense attorneys arrayed against the D.A. weren't about to leave town so
quickly. Gritty Henry Lowenberg was the only attorney hired privately,

took the lead in a battery of vigorous pretrial arguments, challenging the D.A. every step of the way. In a daily, nicotine-fueled resistance, he objected to Gallagher's juror choices, moving to dismiss the entire panel. He then motioned for a mistrial, citing a complicated, little-known Court of Appeals ruling. He didn't succeed, yet nevertheless flustered the court.

Lowenberg was just warming up. He charged that his client had been beaten in police custody for twenty to twenty-four hours, and he demanded a private medical examination for Wade, out of sight of the prosecution. He accused the *Citizen Register* of Ossining and the *Herald Statesman* of Yonkers of "so inflaming the public mind" with sensational news stories and editorials that a fair trial was impossible, and he insisted that a change of venue should be granted. When that failed, he unsuccessfully moved to try Wade separately from the other defendants.

Slowly constructing the centerpiece of his defense, Lowenberg stated that Wade's "bloodstained" clothes had "literally been torn from his body"; then Kiernan's lawyer claimed that *his* client's suit also was "ripped from his body and . . . spattered with blood." The defense lawyers accused Gallagher of illegally withholding the clothing as evidence. Wade's sister Marion Emmet even got into the act. A tough little brunette who had spent much of her life sheltering the wayward baby of the family, she pleaded with the court to allow her to bring Wade a presentable suit of clothes, instead of the county prison uniform. Wade, however, refused his sister's offer, possibly hoping his daily appearances in prison garb would win him sympathy from the jury.

The other three defendants—Whitey, McGale, and Kiernan—sat together in court, blinking at the motions and countermotions flying back and forth between the attorneys' tables and the bench. None of them had been in this much trouble before—facing the death penalty for the first-degree murder of Guard Hartye—and they were clearly out of their depth. But by this point they'd been scrubbed up, at least. According to the *Citizen Register,* Kiernan looked especially "natty [in a] gray-green suit and matching tie," McGale's light gray flannel bagged around his ankles, and Whitey, wearing a dark blue sweater and trousers, must have been sweltering in the summer-like heat. Only the stubborn Wade, in the county's blue and white striped fatigues, looked the part of a reckless criminal.

When court recessed, they were led back to the holding pen, where they dined on ham-and-egg sandwiches, coffee, and cake. After lunch they'd deal a deck of cards and chat with one another or with the guards beyond the bars. These were familiar surroundings, and this was what you did—had lawyers do your talking and got fed at the state's expense. Not all that much had changed, except the life and death part. That was new and different.

Local anticipation for the impending trial was high; newsmen and photographers continued to cluster around the courthouse. The public was barred from the pretrial motions, but crowds gathered outside for a glimpse of the killers, jostling with reporters for shady spots against the building as the afternoons turned hot. A group of young women from nearby Edgewood Park Junior College, in the courthouse to audit a case in a nearby room, gasped upon seeing the chained defendants escorted down the hall. That close to the infamous desperadoes, they groaned in disappointment when they were denied admittance to the trial. A Bronx inventor roamed the courthouse halls, claiming to anyone who'd listen that he could save the county the cost of the trial. He buttonholed Medical Examiner Amos O. Squires coming out of the courtroom and mentioned his discovery of a "secret method" for determining a murderer's guilt by photographing the victim. As Squires rolled his eyes behind his thick glasses, looking for a way out, the inventor apologized for not having his own camera but said he was sure he could borrow a camera from one of the newsmen to prove his theory. As the inventor rushed off to find a reporter, Squires fled down the hall in the other direction.

And just in case anyone thought the proceedings lacked sufficient drama, the prickly Lowenberg outdid even himself. Leaning in on a prospective juror during voir dire, the attorney suddenly swayed in the stifling courtroom, his tobacco-yellow fingers gripping the jury box railing. Judge Coyne, with a cold glance at the fainting lawyer, told the bailiffs to "keep a sharp eye" on the defendants, just in case. Lowenberg collapsed to the floor, and the audience jumped to its feet, reporters penciling madly. The judge called a recess, as gallant Gallagher rushed in and helped his adversary to his feet, steadying him down the hall to a chair and some cool water in the D.A.'s office. For sheer fireworks, Wade was certainly getting his money's worth.

————

On the opening day of testimony, spectators crowded the gallery. Newsmen crammed into the front rows, balancing notebooks and pencils on crossed knees. Whitey, McGale, Wade, and Kiernan sat side by side at a long table in front of the bench, between the prosecution and defense tables. A burly, armed deputy was seated behind each man. The room's windows were open to the humid June air.

Gallagher rightly anticipated Lowenberg and his defense. The D.A.'s opening statement tackled the brutality issue head-on. What else could he do? The *Daily Mirror* had splashed those photographs all over the paper, so many shots one after the other that you could almost flip the pages quickly and watch the beating swing to life—the defendants' bruises and bandages were still plain as day. The defense's only strength was attacking the signed confessions as products of a police third degree. Yes, Gallagher admitted to the jury, Riordan and McGale *were* beaten at the Ossining police station. A detective and a Sing Sing guard had indeed thrown punches—but, adhering to a strict definition, Gallagher told the court that "the proof would show" that the beating wasn't intended to obtain confessions and therefore wasn't the third degree. Gallagher was playing to a sympathetic public by suggesting—but not actually saying—that the police and guards, understandably outraged at the murder of their fellow officers, had been letting off steam. He'd let the sworn denials of the state policemen, scheduled for another day, drive home the point.

After lunch, Whitey's public defender, Gerald FitzGerald, cleared his throat and rose to his feet. He buttoned his jacket over his belly, ran fingers through his white forelock, and faced the jury. He dropped his voice for effect. "We admit everything about the escape," FitzGerald said, "but we will show there was no premeditated murder on the part of Riordan in this case." He had rehearsed his statement for weeks, until the rusty

gestures were well oiled. It must have felt good to the old barrister to be
back arguing such an important case, no matter how hopeless it appeared
on its face. "Waters was the brains and the leader, he made the plan that
dovetailed. I say Waters was the brains," FitzGerald thundered, his voice
rising like a Shakespearean actor's, "and he was the man who killed the
Keeper, and that Riordan took no active part in the preparation of these
plans or the shooting." He paused to sip some water and continued more
quietly, his voice conversational and intimate. He let the jury in on a
secret—Riordan was in bed when the shooting occurred. Yes, FitzGerald
admitted, "Riordan made a mistake." "That mistake was getting up from
bed. He should have stayed in bed." Everybody makes mistakes, FitzGerald seemed to suggest, holding the jury's gaze. Any statements by the
defendant to the contrary, the lawyer said, turning away and declaiming,
were "beaten out of him."

Despite the theatrics, McGale, Wade, and Kiernan listened impas-
sively, their cuffed hands folded in their laps. Only Whitey showed any
reaction, his cheeks reddened, his forehead wrinkled in a frown. FitzGerald's corny antics were sinking him, his anguished face seemed to say.

When Wade's attorney Lowenberg rose to begin his opening statement, everyone in the courtroom sat up, wondering if the woozy lawyer
would stay on his feet. But the rested Lowenberg sucked sustenance from
a pack of Camels and had regained his strength. He stuck firmly to the
third-degree angle, noting how Gallagher's case against Wade fell apart
when one considered the medical evidence. Yes, waving some files,
Lowenberg had proof. Here was a medical report from a "jail physician,"
experienced in detecting such things, as well as one from a private doctor,
hired by the defendant. The marks on Wade's body and on his face were
not self-inflicted but the result of a severe police beating. How can any
statement he gave in custody be believed?

The trial lasted five weeks. The hot weather that had dawned on
Hook Mountain back in April intensified through June. At the end of
each day, sheriff's deputies took to hosing down the transport van in the
cement lot out back before driving the men back to Eastview, ten minutes
away. The prosecution examined forty-one witnesses. The defense called
less than a quarter of that figure. The court transcripts filled four thick,

bound volumes, five if you count the photographic exhibits—everything from Guard Hartye's naked, stitched-up body, to a massive foldout blueprint of Ossining's Depot Plaza.

As the prosecution anticipated, the police witnesses downplayed or completely denied any brutality. The inspector in particular rejected the argument that he'd "laid a hand" on Wade. The Sing Sing personnel who testified, notably the visiting room guard, and especially the officer at the front gate, Harry Effenberger, understandably minimized their responsibility for any security lapse. Warden Lawes, the man in charge of Sing Sing, was never called to testify. He'd been examined during the grand jury hearing, and his statement was admitted into the record. Perhaps believing that the state had sufficient evidence, or maybe in deference to his position, the D.A. did not subpoena him.

Gertrude Carlson, Patches's trusting sweetheart, appeared as a material witness after being rounded up shortly after the escape. She wasn't charged with the crime of aiding and abetting, though she was likely threatened with indictment unless she cooperated. She'd been cooling her heels at Eastview for seven weeks when she was finally called to the stand in mid-June. Gert sat folded in on herself, her shoulders hunched. She was pale and drawn, her voice faint. Bailiffs stood ready with glasses of water.

As fragile as she looked, though, Gertrude held her own. She was savvy enough to testify to what she knew *they* already knew: how many times she visited Waters as his wife, how many times she went alone, and how many times she shared a train ride with Kiernan. When the questions had to do with any arrangements she might have made with Kiernan as to what name he would use, or whether she ever saw Patches's friend Robert Brown or longshoreman Charles Bergstrom in the visiting room, Gert answered with a steady, "I don't remember." And when the D.A. tried to get her to talk about Patches's relationship with both Robert Brown and Charles Bergstrom and asked if Patches had ever threatened to "harm" them, Gert replied firmly, "No."

But the real drama came from the sparring between Gallagher and the accused men. Each one except Kiernan took the stand in his own defense. To start, D.A. Gallagher zeroed in on Wade with a merciless cross-examination, after which he read the sixty-three-page confession Wade had made to police. But the glowering little redhead was adamant in his story of coercion. He ticked off on his fingers a precise catalog of abuse—he was struck 600 times, kicked 300 times, knocked down 100 times, hit over the head with shoes 25 times, and strung up by the wrists 15 times. The reporters in the gallery tallied it up in their notebooks and telephoned it in to their editors. Smooth-faced Gallagher, though, looked on unimpressed.

Henry Lowenberg realized that he couldn't sell the Betty and Peggy pickup story that Wade had told the police. So the gutsy attorney simply changed it. Instead of a complicated story about a bad date, Lowenberg told an equally fantastic tale about a mistaken car sale. Wade and Kiernan hadn't gone to Ossining on a tryst; they'd gone up to get their refund on an automobile that had been wrongfully sold to them. The fact that this trip just happened to coincide with the night their former partners in crime were busting out from the Big House didn't faze the brassy lawyer.

When McGale took the stand, he seemed to blossom in the limelight. At last he had a platform from which to show off his expertise, and the cunning Gallagher drew him out. When questioned about the lock-smithing, McGale straightened up, his voice strong so everyone could hear how clever he'd been. In exquisite detail, McGale explained what he'd done and how he'd done it. The detail was so exact that Gallagher got lost referring to all the scratched, homemade keys, and to the technical differences between the Yale and Sargent door locks and padlocks lined up on the exhibit table. The D.A. pointed. This is a Yale lock, and this is a Yale key. McGale shook his head, no, that is a Sargent. And this one here is a Yale? That is a Sargent also. They are both Sargents? No, that one's a Yale. The jury giggled, and even craggy Judge Coyne had to smile.

Charlie McGale was in his glory. Finally, he could talk about his handiwork; everyone wanted to hear. He took his time and instructed the court, taught them how you go about finessing the mechanics of a mur-derous breakout. All his life, he'd been pushed around by the Army, or the cops, or his probation officer—people with jobs and rank, in uniforms and suits and ties, all these good fine folks telling him what to do and when to do it. And now look, they didn't know zip about what it really meant to survive, what a man needed to do if his back was against the wall. They didn't know how smart you had to be to survive a place like Sing Sing. Well, *this* was how smart. And all the while, the jury watched and listened, and the court reporter calmly tapped down every word into the record.

Whitey Riordan did not consider taking the stand as any shining moment. He jousted with Gallagher, but there wasn't much spirit in his fight. The daring bandit from the Con Ed robbery trial, "with a visage so hard and a gaze so frightening," as the *Herald Tribune* put it, that he'd made a witness against him weak-kneed, had been replaced by a sullen lout with white socks prominent beneath his high-riding cuffs. Whitey told the D.A. that he'd never been on the stand before, trying to make it sound as if this were his first time in a courtroom. When Gallagher questioned him about who had set the "hot car" at the train station, Whitey furrowed his brow and said dumb-faced that he didn't understand the term—do you mean like a car that's on fire? Maybe he was hoping for some of that laughter from the jury that McGale had gotten—but the joke fell flat, and nobody cracked a smile.

Whitey stuck to his guns, though. He'd joined the escape plot only a few weeks before the break, and he was in bed when the shots rang out. Anything else was beaten out of him at police headquarters. Whitey also estimated the number of times he was hit, Gallagher leading him through it, pointing out fluctuations in the score. The totals were comparable to Wade's, but by then, nobody seemed to care that the men had been struck.

FitzGerald tirelessly pressed on, flourishing Whitey's broken dentures before the jury and entering them into evidence as proof of brutality. He then solemnly asked Whitey if anything was different about them. Well, Whitey said, turning the yellowed porcelain over in his hands, they're dirtier. I cleaned them every day, he said, handing them back, as if it were a point of pride with him.

But even if Whitey might have cringed at his counsel's old-fashioned approach, the white-haired barrister managed to lay some solid groundwork. He got Guard Matteo DeSimone and prison nurse David Kaplan to testify that Whitey had saved their lives in the hospital basement.

DeSimone quoted word for word Whitey's assurances that the guard wouldn't be hurt if he cooperated; and Kaplan told the jury, in his thick German accent, how Whitey argued Waters out of killing them both. Whitey could only hope that would be enough to save his life.

————————

After five weeks, the case went to the jury. Judge Coyne, anticipating a quick verdict, held the court open into the evening. But as the hours ticked by, that hope faded. The jurors wanted another look at the exhibits—the defendant statements, the guns, the keys and locks. Then they needed a rereading of the degrees of homicide, as well as statements of witness credibility. By nine o'clock, the forewoman came back from the deliberation room, bleary-eyed and pale, requesting the judge to call it a day. He did.

Midmorning on June 27, refreshed from a night's sleep and breakfast at the Roger Smith Hotel in White Plains, the jury had their verdict. The lawyers stood, the deputies dropped their cigarettes and escorted the defendants into the courtroom from the holding cell, and the newsmen waited. The forewoman read off the counts in a clear strong voice. Billy Wade and Eddie Kiernan were found guilty of aiding escape and received life imprisonment. Whitey Riordan and Charles McGale were found guilty of first-degree murder and sentenced to death by electrocution. Deputies immediately led the four out back to the transport van and drove them to Sing Sing. By lunchtime, Wade and Kiernan were processed into the prison's general population.

But Whitey and McGale were locked into a different sphere—New York State's Death House, Sing Sing's isolated and completely self-contained "prison within a prison."

CHAPTER EIGHTEEN

THE DANCE HALL

TRUE TO HIS WORD, Warden Lawes submitted his resignation to Commissioner Lyons, "effective at the close of business July 15th." As the day approached, Lawes arranged to speak with a reporter from the *Citizen Register.* Cigars were offered, and smoke soon drifted through the air. Leaning back in his chair the warden seemed relieved, as if a stone had been lifted from his shoulders. He told the newsman how he'd been thinking about retiring "for a long time," had even discussed the matter with the commissioner a year ago. Lawes didn't mention the breakout or the recently concluded murder trial. He didn't need to—it was the elephant in the room.

The commissioner's report on the Sing Sing break, to be released a month after Lawes's retirement (conveniently avoiding any appearance of quid pro quo), would find "no maladministration" on the outgoing warden's part. Acknowledging institutional "weaknesses," the report outlined the steps Lawes took to remedy them. Despite the deadliest breakout in Sing Sing's history, with initial evidence pointing to the warden's mistakes, Lawes was exonerated. Besides his $6,000 annual pension, the vindication seemed a reward for thirty-six years of state service.

The reporter, taking a puff of his cigar, was undoubtedly grateful for the exclusive. He asked the warden about the future.

Lawes said he looked forward to time on his Putnam County farm. "I'll probably take a good rest for a couple of months, hoe a few potatoes and get a little exercise. This has been a pretty tough job—they want you here twenty-four hours a day, seven days a week." Of course, the hands-on Lawes wouldn't have had it any other way.

Now, though, with the end in sight, Lawes anticipated his freedom, like everyone else leaving Sing Sing. "I plan to do the things I want to do in the way I want to do them, and not be a part of a mechanized unit—that has always been hard for me." With the trial over, and the whole matter receding into history, the time was well suited for a public relations offensive, and the reporter was a compliant audience.

Lawes mentioned some highbrow offers from Colgate University and Union College—"I can either head a regular course, which I do not want to do, or I can hold seminars, which I may do"—the prospects were boundless. He even let slip that there were overtures for more radio and motion picture possibilities, though he kept the prospects of his bio-picture under his hat. The main point that he wanted the reporter and readers to understand was that his retirement was not a hasty retreat in the dark of night but, instead, a sendoff on a high note.

On Lawes's last day, Big Ben sounded at two o'clock on a sunny afternoon, halting Sing Sing's workshops. The warden made a round of appearances and speeches, stopping first to speak with two hundred employees in the Administration Building. Father Bernard Martin, the Catholic chaplain, presented the warden with a silver service set, in appreciation of his "humane leadership." Shortly afterward, Lawes said goodbye to the guards who couldn't be there earlier. Last but certainly not least in the warden's book, Lawes made his way over to the chapel at about three o'clock to speak to the inmates.

Standing alone on the stage, the warden waited for more than twenty-four hundred men to settle down in the auditorium seats or against the rear wall. When it was quiet, he addressed the boys directly, as he had over twenty years before.

"I am about to join the ranks of the unemployed," he said. That brought a laugh. "Almost anybody likes to get out of prison, and any one of you fellows would like to be in my place." Nods all around. "I have never preached to you men—you have never whined," though he acknowledged there was some injustice in sentencing. But he hoped the men would "keep hate from their hearts." He asked them to award his successor, Warden Robert J. Kirby of Attica prison, "the same coopera-tion . . . you have given me. If you do, he certainly cannot have any kick coming. God bless you," the warden said.

The men broke into cheers and clapping that lasted for minutes. Inmates surrounded him as he made his way out, shaking his hand and patting his back. No matter what the town may have thought, the con-victs whom the warden had kept locked up were giving him a heartfelt goodbye.

The only inmates not allowed to join in the ovation were those being disciplined for unruliness. And the condemned, passing their remaining days sequestered in the state's Death House.

———————

Warden Lawes had constructed a new Death House two years after he arrived. He thought the old one was grotesquely close to the general pop-ulation—a long chamber adjacent to the B-block tiers, complete with a postmortem room. The whining autopsy tools were a cruel disturbance to the men left behind. The new structure, of blank brick and steel, sat in an empty corner by the river. It was a completely separate world, with its own kitchen, exercise yards, visiting rooms, even its own hospital wing. The condemned were kept out of sight from the rest of the population, like an ugly secret hidden from the family.

Upon entry, every condemned man and woman—New York State executed both sexes at Sing Sing—was cataloged. If you'd just broken out of Sing Sing, the procedure must have seemed tedious. It was Bertillon all over again. You were photographed and measured, questioned and exam-ined. When asked why he had committed the crime for which he would receive the death penalty, Whitey repeated that he was innocent.

The Death House consisted of two tiers of cells, twelve top and bot-tom, facing south. Three women's cells lodged on a separate floor, facing west. Twelve years later, in 1953, when two of Sing Sing's most famous death row occupants, Julius and Ethel Rosenberg, were condemned for espionage, measures were taken to further isolate the controversial pair. A specially built stepladder allowed Ethel to climb through a window onto a rooftop and stroll about in the sunshine for her exercise period, away from the other row inmates. The stepladder remains there to this day.

The sun was a constant on nice days, streaming through the barred windows across from the rows of cells. Steamy in the summer; quiet too—only the crying gulls audible when the windows were open for the air. In the winter, though, you welcomed the sunny afternoons, when the radiators hissed beyond the bars and the heat didn't seem to reach the cells.

When the weather allowed, you were let out briefly into the small yard for an hour of exercise, if you could call it that. Otherwise you were locked in for nearly all of every twenty-four-hour period. You could talk to your neighbor, but you couldn't see him except at night—and then only as a watery reflection in the glass panes opposite the lighted cells. You could smoke, but the keeper held the matches, running back and forth like a madman keeping everyone lit.

They took good care of you, the Death House guards, keeping a close watch in case you got any ideas about cheating the state by suicide or escape. Toilets and sinks had their plumbing recessed to prevent monkeying with the pipes. Ceiling bulbs were too high to reach. You ate in the cell, from a tray slipped through a slot in the gate—no silverware, just soft aluminum utensils that the guards made damn sure you returned. In fact, no "moveable objects of any size" were allowed. The deliberately vague phrase gave the guards tremendous leeway when they tossed your cell, which they frequently did.

If you wanted to write a letter, you asked for a pen and paper. If you wanted to read, the prison library loaned you a book, or a newspaper, or a magazine with the staples removed. You didn't wear shoes with laces or with metal in the heels—you wore felt slippers. The administration was deadly serious about keeping you healthy.

Years before Whitey and McGale moved in, a doomed man tried to take the matter into his own hands. X-rays revealed that the fellow had swallowed "a large quantity of sand, wire, rubber and other foreign bodies." But Dr. Sweet, the prison physician at the time, operated quickly, saving the man for the chair. The law proclaimed that a prisoner's life was not his own; and Dr. Sweet's death row oath declared that neither was his death. Whitey and McGale had their appointment with death scheduled for the following month, August 10, 1941. But the date was a formality more than a chiseled-in-stone certainty. All death penalty cases brought automatic appeal.

FitzGerald especially had hope for an appeal. He had some reason. There was corroborating testimony that Whitey Riordan had saved three lives. FitzGerald would have sat across from Whitey in the Death House visiting room—there'd be no more contact with the general population— and convinced his client to have faith. With the automatic appeal, Whitey certainly wouldn't die on the tenth. It would take months for the case to move through the court. Whitey was advised to be optimistic.

Whitey tried.

The memory of his actions on that night probably became a saving grace. He could comfort himself with that thought when summer heat blanketed the cells. He could believe it when winter storms pounded against the windows. Three men were alive because he, Whitey Riordan, who had never amounted to anything, to less than nothing—look where he was—had intervened. He told Waters no, and Waters hadn't. He told McGale stop, and McGale had lowered his gun. A nurse, a guard, a fisherman, all could go on living their lives, thanks to him. Surely the Court of Appeals would agree. In fact, Governor Lehman's policy instantly commuted a death sentence to life imprisonment if just one judge on the court ruled to overturn it.

But Whitey and McGale, tried and convicted together, were hard to isolate on appeal. Gallagher returned to argue that they were both involved in the same bloody crime. A bullet from McGale's gun was found in Hartye's back; Whitey had fired his own revolver three times in the shootout with Officer Fagan. FitzGerald protested that had nothing to do with the Hartye case—the men were never charged with the crimes against Officer Fagan. But the Court of Appeals upheld the conviction. By May 1942, thirteen months after the crash out, the court reset the execution date for June 10, five weeks away.

FitzGerald still kept up a good front. He told Whitey that he had

filed a clemency hearing with Governor Lehman and was summoning
the guard, DeSimone, as a witness on Whitey's behalf. The court may
have ignored the officer's evidence, but surely the governor wouldn't.
Remembering the testimony of the policemen and state troopers,
though, Whitey may not have been so sure.

The Governor's commission, after a short delay, met Whitey, McGale,
and their attorneys in the small visiting room at two o'clock in the afternoon of May 22. As FitzGerald promised, he once again got DeSimone
to admit the truth: "Riordan argued the other escapees out of killing me
and the trusty Kaplan." FitzGerald also reiterated how Whitey was in
bed when Hartye was gunned down. McGale's attorney, with nothing
quite so concrete as a guard's testimony in his client's favor, repeated that
anything McGale had said was the result of a police third degree. And
then they waited for the governor's decision.

They had nineteen days until their scheduled date with the chair.

The electric chair sat in the building's southwest corner, behind four walls
at most, maybe twenty-five yards from where Whitey and McGale
waited on the row. The oak contraption with the wires and leather straps
was supposed to be a modern improvement over hanging, meant to do
away with the grisly scenes of swinging, choking people at the end of the
state's rope. Sing Sing's most infamous piece of furniture was thick-
limbed and sturdy and had a rubber seat and back cushion. People viewing the chair with Lawes's permission sometimes asked to sit in it, and
they found it surprisingly comfortable with its customized footrest. But
that was without the juice. When some unoriginal wag called it "Old
Sparky," the name stuck.

The electric chair was the result of Thomas Edison's ghoulish marketing trick. Dominating the field with his direct current (DC), Edison
feared competition from George Westinghouse's emerging alternating
current (AC). AC had consumer advantages over DC; but Edison, taking
note of a small number of accidental electrocutions attributed to AC, was
determined not to yield the marketplace. He sent a traveling salesman, an
engineer named Harold P. Brown, around the country, demonstrating the

dangers of wiring your home with Westinghouse's alternating current. Plugging wires in before invited audiences, Brown would proceed to electrocute stray dogs and cats onstage. Death was apparently instantaneous, the animals wagging or purring one moment, dropped and curled fetal-like the next. What parent in his right mind would jeopardize his family with Westinghouse's deadly currents, asked the New Jersey inventor's flack. Members of the New York State legislature, catching the show one evening in Albany, decided they'd found the perfect method for delivering painless executions. Despite legal challenges by Westinghouse, his AC became the executioner's current of choice in 1890.

The first try on a human being, though, was a botch. Rather than delivering a quick, painless end, a faulty generator in Auburn's Death House sent less-than-lethal surges buzzing through hatchet-murderer Walter Kemmler's body for over two minutes. Kemmler bled from the face, writhed spasmodically, then caught fire. Editorials as far away as London condemned the "revolting exhibition."

By the time Sing Sing installed the chair a year later, the technology had improved. Harris A. Smiler was the first man shocked to death at Sing Sing, on July 7, 1891, in a fatal charge supposedly quicker than the human nervous system could register pain. Three others followed him that day.

Fifty years later, as Whitey Riordan and Charles McGale waited for Governor Lehman's intervention, electric chair executions had become routine. Four hundred seventy-four men and women had taken their seat in Old Sparky since Smiler was executed—eleven men in the first three months of 1942 alone—always at eleven o'clock on a Thursday night. The method was standardized by then through years of trial and error. A dampened electrode was attached to the condemned's head and to one leg. The executioner, at his control panel in the chamber's side room, turned on the switch and spun the dial that carried an initial three-second, 2,000-volt blast. He then lowered the charge to 500 volts for fifty-seven seconds, ramped it back up to 2,000, then down again to 500 for another near minute, and once more up to 2,000 for the final flourish. The galvanizing seesaw lasted for two full minutes and raised the body temperature to 140 degrees. The brain reached nearly the boiling point of water. Death most likely occurred with the first surge, but given the history, no one wanted to take any chances.

———————

June 9, 1942. Forty-eight hours until Whitey's and McGale's Thursday night appointments. From all appearances they seemed to be "calmly awaiting execution," according to a local report. After a year in the Death House, maybe they'd gotten used to their immediate circumstances. The row's lights might dim briefly, late on certain Thursday nights when the lever was switched, but if you'd managed to fall asleep by then you wouldn't notice.

Or maybe they were genuinely resigned to their fate. Father Martin had made the rounds—it was the worst part of a chaplain's job, but he did it, his lips fluttering with prayers and scripture. Both men received him, Whitey perhaps with a hand on his saint's medallion, McGale less open-armed. But other than hearing their confessions and absolving them of sin, there was little more Father Martin could do. He'd saved one man from the chair. But that was a miraculous exception.

In New York State, at least, Governor Lehman had the final word—and he had yet to give it.

The men had had no visitors so far that week. A woman verifying herself before a judge as Whitey's niece Mary had come up back in March, and Whitey's more immediate family had also made the trip over the months. But that was getting harder to do, this close to his last day. McGale's sister-in-law had visited the previous August, but his brother and father had written Charlie off years ago. Father Martin and the attorneys had seen more of him than his own family.

On the morning of June 11, Whitey and McGale changed out of their prison grays and into black trousers and white shirts, the state's electrocution attire. The guards took them from their cells on the row and marched them to a half ring of six cells known as the Dance Hall. Whitey and McGale would wait out the last dozen hours of their lives in small cages arranged around an open floor area of glazed cement. Rumor persists that Julius and Ethel Rosenberg met in this spot to waltz, but that's not where the nickname comes from. Warden Lawes referred to it as the Dance Hall twenty years before the Rosenbergs, a gallows-humor reference to the area's size and shape.

The half dozen cells angled off a thick black door that opened to what nearly every Hollywood prison picture referred to as "the last mile." It actually took about fifteen steps to cover, sixteen if your strides were short. Transom windows above the cells ventilated the pre-execution area but offered the condemned no view of sky or river. They'd seen the last of the outside world by time they were locked into the Dance Hall.

Customarily a person facing execution is allowed a last meal of whatever he or she wants to eat. A typical menu at Sing Sing might include barbecued chicken, French fries, strawberry shortcake with whipped cream, and cigarettes. Or maybe you preferred lobster, ice cream, a box of chocolate, and cigars. Lawes, a fierce opponent of the death penalty, writes about an inmate requesting a shot of whiskey, which was completely against the rules. But the warden complied, only to have the condemned man hand the shot back to the warden with the words, "Here, you need this more than me." It is unknown what Whitey and McGale ordered. But as a former rabbi at Sing Sing who had accompanied many men on the last mile explained in a television interview, no matter what favorite food the condemned ordered, the rabbi had never seen a single person touch the plate.

Whitey was hangdog, stunned that rescuing three lives hadn't yet gotten him out of there. The guards listened with one ear. "I never croaked anyone," he told them. "I never even tried to fire a shot. I prevented Waters from plugging two other men." The guards nodded, sure, sure. Little sympathy there. But Whitey wouldn't give in. He kept insisting that today, June 11, was his twenty-seventh birthday. Never mind that his birthday was really in February. If that word could get back to Governor Lehman, maybe the governor would have a change of heart. Maybe he'd take pity and pick up the phone. It was worth a shot.

McGale was subdued. He didn't expect any miracles, not this late in the game. But he still backed up Riordan. "If I have to go, then I'll grin and bear it," he told guards. "But Riordan didn't want anyone shot." For all his lifelong haplessness, and his buggy, murderous intent, in the last hours of his life, McGale took responsibility. He wouldn't go to the chair pinning his crimes on anybody else.

The crowd in the execution chamber was standing-room only, eighteen witnesses in a room meant for a dozen. Reporters and lawmen sat shoulder to shoulder with the warden and clergy in four rows of wooden pews. Others stood to the side of the exit in the south wall, near the autopsy room. All of them were quiet as if gathered for a private service in a small chapel. Hundreds of witness applications had poured into Warden Kirby's office. People from all over wanted to see the Sing Sing breakout killers fry in the famous chair bolted to the floor on a rubber mat, under a pitched skylight and exhaust fan. Kirby had been busy that week whittling down the list to those with more than just a prurient interest, and signing permission letters. Officials understood that you would need to approach the night with the proper frame of mind. Seated that close, half a dozen steps away, you'd not only see the strain; you'd be able to smell it.

At eleven o'clock sharp, as the named defendant in the case and with no word from the governor, Whitey Riordan was led from the Dance Hall cell first. Guards at his elbows, Father Martin right behind, he walked his last mile and passed through the thick wooden door, under the sign commanding silence. He hung his head as he always did when he was in a fix, didn't look at all the witnesses, looked at the floor instead, his felt slippers stepping onto a rubber mat. His blond forelock was gone, his hair cut short that afternoon. He sat down and they strapped him in, fastened the electrodes. Warden Kirby, standing by the wall phone just in case, asked if Whitey had anything to say before the guards dropped the leather hood over his face.

Whitey nodded and cleared his throat. Then he glanced up. "So this is Governor Lehman's reward for saving three lives." He didn't mention his birthday; he probably didn't want to go with a lie on his lips.

The executioner threw the switch, and the room buzzed. Four minutes later, the doctor's stethoscope detected no heartbeat. Whitey's body was lifted from the chair onto a gurney and wheeled into the side autopsy room.

At six minutes after eleven, Charlie McGale was brought in. His stoic behavior during the preceding weeks vanished as he came through the door, with the chair right there in front of him. Despite the whirring ceiling fan, the air was still singed. McGale's knees jellied, the guards caught his arms and nearly carried him the last few feet. As they strapped him in and wired him up, the warden asked him for anything he might want to say. But McGale couldn't manage it. By 11:10 P.M. he, too, was dead.

The next afternoon, family members came up and claimed the bodies. Whitey Riordan was brought home to Manhattan, and a funeral Mass in the Catholic church opposite the family apartment on Isham St. in Inwood. Then the Riordan family caravanned behind the hearse out to Queens and the family gravesite in Calvary Cemetery, where Whitey was laid to rest beside his father John and sister Mary. Inwood is a close-knit neighborhood, back then mostly Irish, a definite step up from Hell's Kitchen. But living right across from the church, with its Sunday crowds, meant that keeping news of an execution in the family quiet was nearly impossible. Elizabeth didn't want to live surrounded by whispers, so the Riordans went on the move again, this time to Queens. They couldn't return to Hell's Kitchen and all the knockdown memories.

As for Charlie McGale, he's buried in time. Any Sing Sing records that might point to the fate of his remains are lost. Either destroyed when the old cellblock was gutted by fire in 1981, or just tossed away during continual, facility-wide renovations, McGale's record, along with his body, is gone.

The war detonating across the world the year of their deaths blew away almost everything else. Pearl Harbor had been attacked the previous December, in 1941. The same newspaper pages devoted to the sensational Shopping Bag Gang headlines in the late '30s, the column space lined just fourteen months before with pictures and gripping details of the "bloodiest break in Sing Sing's history," were relatively empty of news about the executions on June 11, 1942. Ossining's *Citizen Register* gave the story some inside pages; but the New York dailies chopped it down to small, forgettable paragraphs. With Americans dying on foreign soil, and the whole country steaming with war effort, people's attention was focused elsewhere. Two-bit bandits and gun-slinging fugitives still blasted away, but their daring and violence seemed petty in comparison with the mayhem on the world stage. Crime changed, too.

Al Capone and Dutch Schultz had built locally powerful empires during Prohibition, but crime in the 1940s reflected a growing, increasingly mechanized mass society. The real money was in criminal syndicates with international reach. The Sicilian mafia dominated, organized like the Guaranty Trust Company or Coca-Cola, with bookmaking wired coast to coast and Mediterranean drug conspiracies managed by neck-tied hierarchies. This wasn't the '30s anymore, when lone wolf packs could make out like, well, bandits. Guys like Rusty and Mac, Lulu and Willie the Greek, would probably have thrown in with the syndicates for a bigger piece of the pie. Small independent mobs like the Shopping Bag Gang, when cooperating with waterfront gangsters like Davie Beadle, were on the cusp of the changes in organized crime. But in the 1940s, unconnected outlaw bands seemed anomalous, almost as passé as the Jesse James gang.

Only Billy Wade, facing a life sentence, got a break with his characteristic Irish luck. Thanks to attorney Lowenberg's nicotine tenacity, Wade's case was appealed three times, all the way up to the U.S. Court of Appeals. In 1958, the court determined that Wade's confession was indeed coerced and thus inadmissible as evidence. After seventeen years in prison, much of the time spent shivering in Clinton near the Canadian border, Wade was released. Then he, too, disappeared from the record.

His childhood buddy Eddie Kiernan wasn't so fortunate. Kiernan never took the stand in his own defense. His version of events wasn't in the trial record, couldn't be molded on appeal. He spent the rest of his useful life in the New York State system.

Little Joe Salvatore adjusted with the times. His months in the Tombs counted toward his year's sentence in state prison, in return for testifying against the Shopping Bag Gang. When he got out, he returned to what he knew best: bookmaking. Throughout the war years he racked up half a dozen gambling convictions. Then his trail went cold as well.

———————

Although four men actually died the night of the break, Guard Matteo DeSimone might be considered the Sing Sing crash out's fifth victim. After testifying on Whitey's behalf before Governor Lehman's commission, DeSimone went back to work. He was reassigned to the Administration Building's front gate, a boring job by some accounts, with little inmate contact. He remained a nervous sort, though, staying aloof from coworkers—probably for a good reason. DeSimone was ostracized by fellow officers for coming to an inmate's defense, especially one convicted in the murder of a guard. Thirty years after the breakout, in 1971, shortly after he had retired and years after his wife had passed away, Matteo DeSimone drove up to his wife's graveside in St. Augustine's Cemetery, not far from where Officer Fagan also lay buried, and put a bullet through his head.

Officer Fagan's memory is more revered by his police colleagues. On Spring Street, in Ossining—near Cliff Ellsworthy's old taxi stand—a large, state-of-the-art police headquarters and court complex is named in Fagan's honor.

Warden Lewis Lawes declined to witness the execution of the men who had hastened his own departure from Sing Sing. Although as warden he had signed off on more than three hundred executions during his career, to an outspoken opponent of capital punishment like Lawes, that was more than enough. Besides, by the summer of 1942, he had moved on.

After his retirement the previous year, with Europe burning, Lawes threw himself into the war effort. In scheduled appearances he rallied against Hitler, exhorting pro-war crowds at Madison Square Garden, and arguing vehemently against alleged Nazi appeasers like aviator Charles Lindbergh. As a member of the War Production Board, he stumped at prisons across the country, congratulating inmates on their steady output of supplies in a time of homeland shortages. But activism didn't pay the bills. His state pension stretched thinner and thinner while he waited for Hollywood to call.

Warner Brothers had been considering his script for over a year—the bio-picture that would at last enshrine him in celluloid, putting a big star's face to his name. But as the rewrites flew back and forth across the country, Lawes became more infuriated with each new adaptation. They were ruining his story, gussying up the stark facts with Technicolor flim-flam. The only way to salvage his picture was to take an express train out there himself and keep an eye over their shoulders.

But Lawes's customary hands-on approach did little good with dom-ineering movie producers. In their view, the bare facts of Lawes's life lacked sufficient drama. A compromise receded out of reach, and the deal ultimately fell through. Anyway, they told him, the country had moved beyond cops and robbers; the war was changing everything. His life story on film, a dream of his for years, would never be.

Still, the bills had to be paid. Lawes relied on what he knew best, lec-turing and writing on juvenile delinquency, crime, and prisons. But with-out the day-to-day experience of Sing Sing to occupy his mind, Lawes seemed to fade. He kept touring the country, the rattling trains and road-house food taking their toll. His health deteriorated, straining his cir-cumstances even further. Finally, though, one last ship sailed in.

In 1946, five years after signing with his new agent, Lawes was back on the air. His new radio show, *Crime Cases of Warden Lawes,* premiered in October, with a contract worth waiting for—an incredible four-year term with a steadily increasing salary. But the show-biz renaissance arrived too late for the ailing Lawes. Six months later, in April 1947, Lewis Lawes died in his bed from a cerebral hemorrhage.

Although his obituaries were glowing tributes, and his funeral was crowded with hundreds of friends and former employees, Lawes's profes-sional reputation was tarnished. Hollywood was right—things *had* changed. Corrections had buckled down since his time, likely starting with Warden Kirby in the summer of '41. Perhaps because of Lawes's fame as a reformer—what many in the department considered prisoner coddling—combined with the murders of Guard John Hartye and Offi-cer James Fagan, not everyone was sorry to see Lawes, and all he stood for, pass on. One startling sign of the fading of his reputation is apparent in *Sing Sing Prison, Ossining, N.Y., Its History, Purpose, Makeup and Pro-gram,* a fifty-three-page New York State Department of Correction handbook published in 1958. The handbook mentions by name many individuals instrumental to the prison's detailed history and outlines improvements that Lawes himself instituted. But just eleven years after the death of the country's most famous warden, the Sing Sing handbook never once mentions Warden Lewis Lawes by name.

Five years later, in 1963, Sing Sing's electric chair embraced its last occupant. Eighteen men were confined on New York's death row that year, but only one man walked the last mile. Thirty-four-year-old Eddie Lee Mays was the 614th—and last—person to die in Old Sparky. For the remainder of the decade, the chair sat unplugged, gathering dust. The death penalty, mired in political and legal challenges, had been abandoned. In 1971, the chair was moved upstate to Greenhaven prison, in Fishkill, New York, then sent to a Virginia museum as a relic of America's colorful past. Sing Sing's infamous Death House, now the prison's "vocational ed" unit, still stands in the compound's most remote corner. Lawes would probably feel justified by the transformation. The Dance Hall is remodeled with a bisecting hallway; the wire cages are storage bins. And in the execution chamber, now cluttered with workbenches and tools, motor parts and lawnmowers, inmates learn a trade.

Hell's Kitchen is nearly gone, too. Area priests and landlords advocated a name change to something less demonic—a name more in keeping with the area's new upscale corporate residents. And the winner was Clinton, after the father of the Erie Canal, De Witt Clinton. The neighborhood's composition soon changed to suit the name. A large section of the residential area had been razed in the 1930s to make way for the Lincoln Tunnel, and today urban renewal and gentrification continue. A Disney store, of all things, holds a commanding post on 42nd Street, and luxury apartment buildings are multiplying throughout the area. Some longtime residents fear the neighborhood's character will be sandblasted off the now-historic tenements still leaning against one another like drunks on the streets west of Tenth Avenue, where the Hudson can be glimpsed, a blue-steel square at the end of the block.

The Riordan family has changed, as well. Hell's Kitchen is in their distant past. Trace the family through the church documents, the file cards and entries of the marriages, baptisms, and confirmations of Whitey's brothers, nieces, and nephews. The close family has grown, come through some of the worst that a family can experience and remain intact. Whitey's death seems to have turned them around. John and his mother followed Whitey out to Queens and settled in a quiet parish in Long Island City. Andrew stayed behind in Inwood. John and Andrew, with police records and on years of parole, worked straight jobs from then on. The waterfront bustled with wartime activity. There was tremendous money to be made, and many Waterfront Crime Commissions were nosing into just how. But the Riordan brothers buried armed thieving as a way of life in the ground with Whitey. They went on to raise families of their own and were godparents to each other's children. Andrew brought his kids up in Inwood. John worked all his life on the docks, raising his family in Queens. Elizabeth, who had borne so much, lived with John until her death in 1963 in a clean brick apartment building nearly identical to the one she had left behind in Inwood. She was especially close to her grandchildren, one of her grand-daughters remembers. "She was a good woman, very good to all of us," she said. "We were all very sad when she died."

According to her grandchildren, Elizabeth Riordan never complained to them about the hard days back in Hell's Kitchen. With their whole lives ahead of them, the kids were best unburdened by what the adults had lived through. Things as ignominious as murder and execution are better left unmentioned.

Perhaps in a way, the Hell's Kitchen code of silence—and persever-ance—worked. In a 1914 essay written the year before Whitey's birth, a city social worker described Hell's Kitchen as a hopeless trap: "There is something in the dullness of these West Side streets that crushes the wish for anything better and kills the hope of change." But the Riordans, like countless other immigrant families who weathered dark times and losses, proved otherwise. The Riordans' current generation appears to be living their parents' dream of steady jobs, growing children, success. Whitey's niece, for instance, has many grandchildren of her own now, and a suc-cessful career in the fashion industry. Together with her husband, she helps to run her parish homeless shelter.

Not all of the children of Hell's Kitchen escaped. But maybe, in a sense, Whitey Riordan has finally crashed out.

NOTES ON SOURCES

I was living in Los Angeles in the 1990s when the inspiration and first source for this book arrived in the mail. My brother—then entering his twenty-fifth year as a Sing Sing officer—had sent me an intriguing piece of prison memorabilia: a Xeroxed copy of a collection of newspaper clippings and photographs that I came to identify as the Patchey scrapbook. The clippings were meticulously compiled by a local news photographer by the name of John Patchey, gathered mostly from Ossining's now-defunct village paper, the *Citizen Register*. The Patchey scrapbook, devoted to the 1941 break, is a unique example of Sing Sing folk art, bound with a black pasteboard cover carved to resemble a cell door with bars. The Ossining Historical Society (OHS) safeguards the huge document in a file drawer. A few clippings are missing their headlines, some their dates (I imagine Mr. Patchey late at night after a long day spent squinting through a lens, too bleary-eyed to scissor within the lines). But the book's battered, dog-eared appearance is a testament to its use as a primary document for anyone researching Sing Sing prison in general, and the 1941 break in particular. As a starting point, it was invaluable.

In reconstructing the context and the story behind the events sketched in the Patchey scrapbook, I relied on more than half a dozen newspapers, including the [New York] *Daily Mirror*, the [New York] *Daily News*, the [New York] *Herald Tribune*, the *New York Journal and American*, the *New York Sun*, and the *New York Times*. All carried gripping accounts of the Shopping Bag Gang robberies as well as the Sing Sing break; the *Mirror* and *Journal and American* in particular are written in a fast-paced, key-clicking style reminiscent of Damon Runyon. Even scrolling through the New York Public Library's microfilm machines, you can almost smell the reporters' cigar smoke. I also consulted feature stories in *Collier's Weekly* and *Harper's* for background information on the New York waterfront. In the following notes, when I use a news story more than once, I shorten the cited headline. Descriptions of weather conditions taken from the New York newspapers are not cited.

A large number of books provide excellent background and insight into the Great Depression, New York's Hell's Kitchen, and crime; a more modest number provide a behind-locked-doors view of Sing Sing prison. Among the most detailed and colorful studies are the (now obscure) Sage Foundation's *West Side Studies* (cited as "Sage" in the notes), the first close-up look at early-twentieth-century living conditions in Hell's Kitchen. Richard O'Connor draws heavily on the Sage Foundation's work for his lively *Hell's Kitchen*. Another contemporary source is *The WPA Guide to New York City*. The guide is a practical walking tour through Whitey Riordan's and Patches Waters's hometown. For background I have also drawn on Frederick Lewis Allen's *Only Yesterday* and *Since Yesterday*, classically great accounts of, respectively, the 1920s and the Great Depression. Herbert Asbury's *Gangs of New York* deserves its fame; less famous but equally informative and entertaining are Malcolm Johnson's *Crime on the Labor Front* and Alan Block's *East Side–West Side: Organizing Crime in New York, 1930–1950*. Lewis E. Lawes's *Twenty-Thousand Years in Sing Sing* is the granddaddy of all prison books; it put Sing Sing on the map. More recent are Ted Conover's gutsy *Newjack: Guarding Sing Sing* and Ralph Blumenthal's absorbing biography of Warden Lawes, *Miracle at Sing Sing: How One Man Transformed the Lives of America's Most Dangerous Prisoners*.

Underpinning the research are numerous files. New York City's Department of Records and Information Services (DORIS) archives the personal data, crimes, and misdemeanors of generations of New Yorkers. My happy trawling through old case files, magnifying glass in hand, occupied my mornings and afternoons for months. The New York State Archives in Albany houses the records of the state prison system, though many of the Sing Sing files disappeared over the years—one source thought they were dumped in the Hudson or destroyed when the old cellblock burned in the early 1980s. The Lloyd Sealy Library at John Jay

College contains Warden Lewis Lawes's papers in its Special Collections. The acquisition is a treasure trove of information on both the man and the prison he managed.

But no tale can rely on dry paper alone; it needs people to bring it alive. Growing up among prison guards gave me an inkling into what it takes to work at Sing Sing. Many others gave me a more detailed perspective. Among the most knowledgeable was Fred Starler. Everyone who wanted to know what the prison had really been like under Warden Lawes spoke to ninety-three-year-old Fred. He was on duty the night of the break and offered the last eyewitness account. My first in-depth interview with him took place at the Ossining Community Center, during morning Jazzercise. In between chilling anecdotes of escaping inmates and murder, Fred, his lanky frame still limber, kept jumping up to dance to the rhythms of the tune "Sex on the Beach." A generous witness to Sing Sing's storied past, Fred Starler passed away in February 2005.

PROLOGUE

xii   probably the only prison: Conover, 5.

xiii   four miles at a northwest diagonal: People vs. Joseph Riordan et al., 1791, Westchester County Clerk.

xiii   buckets of money: "6 Thugs Get $35,000," *Daily News*, May 16, 1939; "5 Gunmen Raid Harlem Office," *New York Times*, May 16, 1939.

PART ONE
THE SHOPPING BAG GANG

Chapter One: **Robbers**

3   Henry Hudson Bridge: *WPA Guide*, 305.

4   last working farm: Kisselhoff, 222.

4   the A train: *WPA Guide*, 403.

4   Irish New Yorkers escaping: Bayor and Meagher, 441.

4   best on the docks: Johnson, 134; "Red Skies over the Waterfront," *Collier's Weekly*, Oct. 5, 1946; "The Pirate's Nest of New York," *Harper's*, Apr. 1952.

5   arrangement was nearly as old: Keating, 90.

5   waterfront rackets were as deeply entrenched: Johnson, 99.

6   pinball racket: "Operation of Pinball Machines in New York City," New York City Commissioner of Investigation, William B. Harlands's report to Mayor Fiorello LaGuardia, Dec. 17, 1941, LaGuardia Archives, LaGuardia Community College.

6   LaGuardia took a sledgehammer: Brodsky, 342.

6   a kid's game like pinball: "Pinball Devices in City Replace Slots," *Herald Tribune,* Dec. 28, 1941.

6   a dollar figure on his past: Sing Sing inmate admission registers, New York State Archives, B0143.

6   Tammany Hall and Mayor Jimmy Walker: Mitgang, 246–65, 273–75, 282–97.

7   the same sharp appearance: "Stickup Mob?" *Daily News,* June 18, 1939.

7   Patches meeting the boys: People vs. Joseph Salvatore, defendant statement, June 15, 1939, DORIS.

7   description of office: "Six Bandits Take $15,000 in Edison Company Holdup," *Daily Mirror,* May 16, 1939; "5 Gunmen Raid . . . ," *New York Times,* May 16, 1939.

8   Jake the Butch: "Audubon Avenue Job," "125th Street Job," People vs. William Athalias and Thomas Gentiles; People vs. William Athalias and William Wade, June 20, 1939, DORIS.

8   the latest GE "Flat Top": www.antiqueappliances.com.

8   Jake's information: People vs. Athalias, DORIS.

8   the large Buick sedan: "6 Thugs . . . ," *Daily News,* May 16, 1939.

8   Fifth and Lenox: "Clews Scant in Edison Holdup," *New York Sun,* May 16, 1939; *WPA Guide,* 259.

9   World's Fair flag: "6 Bandits Get $10,000 with 175 in Office," *Herald Tribune,* May 16, 1939; "5 Gunmen Raid . . . ," *New York Times,* May 16, 1939.

9   Eleanor Roosevelt: "Mrs. Roosevelt Is Guest of Honor," *Herald Tribune,* May 16, 1939; "The Fair Today," *New York Times,* May 16, 1939.

9   "My Day": Allen, *Since Yesterday,* 273.

9   a thousand-acre wasteland: Appelbaum, x; *WPA Guide,* 628.

10   fair's board of directors: Appelbaum, xi.

10   three hundred thousand people: "Bright Day Draws 306,000 to the Fair," *New York Times,* May 14, 1939.

10   wonders like the television: Appelbaum, xiii, 44, 60.

10   a record sixty nations: Ibid., xii.

10   "New York City of Light": Ibid., 48, 49.

11–13   description of the robbery: "6 Thugs Get . . . ," *Daily Mirror*, May 16, 1939; "6 Bandits Get . . . ," *Herald Tribune*, May 16, 1939; "Clews Scant . . . ," *New York Sun*, May 16, 1939; "5 Gunmen Raid . . . ," *New York Times*, May 16, 1939.

13   Emilio Spagniolo: People vs. Athalias, DORIS.

13   Yankees and Athletics: "Yanks Triumph, 3–0, for Fifth Straight," *New York Times*, May 16, 1939.

14   numbers runner: Block, 149–52.

14   Rose Angela: People vs. Athalias, DORIS.

15   He fancied himself a chef: People vs. Thomas Gentles, handwriting evidence, March 7, 1941, DORIS.

15   quoted dialogue: People vs. Athalias, DORIS.

16   the boys . . . muscled: "Four Rob Customs Teller, Get $6,000 and Flee," *Daily News*, Feb. 25, 1939; "Brooklyn Hold-up Nets Thugs $4,500," *New York Times*, Oct. 8, 1938; "Four Gunmen Rob Edison Office," *New York Times*, Dec. 6, 1938; "Clews Scant . . . ," *New York Sun*, May 16, 1939; "Five Gunmen Raid . . . ," *New York Times*, May 16, 1939; "6 Bandits Get . . . ," *Herald Tribune*, May 16, 1939; "Six Bandits Take . . . ," *Daily Mirror*, May 16, 1939.

17   two years . . . Virginia Penitentiary: People vs. Joseph Salvatore, prisoner's criminal record, Police Department, City of New York, DORIS.

18   Rusty the bagman: People vs. Salvatore, defendant statement, ibid.

20   Joe read in the *Journal:* "Bandits Get Big Haul in Customs Duties," *New York Journal and American*, Feb. 24, 1939.

Chapter Two: **Cops**

23   "watch for six men . . .": "Six Bandits Take . . . ," *Daily Mirror*, May 16, 1939.

24   mobbed the courthouse steps: "Dewey Says Capshaw Lied on Stand," *New York Sun*, Feb. 24, 1939; Stolberg, 226–47.

24   all the New York papers: "Kear Chosen as 2nd Deputy to Valentine," *Daily Mirror*, Feb. 25, 1939; "Valentine Promotes Two Ace Detectives,"

Feb. 24, 1939; "Kear Appointed 2nd Police Deputy," *New York Sun,* Feb. 24, 1939.

25   description of investigation: "Six Bandits Take . . . ," *Daily Mirror,* May 16, 1939; "6 Bandits Get . . . ," *Herald Tribune,* May 16, 1939; "Clews Scant . . . ," *New York Sun,* May 16, 1939; "Five Gunmen . . . ," *New York Times,* May 16, 1939; People vs. Athalias, June 20, 1939, DORIS.

25   five years to solve: "Kear Chosen . . . ," *Daily Mirror,* Feb. 25, 1939; "Valentine Promotes . . . ," *New York Journal and American,* Feb. 25, 1939; "Kear Appointed . . . ," *New York Sun,* Feb. 25, 1939.

26   Lexow Committee: Block, 19–20; Ellis, 230–34.

26   Tammany Hall: Ellis, ibid.; Bell, 127.

27   Boss Tweed: Ellis, 330.

27   its own private shillelagh: Ibid., 433.

27   description of Reverend Parkhurst: Ibid., 423–39; O'Connor, 99–115.

29   "Down into the disgusting . . .": Ellis, ibid.

29   thirteen-year-old Fiorello LaGuardia: Ibid., 430.

29   Alexander Williams: Asbury, 217–19, 230–31.

30   "I've had nothing but chuck . . .": Ellis, 430.

30   seventy indictments: Ibid., 434.

30   Tammany mayor was defeated . . . Roosevelt: Ibid.

31   thankful crusaders . . . Parkhurst: Ibid.

31   Mazet Commission: Block, 20.

31   Honest cops . . . variety: "Kear Chosen . . . ," *Daily Mirror,* Feb. 25, 1939; "Valentine Promotes . . . ," *New York Journal and American,* Feb. 25, 1939; "Kear Appointed . . . ," *New York Sun,* Feb. 25, 1939.

31   ratification . . . Eighteenth Amendment: Allen, *Only Yesterday,* 212–18.

32   Midwest politicians . . . Capone's sister: Ibid., 229.

32   a gambling racket . . . $35,000 a day: Stolberg, 226–47.

32   Luciano . . . Unione Siciliane: Ibid., 118–19; Reppetto, 143.

32   federal agents assigned: Allen, *Only Yesterday,* 212–18.

32   ninety-five deaths by starvation . . . sixteen hundred people killed: Ellis, 533–34.

33   Hollywood Production Code: Dooley, 296–97.

33   a missing persons report: Mitgang, 167–68.

33   Samuel Seabury: Ibid., 178–202.

34   Nicknamed "Beau": Ibid., 245.

34   The same mayor: Ellis, 543.

34   a secret safe-deposit box: Mitgang, 247.

34   Equitable Coach Company: Ibid.

34   he wasn't crafty: Ibid.

34   slush fund that financed: Ibid.

34   "Little Boy Blue . . .": Ellis, 546.

34   Seabury scoffed: Mitgang, 247.

35   "What I'm going to do . . .": Stolberg, 47.

35   He appointed . . . Valentine: Lardner and Reppetto, 212.

35   "Blood should be smeared . . .": Brodsky, 343.

Chapter Three: **Hell's Children**

37   the lead of witness descriptions: People vs. Athalias, DORIS.

37   any street cop could tell you: Lardner and Reppetto, 63; "Vast Arsenal Uncovered by Raid," *New York Times*, March 18, 1936.

38   he also kept an apartment: People vs. Gentles, memo to D.A. Thomas E. Dewey from Assistant D.A. Herman T. Stichman, Apr. 7, 1941, DORIS.

38   shacked up with his girlfriend: "G-Men Accuse Crying Dancer of Faking Help," *New York Journal and American*, June 18, 1939.

38   description of Riordan genealogy: Elizabeth Riordan death certificate, Division of Records, New York City Department of Health; John Riordan death certificate, DORIS.

39   "the largest group . . . city": *WPA Guide*, 144.

39   "the highest general . . . mortality": Ibid., 145.

39   Inhabiting tenement basements: O'Connor, 27; Kisselhoff, 549.

39   the Gophers . . . Hudson Dusters: Asbury, 235, 238.

40   One-Lung's claim: Asbury, 235–36.

40   a fearsome women's auxiliary: Ibid.

40   supply of goods: O'Connor, 55.

40   ad hoc security force: Asbury, 322.

40   "from hell to breakfast": Ibid.

41   from colonial times: *WPA Guide*, 145.

41   John Jacob Astor: Homberger, 66–67.

41   a Gilbert Stuart portrait: *Encyclopaedia Britannica.*

42   "landlord of New York": Ellis, 244.

42   a remarkable bargain: Sage, vol. 2, 12; O'Connor, 13.

42   Vanderbilt made his first fortune: Ellis, 212, 240.

42   he shifted his focus: Ibid., 259; *WPA Guide,* 145.

42   the richest man in America: Ellis, 258.

42   row after row: O'Connor, 14; *WPA Guide,* 145.

42   One popular legend: Kisselhoff, 547.

43   the moniker . . . hideout: O'Connor, 12.

43   pastures; limekilns, distilleries: *WPA Guide,* 145.

43   a horseman preceded the train: Ibid., 157; Sage, vol. 1, 4.

44   the steam-powered El: Ellis, 340–41.

44   stray goats wandered: O'Connor, 38.

44   fighting . . . Know-Nothings: Ellis, 340–41.

45   first municipal Board of Health: O'Connor, 19.

45   "[I]n street after street . . .": Sage, vol. 1, 5.

45   the Hell's Kitchen Irish . . . waterfront: Bell, 207.

46   "Hell's Kitchen 1 Bedrooms . . .": *New York Times,* Dec. 5, 2004.

46   death certificate: John Riordan, DORIS.

46   everything from Oregon . . . iron: cargo ship's manifest, Box 8, Fr. Corridan papers, Xavier Institute collection, Fordham University.

47   Neighborhood housewives: Sage, vol. 1, 74–75.

47   Paddy's Market: O'Connor, 188; *WPA Guide,* 157–58.

47   "meets her responsibilities . . .": O'Connor, 189.

47   the concrete apathy: O'Connor, 176.

48   A popular game: Kisselhoff, 571.

48   the waterfront . . . wet relief: Sage, vol. 1, 20–23.

48   the Sanitation Department's dump: Kisselhoff, 566.

48   stained pink by runoff: O'Connor, 177.

48   "You swam with the tide . . .": Kisselhoff, 566.

48   Hell's Kitchen . . . honor code: Sage, vol. 1, 40–54.

49   childhood pranks . . . crime: Ibid.

49   you didn't squeal: Bell, 208; Sutton, 14; "The Pirate's Nest . . . ," *Harper's,* Apr. 1952.

49   criminal acts demanded: O'Connor, 28.

49   description of Clinton family: People vs. Daniel St. John, John J. Clinton statement, Lt. John Cordes statement, Apr. 15, 1941, DORIS.

50   urbane and literate: Sann, 173–75.

50   Jack Diamond: Kennedy, 20; Sann, 186.

50   Coolidge Prosperity: Allen, *Only Yesterday,* 142.

51   Whitey's first conviction: Sing Sing inmate admission registers, New York State Archives, B0143.

51   The nature of the disease: John Riordan, DORIS.

51   Whitey's older brother John: Geraldine Riordan Murphy, telephone interview, Jan. 24, 2005.

51   He made deliveries for a local market: People vs. Joseph Riordan, affidavit, May 9, 1931, DORIS.

Chapter Four: **Welfare Boy**

52   "largest integral housing project": "120-Acre Housing Will Rise in Bronx," *New York Times,* Apr. 8, 1938.

52   "a completely balanced community": Ibid.

52   *Sixty-sixth Annual Report:* New York Catholic Protectory (NYCP) Archives, Lehman College.

53   five new parishes: Sacred Heart Church archive.

53   Temperance Society: Scott, 42.

53   The Protectory was established: NYCP Archives, Lehman College, 8.

53   "idle, truant and vicious": Ibid., 7.

53   nine hundred juvenile delinquents: Ibid., 3.

53   "Flaming Youth": Ibid., 17.

54   "noble conduct": Ibid., 27.

54   notions of childhood corrections: Morris and Rothman, 330.

54   "constant occupation": NYCP Archives, Lehman College, 10.

54   "mechanic arts": Ibid.

54   "great aim . . . practice of virtue": Ibid.

54   Max Hahn: "Rope Breaks, Boy Hurt Fleeing Protectory," *New York Times,* Sept. 5, 1926.

54   "infected with Spring fever": "18 Spring Fever Victims Flee Protectory," *New York Times,* Apr. 21, 1934.

55   "for wanting to go . . . prank": Ibid.

55   "appalling . . . bless themselves": NYCP Archives, Lehman College, 18.

56   lined with butcher shops: Kisselhoff, 569.

56   John was the main breadwinner: Geraldine Riordan Murphy, telephone interview, Jan. 24, 2005.

56   forty, sometimes fifty dollars a week: "Red Skies . . . ," *Collier's Weekly*, Oct. 5, 1946.

56   a postwar shipping slowdown: Ibid.

56   Fords and Chryslers . . . horse carts: Ellis, 462.

56   national unemployment: Ellis, 462.

56   bare-knuckle jobs: Kisselhoff, 552.

57   Twenty-one-year-old John: Geraldine Riordan Murphy, telephone interview, Jan. 24, 2005.

57   The average longshoreman: "Red Skies . . . ," *Collier's Weekly*, Oct. 5, 1946.

57   12:30 . . . May 9, 1931: People vs. Joseph Riordan, affidavit, May 9, 1931, DORIS.

58   the few jobs available: O'Connor, 189–90.

59   The Beadles: "Two Brothers Slain in Speakeasy Fight," *New York Times*, Apr. 10, 1930.

59   C. T. Crain: Mitgang, 207.

59   Whitey and a pal: People vs. Joseph Riordan, affidavit, Sept. 6, 1931, DORIS.

59   a state-of-the-art facility: "Elmira," *D.O.C.S. Today*, www.correctionhistory.org.

59   Many of these programs: "Recreation at Elmira Reformatory," L. Lawes Collection, Box 5, File 26, Lloyd Sealy Library, John Jay College of Criminal Justice.

60   "the worst prison in the world": "M'Cormick Raids Welfare Island, Smashes Gangster Rule of Prison," *Herald Tribune*, Jan. 25, 1934.

60   description of early Roosevelt Island: Ellis, 86; *WPA Guide*, 423.

61   smallpox hospital: "Before Rikers, Blackwell's Was DOC's Island Home," online article, www.correctionhistory.org.

61   a public scandal: *WPA Guide*, 423.

61   The Tombs: Ibid., 103.

61–67   description of Welfare Island: "U.S. May Enter Investigation of Welfare

Island Situation," "Jail Disorders in One Unit Only," *New York Sun,* Jan. 25, 1934; "Welfare Island Raid Bares Gangster Rule over Prison; Weapons, Narcotics Found," "Prison Scandal Typical of City Conditions Inherited by Administration, Mayor Says," *New York Times,* Jan. 25, 1934; "M'Cormick Raids . . . ," *Herald Tribune,* Jan. 25, 1934; New York City Department of Corrections, Commissioner Austin MacCormick's report to Mayor Fiorello LaGuardia about the third grand jury investigation of Welfare Island, Apr. 18, 1934, LaGuardia Archives, LaGuardia Community College.

63   Rao had ridden shotgun: Thompson and Raymond, 132, 309.

65   an old tenement custom: O'Connor, 189–91.

65   Opium had been smoked: Sante, 146.

65   Aspirin maker Bayer: Ibid., 150.

67–68 description of MacCormick: "M'Gahan Gets Budget Post, US Expert to Run City Jail," *Herald Tribune,* Dec. 24, 1933; "Penologist Named City Prison Head," *New York Times,* Dec. 24, 1933.

68   "a gangster's paradise": "Prison Gang Chiefs Served by Valets," *New York Times,* Jan. 25, 1934.

68   "seemed greatly relieved": Ibid.

68   "I'll go along . . . wave": "M'Cormick Raids . . . ," *Herald Tribune,* Jan. 25, 1934.

68   "a typical illustration . . . predecessors": Ibid.

68   *Blackwell's Island:* Dooley, 332–33.

68   "laughable . . . lackeys": Ibid.

69   "repair shop": "City's New Prison to Be Repair Shop," *New York Times,* Apr. 22, 1934.

69   Whitey's next three years: Sing Sing inmate admission registers, New York State Archives, B0143.

Chapter Five: **The Pistol Local**

70   description of early ILA: Johnson, 94.

70   description of Gregory: Ibid.; "Man of Many Arrests Is Shot Four Times," *New York Times,* Nov. 17, 1940; "Union Delegate Shot," *Herald Tribune,* Nov. 17, 1940.

71   "book": Johnson, 94.

71   description of Beadle: Ibid.; "Beadle the Beetle Slain at the Spot," *Daily News,* Dec. 9, 1939; "Man Slain from Ambush After Visiting Barroom," *Herald Tribune,* Dec. 9, 1939; "Davie the Beetle Shot Dead," *New York Sun,* Dec. 9, 1939; "Shot Dead in Street," *New York Times,* Dec. 9, 1939; "Two Brothers Slain . . . ," *New York Times,* Apr. 10, 1930; People vs. Daniel St. John, Apr. 15, 1941, DORIS.

71        $7-billion-a-year empire: Johnson, 92; *WPA Guide,* 54–55.

71–72   description of New York Harbor: Johnson, Ibid.

72   International Longshoreman's Association: Ibid.; Bell, 188, 192.

72   Pulitzer Prize: "Crime on the Waterfront": *New York Sun,* Nov. 8, 1948.

72   "waterfront jungle": Johnson, 92.

72   worker exploitation: Ibid.

72   padded payrolls: Ibid.

73   union book . . . Pier 88: People vs. St. John, DORIS.

73   loan-sharking operation: Ibid.

73   the hiring stevedore: Johnson, 110, 133; Bell, 181.

73   "Central to . . . setup of a city": Bell, 193.

73   one Tammany leader: Ibid.

73   Dutch Schultz: Reppetto, 167.

73   harbor's porous frontier: Bell, 176.

74   For some newcomers: Ibid., 170.

74   description of Paolo Vaccarelli: Asbury, 254–55; Bell, 189–90; Reppetto, 26.

74   even into Puerto Rico: online article, www.ilaunion.org.

75   Collective-bargaining goals: Bell, 197.

75   statistics: "The Pirate's Nest . . . ," *Harper's Magazine,* Apr. 1952.

75        $65 million to $100 million: Ibid.

75   Bandit's arrest: "Man of Many . . . ," *New York Times,* Nov. 17, 1940.

75   Whitey and Bandit: People vs. St. John, DORIS.

76   description of John Riordan crime: first-degree robbery indictment and plea summary/affidavit, Apr. 17, 1936, ibid.

77   description of Waters crime: People vs. Michael McGrath and John Waters, May 17, 1927, ibid.

77   Hudson Hofbrau: People vs. St. John, Frank McCabe statement, Apr. 15, 1941, DORIS; "Man of Many . . . ," *New York Times,* Nov. 17, 1940.

79   Ardsley bank robbery: "Ardsley Bank Robbed," *Daily News,* Dec. 18, 1935.

79   FBI was tracking: Ibid.; "G-Men Accuse . . . ," *New York Journal and American,* June 18, 1939.

80   "John Doe" warrants: "Arsenal Seized, 5 Questioned in 6 Holdups," *Herald Tribune,* June 17, 1939.

80   Fay and Flood: Ibid.

80–81   description of Athalis activities: felony attempted extortion indictment and plea summary/affidavit, Feb. 20, 1937, DORIS.

81   the heady days: Kisselhoff, 595.

81   description of Lulu: felony attempted extortion indictment and plea summary/affidavit, Feb. 20, 1937; People vs. Thomas Gentles, Mar. 7, 1941, DORIS.

83   Milton Kessler: felony attempted extortion indictment and plea summary/affidavit, Feb. 20, 1937.

83   penitentiary population: "City's New Prison . . . ," *New York Times,* Apr. 22, 1934.

84   Lever Bros. robbery: "Brooklyn Hold-Up Nets Thugs $4,500," *New York Times,* Oct. 8, 1938.

84   Wade got locked up: Sing Sing inmate admission registers, New York State Archives, B0143.

84   Wade and Maislich: People vs. Athalias, June 20, 1939, DORIS.

85   description of Picaso robbery: "Hunt 4 in Holdup of Customs Man," *Daily Mirror,* Feb. 25, 1939; "4 Rob Customs Collector, Get $6,000 and Flee," *Daily News,* Feb. 25, 1939; "4 Bandits Get $6,100 Customs Cash in Street," *Herald Tribune,* Feb. 25, 1939; "Bandits Get Big Haul in Customs Duties," *New York Journal and American,* Feb. 25, 1939; "Sluggers Rob Customs Teller," *New York Sun,* Feb. 25, 1939; "Customs Official Robbed of $6,000," *New York Times,* Feb. 25, 1939.

86   "young men of Latin appearance": *New York Times,* ibid.

Chapter Six: **"5 Arrests Smash Mob"**

87   take his mother . . . doctor's: Alice Salvatore to A.D.A. Herman Stichman, Oct. 25, 1940, People vs. Salvatore, DORIS.

87   a three-month suspended sentence: People vs. Athalias, DORIS.

88   Willie the Greek: Ibid.

88   "lumber jacket": Ibid.

88   Coney Island was like Mecca: *WPA Guide,* 471–75.

88   headlines on the newsstand: "French Submarine Down with 63 Lost,"
        New York Sun, June 16, 1939; "Another Sub Disaster," *New York Journal
        and American,* June 17, 1939.

88   The Indians' Al Milner: "Donald Is Chosen for Mound Duty," *New York
        Sun,* June 16, 1939.

89   "more now than ever": Alice Salvatore to A.D.A. Herman Stichman, Oct.
        25, 1940, People vs. Salvatore, DORIS.

89–92   description of investigation and arrests: "Solve $48,000 Holdups with
        Seizure of Five in Brooklyn," *Daily Mirror,* June 17, 1939; "5 Shopping
        Bag Thugs Identified," *Daily Mirror,* June 18, 1939; "5 Arrests Smash
        Mob That Lifted $42,600," *Daily News,* June 17, 1939; "Arsenal Seized,
        5 Questioned in 6 Holdups," *Herald Tribune,* June 17, 1939; "Victims
        View 5 Suspects in Holdup Series," *Herald Tribune,* June 18, 1939; "5
        Suspects Trapped in Big Holdups," *New York Journal and American,* June
        15, 1939; "Trap 5 Suspects in Holdup Series," *New York Journal and
        American,* June 17, 1939; "G-Men Accuse . . . ," *New York Journal and
        American,* June 18, 1939; "Five Seized as Bank Robbers," *New York Sun,*
        June 16, 1939; "Four Identified as Robber Gang," *New York Sun,* June 17,
        1939; "Gang Is Captured in $40,000 Holdups," *New York Times,* June 17,
        1939, DORIS.

89   "excellent police work": "Police Name Bals to Put Out Mobs," *New York
        Times,* Jan. 3, 1946.

89   clean-government reformers': Block, 81–83.

89   Abe "Kid Twist" Reles: Ibid., 84–85.

89–90   million dollars . . . buy protection: "Valentine to Investigate Charge of
        Police Bribe," *New York Times,* Jan. 26, 1941.

90   "The borderline . . . very thin": Lardner and Reppetto, 213.

90   their living arrangement: "Taxi Dancer Bandit Moll Held in $500," *Daily
        News,* June 16, 1939; "G-Men Accuse . . . ," *New York Journal and Amer-
        ican,* June 18, 1939.

91   quoted dialogue: People vs. Joseph Salvatore, June 5, 1939, DORIS.

91   offered to reduce . . . bail: Joseph Salvatore to Herman L. Stichman, Nov.
        28, 1940, People vs. Salvatore, DORIS.

92   "gladly stay until . . .": Ibid.

93   Willie did receive: "Futile Break at Sing Sing Costs 4 Lives," *Herald Tribune,* Apr. 16, 1941.

93   "tricky little hat perched jauntily": "G-Men Accuse . . . ," *New York Journal and American,* June 18, 1939.

93   "the marble corridors . . . wails": Ibid.

93   burgling the safe: Detective Phillips to Mr. Stichman, Oct. 24, 1940, People vs. Athalias, DORIS.

93   transferred to Albany: "Futile Break . . . ," *Herald Tribune,* Apr. 16, 1941.

93   Thomas "Lulu" Gentles: People vs. Thomas Gentles, DORIS.

94   "Green Peppers . . . Veal or Beef": Ibid.

94   William Wade: People vs. William Wade, Apr. 1940, DORIS.

PART TWO
SING SING

Chapter Seven: **The Prison That Lawes Built**

99   on any given summer weekend: Blumenthal, 119.

99   the always-crowded bleachers: Cheli, 86.

99   Warden Thomas McCormick: Lawes, 104.

99   the vision to build: Blumenthal, 117.

100   Babe Ruth: Cheli, 49.

100   one lucky Ossining boy: Blumenthal, 175–76.

100   the boy . . . lost the ball: Roberta Arminio, interview, Jan. 18, 2005.

100   "prisoners should be encouraged . . . recreation": Lawes, 107.

100   description of Sing Sing furniture: Cheli, 33, 34; Lawes, 349.

100   "turning these prisons . . . encouragement": Lawes, 383.

101   "the boys": Blumenthal, xiii.

101   A regular at Manhattan nightclubs: "Warden Lawes' Wife Was Murdered," *Confidential,* July 1956.

101   a nearly $30-million institution: Lawes, 189.

101   over $3 million dollars: Ibid.; Department of Correction (DOC), 39.

101   "there was . . . crowd of men": Lawes, 410.

102   description of Sing Sing's construction: Cheli, 9–10; Conover, 172; DOC, 2–3; Lawes, 72–73.

102   The native inhabitants: Oechsner, 3.

102   a silence enforced: Conover, 175; Lawes, 72–73.

102   within the sights: Cheli, 2–3.

102   Newgate prison was shuttered: Conover, 174.

102   the cellblock's first inmates: Ibid.

102   Built only inches: Cheli, 39.

102   led convicts to risk: Lawes, 75.

102   the state legislature: Ibid., 88.

103   prison keepers who couldn't count: Oechsner, 96.

103   The old cellblock's roof: Cheli, 15.

103   a foul reputation: Lawes, 88.

103   striped uniforms: Ibid., 15.

103   Discipline: Ibid., 74–75, 83, 85.

103   "poor work": "Auburn Inmates Built, Occupied Sing Sing," Facility Spot-
        light, Ossining Historical Society (OHS).

103   Sing Sing's first hundred years: Cheli, 127.

104   description of Lawes and Smith: Lawes, 65–66.

104   quoted dialogue: Ibid.

104   a polite coolness: Ibid.; Blumenthal, 2.

104   "the quickest . . . warden": Lawes, 109.

104   Lawes's predecessor: Ibid., 111.

104   Lawes was raised: Ibid., 12–13; Blumenthal, 69–72.

104   the "Siberia of America": Lawes, 14.

105   the New York School of Social Work: Blumenthal, 82–83.

105   "I was . . . confirmed in my ideals": Lawes, 44.

105   Potter's Field: *WPA Guide*, 551.

105   description of Lawes's first day: Lawes, 66.

105   multicolored silk shirts: Ibid., 125.

105   "a man-sized job": Ibid., 107.

106   description of Lawes's speech: Lawes, 109.

106   Lawes won state appropriation: Ibid., 179.

106–107 A-block and B-block: Officer Andre Varin interview, June 17, 2004.

107   description of Sing Sing expansion: Lawes, 179.

107   "The gesture of trust . . . faith": Ibid., 143.

108   rumors persist: Blumenthal, 207; Sutton, 73.

108   Carlyle, Shaw, and Emerson: Lawes, 340–42.

108   "Guidance . . . answer to crime": Ibid., 411.

108   Warner Brothers: Dooley, 331.

108   filmed on location: "Sing Sing Fact Sheet," DOC.

108   Lawes as technical advisor: Blumenthal, 213.

109   "Truth is . . . fiction here": Dooley, 331.

109   the picture boosted book sales: Blumenthal, 213.

109   broadcast from an old radio console: Officer Andre Varin interview, June 17, 2004.

109   *Invisible Stripes:* Blumenthal, 254.

109   *Chalked Out:* L. Lawes Collection, Box 5, File 22, Lloyd Sealy Library, John Jay College of Criminal Justice.

109   a blizzard of invitations: Ibid.

109   MacCormick's note of apology: Ibid.

109   Zeppo Marks Agency: Ibid.

109   *You Can't Get Away with Murder:* Dooley, 333.

110   ever-popular genre: Ibid., 328.

110   "stir" and "chow": Ibid., 329.

110   Twenty-seven prison films: Ibid., 331–2.

110   movies filmed at Sing Sing: "Sing Sing Fact Sheet," DOC.

110   payment to inmates: Blumenthal, 213.

110   a regulation-size gymnasium: Cheli, 75.

110   wife and three daughters: Blumenthal, 130–31.

111   the only child ever born: Lawes, 142.

111   photo of Cherie: Lawes, facing page 183.

111   description of house staff: Blumenthal, 131.

111   "old time . . . mother love": "Convicts at Lawes Bier," *New York Times,* Nov. 2, 1937; "Many at Funeral of Mrs. Lewis E. Lawes," *New York Times,* Nov. 3, 1937.

112   "general publicity . . . Productions": "Warden Lawes Married," *New York Times,* June 12, 1939.

112   "formal announcement": Ibid.

112   requests for magazine stories: L. Lawes Collection, Box 1, File 9, Lloyd Sealy Library, John Jay College of Criminal Justice.

113   *Lawes of Sing Sing:* L. Lawes Collection, Box 3, File 82, ibid.

Chapter Eight: **In the Big House**

114   "yard-out": Sutton, 124.

114   personal items of clothing: Lawes, 121, 125.

114   Charles Chapin photo: Morris, plate 15.

115   On weekends: Sutton, 124.

115   A man's old life: Ibid., 70.

115   former Tammany boss Hines: Stolberg, 246.

115   Louis "Lepke" Buchalter: Reppetto, 228.

115   the Bertillon Department: Lawes, 184–85.

115   anthropometrics: "The Identification of the West Brothers: Why the Bertillon Anthropometric System Failed," http://www.members.aol.com/SVG2254/West.htm

115   description of the chief clerk: Cheli, 80–81.

115–116 description of inmate processing: Lawes, 180–86.

117   The routine was similar to Elmira's: Register of men returned for violation of parole, New York State Archives, B0130-80.

117   "a thorough understanding . . . on life": Lawes, 185.

117   the state of Texas: Hallinan, 105.

117   MacCormick had been appalled: "M'Cormick Raids . . . ," *Herald Tribune,* Jan. 25, 1934.

117   masturbation was punished: Blumenthal, 70; Hallinan, 71.

117   "Self-abuse . . . admit": Blumenthal, 196.

117   "seventy-five percent . . . one cell": Lawes, 246.

117   policy of one man per cell: Lt. Kenneth Goewey, telephone interview, Feb. 9, 2005.

118   "Sunday letter": Lawes, 184.

118   sign-painting at Elmira: Register of men returned for violation of parole, New York State Archives, B0130-80.

118   prison food: Fred Starler interview, Feb. 20, 2003.

118   radios in the cell: Sutton, 123.

118   He'd been going to Mass: Inmate admission registers, New York State Archives, B0143.

118   Father Bernard Martin: Patchey, photo caption "In Appreciation . . . ," OHS.

119–120 description of early prison history: Morris and Rothman, 100–16.

119   "barbarous usages . . . principals": Ibid.

120   sketched the blueprint: "Sing Sing: Study of Contrasts, the Old and the New," Facility Spotlight, OHS.

120–121 the country's first prison systems: Morris and Rothman, 100–16.

121   "congregate": Ibid., 105.

122   the concept of the Big House: Ibid., 165–66.

123   record incarceration rates: DOC, 32; Hallinan, xiii.

123   experimenting with medicine and psychiatry: Morris and Rothman, 158–60.

123   Whitey would later testify: People vs. Joseph Riordan, 2204, Westchester County Clerk.

124   the New York Central: Cheli, 91; Lt. Kenneth Goewey, telephone interview, Feb. 19, 2005.

124   they'd even done short stretches together: Inmate admission registers, New York State Archives, B0143.

124   "buggy": People vs. Joseph Riordan, 2120, Westchester County Clerk.

125–126 quoted dialogue: Ibid., 2285–87.

126–128 description of Whitey and Patches meeting: Ibid., 2204.

127   "too many ears around": Ibid., 317.

128   Lawes's picture on the cover of *Time:* Blumenthal, 178.

Chapter Nine: **From Saint Peter to Patches**

129   From about 2000 B.C.: Morris and Rothman, 8.

129   the Middle Ages: Ibid., 32.

130   Colorado State Prison: Blumenthal, 176.

130   Clinton Prison riot: Sutton, 82–83.

130   Auburn prison: "The Best Prison in the World," online article, www.geocities.com/MotorCity/Downs/3548/facility/auburn.html

131   "Everything changed . . . Attica": Lt. Kenneth Goewey telephone interview, July 29, 2003.

131   Dillinger's professional bank robbing: Toland, 28.

131   "wheelman": Ibid.

131   description of Indiana State Prison escape: Ibid., 112–18.

131   description of Allen County Jail escape: Ibid., 128–31.

131   Dillinger's most legendary escape: Ibid., 209–16.

132   escape from Eastern State: Sutton, 185.

132   thirty incomplete tunnels: Hallinan, 65.

132   escape from Holmesburg prison: Sutton, 191–213.

132   "the most horrible . . . been in": Ibid., 70.

132   tightened overall security: Ibid., 123.

132   night staff: Lt. Kenneth Goewey, telephone interview, July 29, 2003.

132   empty tower behind A-block: Sutton, 128.

133   an overall drop: L. Lawes Collection, Box 12, File 62, Lloyd Sealy Library, John Jay College of Criminal Justice.

133   one fugitive's skeleton: Blumenthal, 155.

133   towers held high powered arsenals: Lt. Kenneth Goewey, telephone interview, Feb. 19, 2005.

133   description of Thompson submachine gun: www.nfatoys.com.

133–134 November 1930 escape: Patchey, untitled, OHS.

134   "These crooks . . . something": Lt. Kenneth Goewey, telephone interview, July 29, 2003.

134   Harry Kagel Jr. escape: "Sing Sing Fugitive Caught," *New York Times,* Apr. 7, 1933.

134   George Donaldson escape: "4 at Sing Sing in Tunnel Bolt Seized in River," *Herald Tribune,* Aug. 14, 1932; "Four Convicts Captured Fleeing Sing Sing," *New York Times,* Aug. 14, 1932.

135   "Mr. Hickey of Yonkers": *Herald Tribune,* ibid.; *New York Times,* ibid.

135   Lawes fastened a steel plate: "Sing Sing Tunnel Sealed," *New York Times,* Aug. 15, 1932.

135   "commenced making arrangements": New York State Police (NYSP) Summary of Indictment Re: Edward J. Kiernan, July 1, 1941.

135   According to McGale: People vs. Joseph Riordan, 2285–87, Westchester County Clerk.

136   width of the cells: Cheli, 79.

136   Cells were single: Lawes, 246.

137   "the strange tie . . . gratitude": "Docks Combed for Gangster Aides in Break," *New York Journal and American,* Apr. 15, 1941.

139–141 description of Sing Sing visiting procedure: Deputy Commissioner William Leonard to All Wardens and Superintendents, Re: General

Order #11, Aug. 5, 1936, L. Lawes Collection, Box 1, File 5, Lloyd Sealy Library, John Jay College of Criminal Justice; Leonard to Wardens and Superintendents, Re: General Order #11, Aug. 10, 1936, ibid.; Commissioner Edward P. Mulrooney to Wardens and Superintendents, Re: Amending General Order #11, Sept. 23, 1936, ibid.; Commissioner John A. Lyons Re: General Order #8, July 12, 1939, ibid.; Commissioner of Correction to Sup't. Mattewan State Hospital, Re: General Order #11, Sept. 14, 1939, ibid.; Lyons to Lawes, Re: Sing Sing escape, Apr. 24, 1941, ibid.

137   Kiernan's release: Inmate Admission Registers, New York State Archives, B0143.

137   Kiernan could easily pass: Visiting Desk Officer Paul Wilson to Lawes, May 6, 1941, Box 1, File 5, L. Lawes Collection, Lloyd Sealy Library, John Jay College of Criminal Justice.

137   Kiernan and Wade: NYSP Summary of Indictment Re: Kiernan, July 1, 1941.

138   his most regular visitor: People vs. Joseph Riordan, 1710–19, Westchester County Clerk.

138   practiced in stealth: Lt. Kenneth Goewey, telephone interview, Feb. 9, 2005.

138   Ma Barker: Toland, 44.

138   Bonnie Parker: Ibid., 39.

138   Willie Sutton's loyal wife: Sutton, 133–34.

138   tailored sharkskin suits: "Stickup Mob?" photo caption, *Daily News,* June 18, 1939.

138   the Nickel Dump: Kisselhoff, 574.

139   Anchor Café and Jack Dempsey's: *WPA Guide,* 22–23.

139   description of visiting room: Sutton, 132–33.

140   "For years and years": Parsons to Lawes, May 6, 1941, L. Lawes Collection, Box 1, File 5, Lloyd Sealy Library, John Jay College of Criminal Justice.

140   description of Gertrude's visit: People vs. Joseph Riordan, 1710–19, 1721–29, Westchester County Clerk.

141   Patches's nearest living relatives: Inmate Admission Registers, New York State Archives, B0143.

141   ex-cons weren't allowed to visit: Lawes to Lyons, May 6, 1941, Box 1, File 5, Lloyd Sealy Library, John Jay College of Criminal Justice.

141   Kiernan photos: Patchey, untitled, OHS.

142   Kiernan's parole: Inmate Admission Registers, New York State Archives, B0143; NYSP Summary of Indictment Re: Kiernan, July 1, 1941.

143   *Rules and Regulations Governing Inmates of the New York State Penal Institutions, December 1, 1940*, OHS.

Chapter Ten: **The Steam Vault**

145   McGale hadn't had a single visitor: "Gallagher Claims McGale Confessed," Patchey, OHS.

145   "nearest living relative": Inmate Admission Registers, New York State Archives, B0143.

146   "baggage agent": Ibid.

147   "bugs": People vs. Joseph Riordan, 2120, Westchester County Clerk.

147   descriptions of work at Sing Sing: Fred Starler interview, Feb. 20, 2003; Lt. Kenneth Goewey, telephone interview, Jan. 26, 2005; DOC, 37; Blumenthal, 119, 174.

147   all the prison's mechanics: Lawes to Lyons, Apr. 28, 1941, L. Lawes Collection, Lloyd Sealy Library, John Jay College of Criminal Justice.

148   partly responsible: People vs. Joseph Riordan, 2333, 2335, Westchester County Clerk.

149   "ice house": "Gallagher Claims McGale Confessed," Patchey, OHS.

149   steamfitter experience: People vs. Joseph Riordan, 2333, Westchester County Clerk.

151   "laying around": Ibid., 2325.

151   inmates with keys: Lt. Kenneth Goewey, telephone interview, Jan. 26, 2005.

151   Newspapers afterward: "Gallagher Claims . . . ," Patchey, OHS.

151   McGale told another tale: People vs. Joseph Riordan, 2340, Westchester County Clerk.

152–158 description of McGale's procedure: Ibid., 2319–38.

156   a stack of old mattresses: Ibid., exhibit photo.

158   the crumbling cellblock: "Sing Sing Inmates Moved," *New York Times*, Aug. 23, 1940.

Chapter Eleven: **Machine Guns and Milk Trucks**

160   Patches wanted a Tommy gun: "Motion for Mistrial in Sing Sing Murder Case Denied," Patchey, June 17, 1941, OHS.

160   Thompson submachine guns: www.nfatoys.com.

161   Alfred Catelan: "Motion for Mistrial . . . ," Patchey, June 17, 1941, OHS.

161   He had positioned himself: "Futile Break . . . ," *Herald Tribune,* Apr. 16, 1941; "Four Dead, 2 Captured in Sing Sing Break," *New York Times,* Apr. 15, 1941.

162   Crowley's Dairy: "Convict Aides . . . ," *Citizen Register,* Apr. 15, 1941.

162   the warden suspected: Lawes, 284.

162   a trucker's helper: People vs. Joseph Riordan, 1006, Westchester County Clerk.

163   quoted dialogue: NYSP Summary of Indictment Re: Kiernan, July 1, 1941.

163   pictures of Wade: "Stickup Mob?" photo caption, *Daily News,* June 18, 1939; "Taken into Custody" photo caption, Patchey, OHS.

164   description of milk truck surveillance: "Convict Aides . . . ," *Citizen Register,* Apr. 15, 1941.

164   the tenth of March: People vs. Joseph Riordan, 1716, Westchester County Clerk.

165   quoted dialogue: Ibid., 2205.

166   quoted dialogue: Ibid., 283.

166   the early morning of March 22: "Convict Aides . . . ," *Citizen Register,* Apr. 15, 1941.

168   description of prison milk route: People vs. Joseph Riordan, 1921–49, 2297–2308, Westchester County Clerk.

168   "horse block gate": Officer Andre Varin interview, June 17, 2004.

168–169 description of gun removal: "Futile Break . . . ," *Herald Tribune,* Apr. 15, 1941; "Gallagher Claims . . . ," Patchey, OHS; People vs. Joseph Riordan, 2289, Westchester County Clerk.

Chapter Twelve: **To the Hospital**

170   quoted dialogue: People vs. Joseph Riordan, 2205–06, Westchester County Clerk.

171   quoted dialogue: Ibid.

171   scores of monthly surgeries: Cheli, 74.

171   fifteen inmate nurses: Lawes, 205.

172   bronze inscription: Ibid., 204.

172   African American inmates: Fred Starler interview, Feb. 20, 2003.

173   She would turn sixty-five: Elizabeth Riordan death certificate, Division of Records, New York City Department of Health.

173   William Taylor: People vs. Joseph Riordan, 1562–68, Westchester County Clerk.

174   quoted dialogue: Ibid., 284.

174   checked in at 11:45: Ibid., 2290.

174   Whitey's temperature: "Ossining Officer Takes Credit as He Testifies," Patchey, OHS.

175   variable number of patients: "Futile Break . . . ," *Herald Tribune*, Apr. 15, 1941; "Four Dead . . . ," *New York Times*, Apr. 15, 1941.

175   Martin's own headline: "Prison Priest Ran Down Clews That Brought Davino's Freedom," *New York Times*, Nov. 11, 1941, Archdiocese of New York Archives, St. Joseph's Seminary, Yonkers, NY.

176   the sports pages: "Yanks Win, 3–2, Halt Dodger Rally in 9th," *Daily News*, Apr. 13, 1941.

177   description of gun handoff: People vs. Joseph Riordan, 286–88, Westchester County Clerk.

PART THREE
CRASH OUT

Chapter Thirteen: **Murder and Reprieve**

181   Tappanese Zee: Oechsner, 3.

181   the river had always been: Ibid., 11.

181   farmers and local manufacturers: Ibid., 102; OHS, 118.

181   Isaac Smith & Sons: Oechsner, 80.

181   spring thaw . . . impassable: Ibid., 46.

181   one hundred saloons: Ibid.

182   Hudson River Railroad: Ibid., 80; OHS, 118.

182   entrepreneurs seized the opportunity: Ibid., 125, 126.

182   a red-brick train station: Ibid.

183   "unsightly and unsanitary": untitled, Patchey, Sept. 9, 1922.

183   Cinders from the coal: Fred Starler interview, Feb. 20, 2003.

183   movies at Sing Sing: Ibid.; G.F.C., Director of Recreation to Ralph Daigh, Fawcett Publications, July 29, 1938, L. Lawes Collection, Box 1, File 9, Lloyd Sealy Library, John Jay College of Criminal Justice.

183   state required . . . confines of Ossining: Lt. Kenneth Goewey, telephone interview, Feb. 21, 2005.

183   town's large employers: OHS, 118, 119, 121, 124.

183   The Prison Keepers: "St. Ann's, Keepers Battle for 2d Half Title at Park Tonight," Citizen Register, Sept. 3, 1940; Cheli, 85.

183   pistol marksmanship contests: untitled, Patchey, OHS.

184   monthly parades: OHS, 36, 82, 126.

184   description of 1980s search: Lt. Kenneth Goewey, telephone interview, July 29, 2003.

184   official police version: NYSP Summary of Indictment Re: William Wade, July 1, 1941; NYSP Summary of Indictment Re: Edward Kiernan, July 1, 1941.

185   A later photo: "Taken into Custody . . . ," photo caption, Citizen Register, Apr. 15, 1941; "3 Slain, 2 Caught in Prison Break," New York Journal and American, Apr. 14, 1941.

185   a pair of license plates: "Escape Plot to Be Given to Grand Jury Friday," Patchey, OHS; "Four Dead . . . ," New York Times, Apr. 14, 1941.

185   Charles Bergstrom and Robert Brown: NYSP Summary of Indictment Re: Wade and Kiernan, July 1, 1941.

185   Bergstrom's record: Inmate Admission Registers, New York State Archives, B0143.

186   Brownie secured a hideout: People vs. Joseph Riordan, 1954–59, Westchester County Clerk.

187   description of hospital ward: Ibid., 2207–08.

187   "[lay] in bed . . . 2:30": Ibid., 2209.

187   "had hollered on somebody": Ibid., 318.

188   "best conditioned club . . . league": "The Roundup," Daily News, Apr. 13, 1941.

188   unannounced visits to posts: Lt. Kenneth Goewey, telephone interview, Jan. 26, 2005.

189   description of Hartye: "Hartye First Gun Victim," Patchey, OHS; "Trib-

ute Paid to John Hartye, ibid.; "Plaque Honors John Hartye," ibid.; "Sing Sing Guards Honor Veteran," ibid.

189   "had custodial . . . over inmates": DOC, 13.

190–196 description of escape: "Hunt Bag Gang in Sing Sing Escape Causing 4 Deaths," *Daily Mirror*, Apr. 15, 1941; "Two Seized in Break," *Daily News*, Apr. 15, 1941; "Futile Break . . . ," *Herald Tribune*, Apr. 15, 1941; "3 Die in Sing Sing Break, 2 Caught," *New York Journal and American*, Apr. 14, 1941; "Escape Plot . . . ," Patchey, OHS; "2 Cross River but Give Up in Palisades Park," *New York Sun*, Apr. 14, 1941; "4 Dead . . . ," *New York Times*, Apr. 15, 1941.

190   never mentioned hearing anything: People vs. Joseph Riordan, 2209, Westchester County Clerk.

190   "everything . . . mind": Ibid.

191   "What the hell . . . here?": Ibid.

191   "Officer Hartye . . . side of a bed": "Ossining Officer . . . ," Patchey, OHS.

192   quoted dialogue: People vs. Joseph Riordan, 2209, Westchester County Clerk.

193   quoted dialogue: Ibid., 2293.

193   Daniel McCarthy murder: "Officer McCarthy Dies, Martyr to Prison Duty," *Democratic Register*, July 1, 1916.

193   Edwin Craft murder: www.correctionhistory.org.

193   description of DeSimone: Fred Starler interview, Feb. 20, 2003; untitled, Patchey, OHS.

193   a hardwood club: Conover, 49.

193   "This is a break": People vs. Joseph Riordan, 2210, Westchester County Clerk.

194   "Let's kill the screw": "Two Seized . . . ," *Daily News*, Apr. 15, 1941.

194   "Let's give it to them": Ibid.

194   "For what . . . out now": "Futile Break . . . ," *Herald Tribune*, Apr. 15, 1941.

194   "We got no time": "Ossining Officer . . . ," Patchey, OHS.

195   "If we do that . . . Let's go": Ibid.

Chapter Fourteen: **A Crack Shot**

198   the phone just kept ringing: "3 Die . . . ," *New York Journal and American*, Apr. 14, 1941.

198   evidence points to: Fred Starler interview, Feb. 20, 2003.

198   Darrow used the stairs: Ibid.

198   Lawes's Easter party: "Futile Break . . . ," *Herald Tribune*, Apr. 15, 1941.

199   "They can't get out . . . have them": Fred Starler interview, Feb. 20, 2003.

199   Only three men: Blumenthal, 155.

199   Big Ben: Lawes, 286.

199   policy on Big Ben: "Prison Machinery Failed Warden Lawes Admits," Patchey, OHS.

199   complete confusion: Fred Starler interview, Feb. 20, 2003.

200   flush toilets: Lt. Kenneth Goewey, telephone interview, Feb. 21, 2005.

200   "characters": "Two Escaped Convicts Caught, Patrolman Fagan, Guard Slain," *Citizen Register*, Apr. 14, 1941.

201–202 description of Officer Fagan: "In Line of Duty," Patchey, OHS; "Shot Convict" photo caption, ibid.; "Police Will Honor Fagan," ibid.; "Pays Tribute to Patrolman," ibid.; "Fagan Nonchalant About Badge Number 13," ibid.; "Fagan and Prisoner Die in Battle on Street," *Citizen Register*, Apr. 14, 1941; "Patrolman Noted in Sports Here," ibid.; "12 Perish, 4 Dying, 25 Hurt as Bus Leaps from Ramp, Explodes," *Citizen Register*, July 22, 1934; "Death List Mounts to 16 in Bus Explosion," ibid., July 23, 1934; "Indictment of Several Persons to Be Sought in Bus Fatality; Damaging Evidence Is Given," ibid., July 24, 1934; "Police Recover Body of Man from River," ibid.

202   The fog was dense: "3 Die . . . ," *New York Journal and American*, Apr. 14, 1941; "Futile Break . . . ," *Herald Tribune*, Apr. 15, 1941.

203   "Hey, you . . . guys": "3 Die . . . ," *New York Journal and American*, Apr. 14, 1941.

206   quoted dialogue: Ibid.; "2 Cross River . . . ," *New York Sun*, Apr. 14, 1941.

207   "know his potatoes": untitled, *Citizen Register*, Sept. 3, 1940.

207   quoted dialogue: "2 Cross River . . . ," *New York Sun*, Apr. 14, 1941.

Chapter Fifteen: **Hook Mountain**

209   "shad brigade": "Shad Run on the Hudson," *Citizen Register*, Apr. 17, 1941.

209   Rohr's news photo: "One Way Ride" photo caption, Patchey, OHS.

210   quoted dialogue: "Two Seized . . . ," *Daily News*, Apr. 15, 1941; People vs. Joseph Riordan, 362–63, 2241–2, Westchester County Clerk.

211   procedure for twenty-one years: "Prison Whistle to Blow Only If Men Are Outside," Patchey, Apr. 21, 1941, OHS.

211   fifty-man Ossining police force: "Futile Break . . . ," *Herald Tribune*, Apr. 15, 1941.

212   90 percent of the men: "New Break Rumor Arouses Sing Sing," *New York Times*, Apr. 16, 1941.

213   quoted dialogue: "Two Seized . . . ," *Daily News*, Apr. 15, 1941.

213   "river-that-flows-two-ways": Carmer, 9.

214   quoted dialogue: People vs. Joseph Riordan, 363, Westchester County Clerk.

215   the State Police contacted: NYSP Superintendent John A. Warner to Police Commissioner Lewis J. Valentine Re: New York City Police Airplane, Apr. 17, 1941, NYSP file.

215   Trooper W. W. Horton: untitled, Patchey, Mar. 1, 1942, OHS.

215–216 description of bloodhounds' prowess: Ann Brooks Holt, DVM, "Bloodhounds: An Underutilized Resource," online article, www.midatlantic-dogs.org.

216   Major John Warner: online profile, www.nysp.gov.

216   fearsome reputation: untitled, Patchey, Mar. 1, 1942, OHS.

216   quoted dialogue: Ibid.

216–218 quoted dialogue: People vs. Joseph Riordan, 363–64, 2242–43, Westchester County Clerk; "Two Seized . . . ," *Daily News*, Apr. 15, 1941.

218   manhunt . . . twenty-six air miles: "3 Die . . . ," *New York Journal and American*, Apr. 14, 1941.

218   Coast Guard station was radioed: Capt. R. W. Dempwolf, USCG, to Supt. Warner, Apr. 23, 1941, NYSP file.

218   one thousand officers: "4 Dead . . . ," *New York Times*, Apr. 15, 1941.

221   "You'll find . . . somewhere": untitled, Patchey, Mar. 1, 1942, OHS.

222   quoted dialogue: "Futile Break . . . ," *Herald Tribune*, Apr. 15, 1941; "3 Die . . . ," *New York Journal and American*, Apr. 14, 1941.

Chapter Sixteen: **The Third Degree**
223   One lucky photographer: "End of Desperate Break" photo caption, *Daily News*, Apr. 15, 1941; "A Clearing on Hook Mountain" photo caption,

New York Journal and American, Apr. 14, 1941; "Tired Convicts in Hands of Police" photo caption, *New York Sun,* Apr. 14, 1941.

224   three officers moved in: "Two Lives for Four," *Citizen Register,* Apr. 15, 1941.

224   *Daily Mirror* photographer: "7," "8," "9" photo captions, *Daily Mirror,* Apr. 15, 1941.

224   "Stand up . . . you": People vs. Joseph Riordan, 754, Westchester County Clerk.

225   "Stop . . . Gallagher": "Beatings Began Here," Patchey, OHS.

225   The photographer took one last: "Killers and Captors" photo caption, *Citizen Register,* Apr. 15, 1941.

225   The term traces back: www.etymonline.com.

226–227 description of third-degree techniques: Steve Irsay, "Fear Factor: How Far Can Police Go to Get a Confession?" online article, www.courttv.com.

226–230 description of NYSP interrogation: People vs. Joseph Riordan, 756–62, Westchester County Clerk; "Beatings Began . . . ," Patchey, OHS.

227   "I don't know . . . wise guy": Ibid.

228   quoted dialogue: Ibid.

229–230 quoted dialogue: Ibid.

230   Supreme Court decisions: Steve Irsay, "Fear Factor . . . ," online article, www.courttv.com.

230   Billy Wade's story: "Wade Sticks to Story That Confession Was Forced by Third Degree," Patchey, OHS.

231   quoted dialogue: Ibid.

232   "We want . . . Shopping Bag gang": "Docks Combed for Gangster Aides in Break," *New York Journal and American,* Apr. 14, 1941.

233   photo caption: "End of Desperate Break," *Daily News,* Apr. 15, 1941.

233   Lawes stands: "The Tragic End of an Attempt For Freedom," *Citizen Register,* Apr. 15, 1941.

Chapter Seventeen: **"Look Out Warden"**

234   "without unnecessary delay": Lyons to Lawes, Apr. 24, 1941, L. Lawes Collection, Box 1, File 5, Lloyd Sealy Library, John Jay College of Criminal Justice.

234 "Ossining police . . . the escape": "Wants Prison to Explain," *Citizen Register,* Apr. 15, 1941.

235 "were not . . . immediately": "Prison Machinery Failed Warden Lawes Admits," *Citizen Register,* Apr. 15, 1941.

235 "machinery . . . function": Ibid.

235 "locked in . . . into the basement": Ibid.

235 "as soon . . . were notified": Ibid.

235 "tried in vain . . . did get one": Ibid.

235 blizzard of internal memos: L. Lawes Papers Supplemental I, Box 3, Folder 61, Lloyd Sealy Library, John Jay College of Criminal Justice.

236 "with the . . . mother": Lawes to Lyons, May 6, 1941, Box 1, File 5, ibid.

236 "a man or men . . . the count": Lawes to Principal Keeper John J. Sheehy, Re: prison whistle, Apr. 22, 1941, Box 3, Folder 61, ibid.

236 "medium security . . . prison": Lawes to Lyons, Apr. 38, 1941, Box 1, File 5, ibid.

236 "cheap, low fence": Ibid.

236 "weak and inefficient": Ibid.

237 "the responsibility should be placed": Ibid.

237 "are . . . secure": Ibid.

237 "an insecure plant . . . poorly located": Ibid.

237 "Look Out Warden": Patchey, OHS.

237 a petition was circulating: L. Lawes Collection, Box 2, File 18, Lloyd Sealy Library, John Jay College of Criminal Justice.

237 "available to do . . . you did before": Frank Cooper, General Amusement Corp. to Lawes, Apr. 15, 1941, L. Lawes Collection, Box 1, File 10, Lloyd Sealy Library, John Jay College of Criminal Justice.

237 "some excellent . . . presentation": Lawes to Cooper, Apr. 16, 1941, ibid.

237 "considerable fireworks": Ibid.

237 "tremendous . . . material": Ibid.

238 a national star: Reppetto, 178.

238 an investigation into corruption: "350 Rounded Up in Racket Probe," *New York Journal and American,* July 16, 1941.

238 the first city D.A.: "Dewey Raids Piers as Aid to Defense," *New York Times,* July 17, 1941.

238   "worst criminals": "Murder Tops Careers of 3 in Break," *New York Journal and American*, Apr. 14, 1941.

238   description of court appearance: "Gallagher Seeks Trial May 19," Patchey, Apr. 21, 1941, OHS.

239   "not guilty": Ibid.

239   "she didn't have no money": People vs. Joseph Riordan, 2270, Westchester County Clerk.

240   "wasn't interested": Ibid.

240   "never heard of him": "Kiernan Writ Is Withdrawn," Patchey, Apr. 16, 1941, OHS.

240   "with the other defendants": "Comb Jersey for Sing Sing Killers' Hidden Arsenal," *Daily Mirror*, Apr. 16, 1941.

241   Gallagher's juror choices: "Avoid Mistrial of Four in Guard Murder," Patchey, OHS.

241   motioned for a mistrial: Ibid.

241   client had been beaten: "Wade Charges Police Beatings," Patchey, May 7, 1941, OHS.

241   "so inflaming the public mind": "Court Denies Wade Plea for New Venue," Patchey, May 12, 1941, OHS.

241   "bloodstained . . . from his body": "First Talisman Called Up for Examination," Patchey, May 26, 1941, OHS.

241   "ripped . . . spattered with blood": Ibid.

241   Marion Emmet: Ibid.

241   "natty . . . matching tie": "2 Women and a Man Now on Jury," Patchey, May 28, 1941, OHS.

242   group of young women: "Girl Students Barred from County Court," Patchey, Apr. 21, 1941, OHS.

242   "secret method": "Many Called to Tell of Crime," Patchey, OHS.

242   "keep a sharp eye": "Wade's Counsel Collapses," Patchey, June 3, 1941, OHS.

243   "the proof would show": "Convicts Hit by Policemen, Guards, Gallagher Admits in Opening Speech," Patchey, June 9, 1941, OHS.

243   "We admit everything . . . this case": Ibid.

244   "Waters was . . . the shooting": Ibid.

244   "Riordan made a mistake . . . stayed in bed": Ibid.

244   "beaten out of him": Ibid.

244   "jail physician": Ibid.

244   hosing down the transport: untitled, Patchey, OHS.

245   "laid a hand": "Inspector Nugent Denies He Laid a Hand on Wade After Arrest," Patchey, June 13, 1941, OHS.

245   Bailiffs stood ready: "Ossining Policeman Who Struck McGale Identified by Lieutenant Mead," Patchey, June 19, 1941, OHS.

245   "I don't remember": People vs. Joseph Riordan, 1727, Westchester County Clerk.

245   "harm . . . No": Ibid.

246   a precise catalogue: "Holds Firm Under Stiff Questioning," Patchey, OHS.

246   an equally fantastic tale: Ibid.

246   seemed to blossom: People vs. Joseph Riordan, 2319–38, Westchester County Clerk.

247   "with a visage . . . so frightening": "Futile Break . . . ," *New York Herald Tribune,* Apr. 15, 1941.

247   "hot car": People vs. Joseph Riordan 2220–21, Westchester County Clerk.

247   I cleaned them every day: Ibid., 268.

248   DeSimone quoted word for word: "Lt. Carlson Claims Capture," Patchey, OHS.

248   another look at the exhibits: "Added Exhibits Asked," Ibid.

248   Roger Smith Hotel: Ibid.

248   "prison within a prison": Cheli, 113.

Chapter Eighteen: **The Dance Hall**

249   "effective . . . July 15th": "To Build Home in Ossining," Patchey, OHS.

249   "for a long time": Ibid.

249   "no maladministration": "Lawes Cleared in Break Quiz," Patchey, Aug. 1941, OHS.

249   "I'll probably . . . seven days a week": "To Build . . . ," Patchey, OHS.

250   "I plan to . . . hard for me": Ibid.

250   "I can either . . . may do": Ibid.

250   "humane leadership": "In Appreciation" photo caption, Patchey, OHS.

250   "I am about . . . God bless you": untitled, Patchey, OHS.

251   a cruel disturbance: Conover, 192.

251   every condemned man and woman: Christianson, 21.

251   description of Death House: Cheli, 113.

252   A specially built stepladder: Officer Andre Varin interview, June 17, 2004.

252   the sun was a constant: Blumenthal, 100.

252   exercise period: DOC, 52.

252   couldn't see neighbor: Christianson, 17.

252   keeper held the matches: DOC, 53.

252   "moveable objects of any size": Ibid.

252   "a large quantity . . . foreign bodies": Ibid.

253   automatic appeal: Lawes, 300.

253   corroborating testimony: People vs. Joseph Riordan, 1587–96, Westchester County Clerk.

254   "Riordan argued . . . trusty Kaplan": "Sing Sing Guard Admits Riordan Saved His Life," Patchey, May 23, 1942, OHS.

254   meant to do away with: Conover, 186.

254   people viewing the chair: Blumenthal, 102.

254   ghoulish marketing trick: DOC, 51.

255   "revolting exhibition": Conover, 187, 188.

255   method was standardized: DOC, 51.

256   "calmly awaiting execution": "No Visitors This Week for Killers," Patchey, June 10, 1942, OHS.

256   Whitey's niece Mary: Log of Actions Relating to Inmates Scheduled for Executions, New York State Archives, B1244.

256   McGale's sister-in-law: Ibid.

256   Rumor persists: Officer Andre Varin interview, June 17, 2004.

257   the dance hall: Lawes, 299.

257   a typical menu: Christianson, 117.

257   "Here, you need this more than me": Lawes, 302.

257   a former rabbi: History Channel, "The Big House."

257   "I never croaked anyone . . . two other men": "Two Waiting Death Tonight," Patchey, June 11, 1942, OHS.

257   "If I have to . . . anyone shot": Ibid.

258   Hundreds of witness applications: "Riordan, McGale Pay Penalty June 10," Patchey, May 4, 1942, OHS.

258   Officials understood: Christianson, 1, 121.

258   "So this is . . . saving three lives": "Two Pay Penalty in Chair," Patchey, June 12, 1942, OHS.

260   increasingly mechanized mass society: Bell, 130–36.

260   U.S. Court of Appeals: Wade vs. J. Vernal Jackson, Warden of Clinton Prison and the People of the State of New York, May 19, 1958, West-Law.

260   adjusted with the times: People vs. Joseph Salvatore, June 15, 1939, DORIS.

261   reassigned to the front gate: Fred Starler interview, Feb. 20, 2003.

261   Lawes in the war effort: Blumenthal, 270–71.

262   description of Lawes's final years: Ibid., 269, 271–74, 279–80.

263   electric chair embraced: "Last Murderer on Death Row Prepares to Leave Sing Sing," Aug. 27, 1969, OHS.

263   sent to a Virginia museum: Christianson, 4.

263   "vocational ed" unit: Officer Andre Varin interview, June 17, 2004.

263   landlords advocated a name change: O'Connor, 234.

263   Lincoln Tunnel: WPA Guide, 156.

263   Riordan family: Geraldine Riordan Murphy, telephone interview, Jan. 24, 2005.

264   "She was . . . she died": Ibid.

264   "There is something . . . hope of change," Sage, vol. 1, 8.

SELECTED BIBLIOGRAPHY

Allen, Frederick Lewis. *Only Yesterday: An Informal History of the 1920's*. New York: Harper & Row, 1931; reprint ed., New York: Perennial Classics, 2000.

Allen, Frederick Lewis. *Since Yesterday: The 1930s in America, September 3, 1929– September 3, 1939*. New York: Harper & Row, 1939: reprint ed., New York: Perennial Library, 1986.

Appelbaum, Stanley. *The New York World's Fair 1939–1940 in 155 Photographs by Richard Wurts and Others*. New York: Dover, 1977.

Asbury, Herbert. *The Gangs of New York: An Informal History of the Underworld*. New York: Knopf, 1927; reprint ed., New York: Thunder's Mouth Press, 2001.

Bayor, Ronald H., and Timothy J. Meagher, eds. *The New York Irish*. Baltimore: Johns Hopkins University Press, 1996.

Bell, Daniel. *The End of Ideology: On the Exhaustion of Political Ideas in the Fifties*. New York: Collier, 1962.

Block, Alan. *East Side–West Side: Organizing Crime in New York, 1930–1950*. New Brunswick, NJ: Transaction, 1999.

Blumenthal, Ralph. *Miracle at Sing Sing: How One Man Transformed the Lives of America's Most Dangerous Prisoners*. New York: St. Martin's Press, 2004.

Brodsky, Alyn. *The Great Mayor: Fiorello LaGuardia and the Making of the City of New York*. New York: St. Martin's Press, 2003.

Carmer, Carl. *The Hudson*. New York: Farrar & Rinehart, 1939.

Cheli, Guy. *Images of America: Sing Sing Prison*. Portsmouth, NH: Arcadia, 2003.

Christianson, Scott. *Condemned: Inside the Sing Sing Death House*. New York: New York University Press, 2000.

Conover, Ted. *Newjack: Guarding Sing Sing*. New York: Random House, 2000.

Department of Correction. *Sing Sing Prison, Ossining, N.Y.: Its History, Purpose, Makeup and Program*. Albany, 1958.

Dooley, Roger. *From Scarface to Scarlett: American Films in the 1930s*. San Diego: Harcourt Brace Jovanovich, 1984.

Ellis, Edward Robb. *The Epic of New York City: A Narrative History.* New York: Kodansha, 1997.

English, T. J. *The Westies: The Irish Mob.* New York: St. Martin's Press, 1991.

Federal Writers' Project. *The WPA Guide to New York City.* New York: Guilds Committee for Federal Writers' Publications, 1939; reprint ed., New York: New Press, 1992.

Hallinan, Joseph T. *Going Up the River: Travels in a Prison Nation.* New York: Random House, 2001.

Homberger, Eric. *The Historical Atlas of New York City: A Visual Celebration of Nearly 400 Years of New York City's History.* New York: Owl Books, 1998.

Johnson, Malcolm. *Crime on the Labor Front.* New York: McGraw-Hill, 1950.

Keating, William, with Richard Carter. *The Man Who Rocked the Boat.* New York: Harper & Bros., 1956.

Kennedy, William. *Legs.* New York: Penguin, 1982.

Kisselhoff, Jeff. *You Must Remember This: An Oral History of Manhattan from the 1890s to World War II.* New York: Harcourt Brace Jovanovich, 1989.

Lardner, James, and Thomas Reppetto. *NYPD: A City and Its Police.* New York: Owl Books, 2001.

Lawes, Lewis. *Twenty-Thousand Years in Sing Sing.* New York: Ray Long & Richard R. Smith, 1933.

Mitgang, Herbert. *The Man Who Rode the Tiger: The Life and Times of Judge Samuel Seabury.* New York: William Nelson Cromwell Foundation, 1963; reprint ed., New York: Fordham University Press, 1996.

Morris, James McGrath. *The Rose Man of Sing Sing: A True Tale of Life, Murder, and Redemption in the Age of Yellow Journalism.* New York: Fordham University Press, 2003.

Morris, Norval, and David J. Rothman, eds. *The Oxford History of the Prison: The Practice of Punishment in Western Society.* New York: Oxford University Press, 1998.

New York Catholic Protectory. *A Short Sketch of the New York Catholic Protectory from its Origins to the Present.* West Chester, NY, 1885.

New York Catholic Protectory. *Sixty-sixth Annual Report of the New York Catholic Protectory.* New York, 1928.

O'Connor, Richard. *Hell's Kitchen: The Roaring Days of New York's Wild West Side.* Philadelphia: J. B. Lippincott, 1958.

Oechsner, Carl. *Ossining, New York: An Informal Bicentennial History.* Croton-on-Hudson, NY: North River Press, 1975.

Ossining Historical Society. *Images of America: Ossining Remembered.* Charleston, SC: Arcadia, 1999.

Reppetto, Thomas. *American Mafia: A History of Its Rise to Power.* New York: Owl Books, 2005.

Sann, Paul. *The Lawless Decade: A Pictorial History of a Great American Transition: From the World War I Armistice and Prohibition to Repeal and the New Deal.* New York: Bonanza, 1957.

Sante, Luc. *Low Life: Lures and Snares of Old New York.* New York: Farrar, Straus, Giroux, 1991.

Scott, Fr. Joseph, CSP. *A Century and More of Reaching Out: An Historical Sketch of the Parish of St. Paul the Apostle.* The Missionary Society of St. Paul the Apostle in the State of New York, 1983.

Stolberg, Mary M. *Fighting Organized Crime: Politics, Justice, and the Legacy of Thomas E. Dewey.* Boston: Northeastern University Press, 1995.

Sutton, Willie, with Edward Linn. *Where the Money Was: The Memoirs of a Bank Robber.* New York: Viking Press, 1976.

Thompson, Craig, and Allen Raymond. *Gang Rule in New York: The Story of a Lawless Era.* New York: Dial Press, 1940.

Toland, John. *The Dillinger Days.* New York: 1963; reprint ed., New York: Da Capo Press, 1995.

West Side Studies, carried on under the direction of Pauline Goldmark, 2 vols. New York: Russell Sage Foundation Publications, Survey Associates, 1914.

ACKNOWLEDGMENTS

In the early stages of this process, I was lucky to receive generous and much-needed critical advice. I am indebted to Steve Adams, John Aiello, Bob Kulesz, and Diana Schwaeble, talented writers all. The Group read the earliest drafts of this manuscript with great care, discussing details and directions over monthly Budweiser and sangria. Thanks for everything, guys.

Thanks, too, to Charlotte Gordon. This book would never have gotten off the ground in the first place without her kind-hearted encouragement.

My gratitude also to Ellen Belcher, Special Collections Librarian for the Lewis E. Lawes papers, Lloyd Sealy Library, John Jay College of Criminal Justice, who always provided me with extra material above and beyond my many requests; Kenneth Cobb, Assistant Commissioner, New York City Municipal Archives, Department of Records and Information Services, for his kind attention and assistance; James Fisher, Center for American Catholic Studies, Fordham University, who shared his expertise with me; Professor Bob Fitch, LaGuardia Community College, who spent an afternoon with me illuminating the finer points of street crime and waterfront labor unions; the busy folks at the New York State Archives, especially Jim Folts, Bill Gorman, and Jack McPeters, who accommodated my every telephone and e-mail query; Patrice Kane, Special Collections archivist for the St. Xavier Labor College, Rose Hill Library, Fordham University, who revealed for me the collected papers of Fr. John Corridan, the cigarette-smoking waterfront priest characterized by Karl Malden in *On the Waterfront;* Scott Kelly, American Irish Historical Society, who introduced me to their magnificent Fifth Avenue mansion library; Joseph Margolis, archivist extraordinaire at the LaGuardia and Wagner Archives, LaGuardia

Community College; Geraldine Riordan Murphy for sharing her family memories; Mary Ann Roberts, Ossining Town Clerk, for finding John Waters's death certificate; Sister Marguerita Smith, archivist at the Archdiocese of New York Archives, St. Joseph's Seminary, who sat by patiently while I perused the materials she had so carefully laid out; Lt. Laurie M. Wagner, Records Access Officer, New York State Police, for providing me with the necessary documents; and the unnamed staff of the newspaper and periodical archives at the New York Public Library, who practically run to assist every customer fumbling with the microfiche machines.

A special thanks to Roberta Arminio, curator of the Ossining Historical Society Museum, historian, and living encyclopedia on all things Ossining. Roberta is a treasure—no book on the town, or the prison, is possible without her warm and generous help. My gratitude also to Peter Kanze for his old photo wizardry.

Special thanks are due also to Sing Sing Correctional Facility Superintendent Brian Fisher, and First Deputy Superintendent Paul Kikendall, for inviting me to the April 14 memorial service, and for their indulgence and permission in allowing me an unforgettable, all-day tour of the prison; Officers Andre Varin and Art Wolpinsky for their help and insight; and especially Fred Starler, for his razor-sharp memory after all those years—rest in peace, Fred.

Thanks also to my sister Linda Stow for her help, undying zeal, and her many prayers. I owe a particular debt of gratitude to my brother, Lt. Kenneth J. Goewey, who first brought this story to my attention, and whose hard-won knowledge helped iron out the details.

I cannot imagine that any first-time author was ever blessed with a more supportive working team. First and foremost, my courageous agent Brettne Bloom, whose tireless enthusiasm, wise counsel, and generous spirit brought this book to fruition; my truly great editor, Shana Drehs, whose brilliant eye and gently targeted questions strengthened the narrative way beyond my expectations; and to all the good people at Crown Publishers, especially the book's amazing designers, Leonard Henderson and Whitney Cookman.

Finally, my warmest, heartfelt thanks go to Anne. You *know* this could never have happened without you.

ABOUT THE AUTHOR

DAVID GOEWEY was born and raised in Ossining, New York, the grandson, son, and brother of Sing Sing officers. He received his MFA from the New School University, and has taught writing at CUNY and in the New York City Department of Corrections, Rikers Island Inmate Education program. He lives in New York City.